# The OLYMPIC SPIRIT

## 100 YEARS OF THE GAMES

**100**

**Atlanta 1996**

TM, © 1992 ACOG

The Olympic Spirit was made possible through the generous support of the following Olympic Sponsors.

Thanks to their commitment, the memories of millions will live on.

# THE OLYMPIC SPIRIT

## 100 YEARS OF THE GAMES

BY SUSAN WELS

Southern Living®

Official Worldwide Olympic Sponsor

*The Olympic Spirit* is published through *Southern Living* magazine, an Official Worldwide Sponsor of the 1996 Atlanta Centennial Olympic Games. *The Olympic Spirit* is published with the permission of the Atlanta Committee for the Olympic Games and bears its official marks.

*The Olympic Spirit* was conceived and produced by Tehabi Books, Del Mar, California.
Nancy Cash–*Managing Editor;* Andy Lewis–*Project Art Director;* Sam Lewis–*Art Director;*
Tom Lewis–*Editorial and Design Director;* Sharon Lewis–*Controller;* Chris Capen–*Project Director and President.*
Additional support for *The Olympic Spirit* was also provided by Debbie Fife–*Editor;* Kathi George–*Copy Proofer.*

For more information on the Olympic Museum, Lausanne, Switzerland please contact the Museum directly at 4121.621.66.10. For more information on *The Olympic Spirit,* including corporate customized copies, please contact Chris Capen, Project Director, Tehabi Books, 13070 Via Grimaldi, Del Mar, California 92014 USA. Telephone: (619) 481-7600.

Tehabi Books, in association with The Basic Foundation, a not-for-profit organization whose primary mission is reforestation, will facilitate the planting of two trees for every one tree used in the manufacture of this book.

Library of Congress Cataloging-in-Publication Data
Wels, Susan.
The Olympic spirit : 100 years of the games / by Susan Wels.
      p.   cm.
    Includes index.
    ISBN 0-00-638279-7 (Softcover - U.S. Edition)
    ISBN 0-00-649054-9 (Softcover - Int'l Edition)
    ISBN 0-8487-1504-7 (Hardcover Edition)
    1. Olympics—History—Pictorial works.  I. Title.
GV721.5.W36  1995
796.48'022'2—dc20
                         95-17442
                          CIP

10 9 8 7 6 5 4 3 2 1

This edition is printed on acid-free paper that meets the American National Standards Institute Z39.48 Standard.

Photography provided by:     Olympic Museum, Lausanne, Switzerland.
                               Duomo Photography Inc., New York, New York.
                               Allsport Photography Inc., Los Angeles, California.

Color separations and film provided by Digital Pre-Press International through PrintNet.

Printed in Hong Kong through Mandarin Offset.

*Photos: Cover photo design by Tehabi Books, © Duomo, David Madison, Al Tielemans;*
*Page 2 and opposite page: Archives, Olympic Museum Lausanne.*

# CONTENTS

# CELEBRATING THE CENTENNIAL

As the world celebrates the one-hundredth anniversary of the modern Olympic Movement with the 1996 Centennial Olympic Games in Atlanta, it is profoundly clear that the true spirit of the Olympics—the union of sport, art, and culture—has flourished beyond the greatest dreams of their founder, Baron Pierre de Coubertin.

## THE FOUNDING VISION

When Coubertin established the International Olympic Committee (IOC) in 1894 in Paris, his goal was to encourage a better understanding among nations through the linking of sport, education, art, and culture. The modern Olympic movement evolved from the ideals celebrated by the ancient Greeks, who devoted themselves to the harmonious pursuit of physical, moral, cultural, and artistic excellence and regarded the Olympic Games as the greatest expression of those values.

In 1896, the first of the modern Olympic Games were held in Athens, Greece. Since then, as Coubertin had hoped, the long tradition of the modern Games has offered an opportunity for the world's youth to gather in the spirit of friendship and learn the importance of values that transcend differences in nationality, geography, and culture.

Now, as the world gathers in Atlanta, the Centennial Games will again honor the great Olympic tradition established by Coubertin. I join you in looking forward to this exciting celebration.

*Juan Antonio Samaranch*
*President of the International Olympic Committee*

## JUAN ANTONIO SAMARANCH

*Perpetuating the vision of Olympic founder Pierre de Coubertin (above), Juan Antonio Samaranch (below) has guided the IOC since his election to the presidency in 1980.*

*Opposite: Seoul, 1988.*

*Following spread: Barcelona, 1992.*

# OLYMPIC DREAMS

Streams of color streak the sky. Doves scatter over a field surging with athletes, Herculean heroes, and rippling flags. And in the black Catalan night, thousands watch a white-clad archer draw his bow; a fiery arrow flashes through the dark and fills the vast Olympic cauldron with a burst of flame. With blazing symbol and ceremony, the 1992 Summer Olympics

### THE PASSION TO COMPETE

opened in Barcelona, Spain. Now the torch passes to the city of Atlanta for the 1996 Centennial Olympic Games.

With their sweeping pageantry, the Olympics have remained, for the past one hundred years, one of the few rituals that regularly bring the people of the world together. During the Games, nations gather, not for combat or debate, but to celebrate the hope of peace and the shared love of competition. In the Olympics, as in any ritual, there has sometimes been friction between ideals and reality. But often enough we witness the ideal, and it never fails to astonish and move us.

The world holds its collective breath as athletes hurtle down the track, plunge perilously down mountain slopes, and flout gravity on the balance beam, the springboard, and the ice. Billions are riveted by these glimpses of pure, realized potential. In a world of virtual reality, the Olympics are one arena in which real human heroes reach levels of physical performance that the rest of us can only dream of. It's a dream that pulls us back, again and again, no matter how strident the politics of the moment or how vast the challenge of gathering together the world's family, once again, for this ultimate spectacle of sport.

### LET THE GAMES BEGIN

*The massive spectacles of the Olympic Opening Ceremonies rivet audiences around the world with their powerful displays of sport, art, and culture.*
*Opposite: Calgary, 1988.*
*Following spread: Los Angeles, 1984.*

Photos: *Above © Duomo, David Madison; Below © Duomo; Opposite © Duomo, Steven E. Sutton; Following spread © Duomo, Paul J. Sutton.*

A century after the birth of the modern Games, the power of the Olympics is still rooted in ideals of heroism, sacrifice, and the human struggle for perfection—just as it was for the ancient Greeks, who invented the Olympic idea almost 2,800 years ago. For us, as for the Greeks, these emotional currents are stirred by the intoxicating Olympic blend of physical contests, pageantry, and art. Olympic imagery is as powerful as any secular devotion could inspire: the lighted torch, a flickering link between the modern Games and the ruins of Olympia in Greece; the cluster of five Olympic rings, a symbol taken from the ancient shrine of Apollo at Delphi; the flags and banners; and the massive, moving spectacles of the Opening and Closing Ceremonies.

But it's always the athletes—the hundreds who medal and the thousands more who don't—who make the Olympic dream personal and real. Their moments on the Olympic stage are dramatically unscripted. For those who win, it's a fragile, fleeting instant at the top. Even for an athlete like Austria's Franz Klammer, a skier who won almost every World Cup downhill race in 1975, the Olympics are the peak. "Now I've got everything," he said after winning the downhill gold in 1976. "I don't need anything else."

"There's no other feeling like winning the Olympic Games," reflected Darrell Pace, a gold-medaling archer in 1976 and 1984. "You stand on the podium and know that you are the best in the world, but you also know that you may never be there again."

For many, the journey to the Games comes at a high personal cost. "People forget how many times you lost on your way there…[and] how much training takes out of you. It's lonely in that pool," remembered swimmer Cathy Ferguson, who won twin golds in 1964. Time and youth pass quickly, too, for athletes who may wind up empty-handed at the end of their Olympic quest. Ye Qiaobo, a Chinese speed skater, wept with grief when she took the silver medal, not the gold, at the 1992 Winter Games in Albertville. "I spend so many times for skating, and I gave up so many hobbies for this," she sobbed. And now, she despaired, "I am old."

But still, the Olympic dream drives them to compete, despite the stakes and sacrifices. "These are the Olympics. You die for them," declared discus thrower Al Oerter, who competed for his third Olympic gold while suffering from agonizing injuries.

Like the athletes, the rest of us are drawn in, time and time again, by the mesmerizing spectacle and celebration of the Games—by the glory, the magic, and the hope.

## BARON PIERRE DE COUBERTIN

*The man who almost single-handedly willed the modern Olympics into being at the end of the last century was a canny, idealistic French aristocrat, Baron Pierre de Coubertin. Born in Paris in 1863, Coubertin was inspired by the archaeological excavations of ancient Greece and concerned about the lack of physical training among French youth. He pressed for the revival of the ancient Olympic Games and won support for launching a modern Olympic festival. In 1896, the first of the reborn Olympic Games was held in Athens. Coubertin continued to guide the Games as president of the International Olympic Committee until 1925. Opposite: Montreal, 1976. Following spread: Moscow, 1980.*

Photo: Opposite and following spread © Duomo.

When the Olympic torch relay was introduced in 1936, 3,000 runners carried torches from Olympia in Greece to the host city of Berlin. Produced by the firm of Friedrich Krupp, the stainless steel torch

## OLYMPIC TORCHES

holders were more than two feet long and weighed 1 1/2 pounds, with specially designed wicks of incendiary magnesium. Since 1936, Olympic torches have been created for every host city, incorporating a range of technologies and cultural and design influences. For the Lillehammer Games in 1994, runners carried a curved, four-foot-long torch on a 5,000-mile relay around Norway. The Olympic flame was kept burning by six wicks in a 10-pound holder made of silver and white Norwegian fir.

Photos: Archives, Olympic Museum Lausanne

Helsinki 1952

Montreal 1976

Sarajevo 1984

Tokyo 1964

Lillehammer 1994

Lake Placid 1980

Barcelona 1992

Innsbruck 1976

Sapporo 1972

Innsbruck 1964

Grenoble 1968

Moscow 1980

Los Angeles 1984

Munich 1972

Calgary 1980

Rome 1960

Mexico 1968

Berlin 1936

Albertville 1992

Melbourne 1956

London 1948

Cortina d'Ampezzo 1956

Squaw Valley 1960

Seoul 1988

Oslo 1952

# THE LEGACY OF OLYMPIA

In the ancient Greek world, there were few qualities more prized than *arete,* the perfection of physical performance, and *kalòk'agathía,* the combination of beauty and goodness. For more than a thousand years, there was no higher expression of those virtues than victory in the sacred Games at Olympia—an athletic and religious spectacle that was

## THE ANCIENT GAMES

venerated from Athens and the Aegean Islands to the Hellenic outposts of the Near East and Asia Minor.

From their historical beginnings in 776 B.C. until they were banned in A.D. 394, the ancient Games at Olympia were held every four years without interruption, despite grave threats of invasion and nearly constant warfare among the city-states of Greece. In 480 B.C., the seventy-fifth Olympic Games went on as scheduled, even while a small heroic force of Spartans struggled, unsuccessfully, to repel invading Persians at the Battle of Thermopylae. When the Persian general Mardonius wondered where the rest of the Greek forces were, he was informed that they were "celebrating the Olympic Games and watching gymnastics and horse contests." Ironically, it was in part the superb physical conditioning of the Greeks, achieved through exercise and competition, that enabled them ultimately to drive out the Persians at Plataea, near Thebes, in 479 B.C.

The Games held such a pivotal position in Hellenic life that the Greeks used the Olympic contests and the Olympiad—the four-year period between Games—as a method of dating historical events. To win a contest in the Games made the champion a hero for life, immortalized

### THE PENTATHLON

*In the ancient Greek Olympics, the five events of the pentathlon included running, wrestling, discus, javelin throwing, and long jump— an event in which the athletes carried semicircular jumping weights, as illustrated on this eighth-century B.C. amphora (opposite).*

Photos: *Above © Hermitage Museum, Saint Petersburg; Below © George Ortiz Collection, Patrick Goetelen, Geneva; Opposite © Rijks Museum van Oudheden, P.T. Bomhof.*

in poetry and sculpture and entitled to free food and lodging. Even to attend the Games was considered a high honor, despite the long journey and frequently uncomfortable living conditions at Olympia. The Games attracted citizens from Greek towns and city-states, and later from colonies in Sicily, the south of Italy, Asia Minor, Spain, and Africa. The most famous artists, poets, writers, and sophists gathered at the Games, including the sculptor Phidias, whose works included the colossal statues of Zeus at Olympia and Athena at the Parthenon in Athens, the poet Pindar, and the historian Herodotus. Every four years, as many as 40,000 people made their way to Olympia, by land and by sea, from all over the Hellenic world.

To protect all the competitors and spectators on their journeys to and from the Games, a sacred truce, the *ekecheiria*, was declared by heralds throughout Greece before every Olympic festival. The truce was strictly enforced by Olympic officials, who levied fines on anyone who broke the peace. In 420 B.C., according to Thucydides, Spartans were barred from the Games after they launched an attack during the *ekecheiria* and balked at paying the penalty demanded by officials.

Olympia itself, a fertile valley in the remote northwest corner of the Peloponnesus, was acknowledged by all Greeks to be a neutral precinct, where free citizens from every city-state could compete peacefully. No town or village had ever been established at Olympia; its groves and fields had, as early as the tenth century B.C., been set apart as the most sacred center for the worship of Zeus, the supreme god in the Greek pantheon.

Apart from Olympia's religious importance, the sanctuary had plenty of natural advantages. Unlike much of the rough and rocky landscape of Greece, Olympia was a lush, green valley watered by two rivers, the Alpheus and the Kladeus. Spreading out from the banks of the rivers was a broad plain, flanked by evergreen hills and shaded by groves of plane trees, pines, oaks, and wild olives.

## THE GREEK IDEAL

*Physical beauty, paired with a well-developed mind, was the epitome of masculine virtue in classical Greece. "From the love of the beautiful," Plato counseled in the* Republic, *"comes every good thing in heaven and earth." To cultivate the Hellenic ideal of* kalòk'agathía—*the combination of beauty and goodness—Greek boys from the age of seven studied literature, music, and art and increased their grace and strength through athletic exercises. Older teenage boys, the* epheboi, *spent time in the* palaestra *and* gymnasium—*public athletic complexes established throughout Greece. There, strict instructors, called* paidotribai, *drilled them in running, wrestling, discus and javelin throwing, boxing, jumping, and ball sports, to the accompaniment of music. The Greek preoccupation with physical training had its roots in the constant warfare between small city-states. Each state needed a supremely fit and battle-ready corps of warriors, kept in peak condition during peacetime through rigorous athletics.*

According to legend, wild olive trees were once so plentiful at Olympia that Herakles made beds of their foliage to sleep on. It was a wreath woven from the branches of one of these trees, called the Crown Olive, that was the prize bestowed on every Olympic victor—the most coveted honor in all of Greece. At Thermopylae, Herodotus writes, one of the Persian leaders was amazed that Greek athletes would compete so passionately for a prize that was apparently so worthless. "What sort of men," he asked Mardonius, "have you led us to fight against, who contend not for money but purely for the sake of excelling?"

That conclusion was somewhat inaccurate, since Olympic victors actually received substantial material rewards from their city-states—including, in some cases, lifetime pensions and lavish payments for appearances. At Olympia, however, the garland of wild olive was the only reward for victory—and it was victory alone that counted. There was no prize for second or third place, and athletes prayed for "the wreath or death." Epictetus, a Greek philosopher writing in the first and second centuries A.D., described the ultimate humiliation of failure at Olympia: "In the Olympic games it is not possible for you merely to be beaten and then leave; but…you…disgrace yourself in the sight of the whole civilized world.…"

For the athletes, the journey to Olympia began in the wrestling schools (*palaestrae*) and *gymnasia* found in nearly every city in Greece. In these public complexes, equipped with exercise rooms, baths, and outdoor training grounds, young men were drilled in athletics to prepare and harden them for armed combat. Those athletes who had the potential to be champions put themselves under the strict supervision of their trainers (*paidotribai*), who prescribed a demanding regimen: "You have to submit to discipline, follow a strict diet, give up sweet cakes, train under compulsion, at a fixed hour, in heat or cold; you must not drink cold water, nor wine just whenever you feel like it; you must have turned yourself over to your trainer precisely as you would to a physician."

---

### THE OLYMPIC FLAME

*Torch races—short-distance local relays of purely religious significance—were occasionally included in Greek athletic festivals, but they were never part of the Olympic program. Nevertheless, since 1936, the modern Olympic flame relay has symbolically linked the modern Games with their ancient past. At Olympia in Greece, classically robed women (following spread) ignite the flame with a parabolic mirror that focuses the rays of the sun. The flame is then traditionally passed hand to hand by torch-bearing runners until it reaches the site of the Olympic Games.*

Photos: Above, Archives,
Olympic Museum Lausanne, Stram;
Below © Hermitage Museum, Saint Petersburg;
Following page © Duomo, William R. Sallaz.

## THE CROWN GAMES

*The glory of the Greek gods Zeus, Poseidon, and Apollo was celebrated at the four Crown Games, the most important of all the Greek athletic festivals. Together, these Panhellenic Games, which attracted athletes from all over the Greek world, were called the* periodos, *or circuit. The Olympic festival and the Nemean Games held at Nemea honored Zeus. The Isthmian Games at Corinth were held at a sanctuary of Poseidon, and the Pythian Games at Delphi were consecrated to the god Apollo. Each of these festivals featured running events, as well as the pentathlon, wrestling, boxing, the fierce* pankration, *and equestrian contests. Only the lesser Crown Games—the Pythian, Isthmian, and Nemean—included musical competitions in singing and the playing of the lyre and the flute.*

*The prize at each of the Panhellenic Games was a simple crown of leaves: a wreath of laurel at the Pythian festival, a garland of pine branches at the Isthmian, a crown of wild celery at the Nemean, and a wreath of wild olive at Olympia. An athlete who won a crown at each of the four Games was immortalized as a hero and honored with the title* periodonikos, *the "winner of the circuit."*

Photos: Above and right, Archives, Olympic Museum Lausanne, Strahm.

ANCIENT GREECE

There were ample opportunities for athletes to compete in local contests and athletic festivals. In 500 B.C. there were some fifty regularly scheduled games, and the number climbed to more than three hundred in the first century A.D. By far the most important of these contests was the *periodos,* the circuit of Crown Games: the Pythian, Isthmian, Nemean, and Olympian festivals. The greatest of all these events, which drew the very best competitors in Greece, were the Games at Olympia, dedicated to Zeus.

Six months before every Olympic festival, official heralds (*spondophoroi*) would travel throughout Greece to announce the exact dates for the coming Games—which always coincided with the second or third full moon after the summer solstice—and to declare the sacred truce to protect all travelers. The arrival of the *spondophoroi* marked the beginning of intensive athletic training and competition in every town and city. Local judges selected the athletes who would compete at Olympia—all, by requirement, free-born citizens of pure Greek lineage who had committed no crimes of violence. About two months before the Games, these hometown champions—accompanied by a colorful procession of leading politicians, artists, merchants, and intellectuals—set off, with great pomp and circumstance, for Olympia and the city of Elis, the district that retained official control over the Games.

Situated some thirty-five miles north of Olympia, Elis was an independent, agrarian backwater. Its government oversaw the codifying of Olympic rules and appointed the Hellenodikai—judges who were the arbiters and umpires of the Olympic Games. To the Eleans' credit, they managed the Games, for the most part, strictly and fairly, even during the corrupt years of the Roman Empire; they made "painstaking and orderly arrangements; they seemed to feel themselves to be on their trial quite as much as the athletic competitors, and to be determined to make no mistakes...."

According to Olympic rules, athletes had to train in Elis, under the eyes and flashing whips of the Hellenodikai, for a period of thirty days before the Games. The judges checked athletes' qualifications, permitted them to compete or disqualified them from the Games, fined or whipped competitors for misbehavior, made sure they slept on skins on the hard ground, and enforced an austere diet of dried figs, nuts, barley bread, porridge, and fresh cheese. On the training grounds of Elis, lined with tall plane trees, the Hellenodikai also set up trial matches and paired wrestling and boxing contestants by age and ability, since there were no weight classes at Olympia.

Three days before the Games, those competitors who had successfully made it through the rigorous month of training set out by foot on a two-day procession to Olympia. By the time the athletes, judges, trainers, and other officials arrived at the sacred valley, the grounds were already teeming with spectators who had traveled to the Games from every corner of Hellas. There were few facilities to house and feed the crowds, who paid no admission for the Games and for the most part camped in tents or slept out under the stars.

The shouting, jostling crush was compounded by legions of food and drink vendors, peddlers, singers, dancers, touts, conjurers, and fortune-tellers who worked the crowd. The high-spirited scene was probably similar to the noisy chaos that one spectator observed at the Isthmian Games: "You could see and hear the accursed sophists shouting and abusing one another, and their so-called pupils fighting one another, many authors giving readings of their works which no one listens to, many poets reciting their poems..., many conjurers performing their tricks and many fortune-tellers interpreting omens, thousands of lawyers arguing cases and a host of cheap jacks selling everything under the sun."

## THE FIRST FOOT RACE

*The first official Olympic Games, held in 776 B.C., reportedly consisted of a single foot race. The competition, a 192-meter dash, was won by Koroibus, a cook from nearby Elis. Thirteen Olympiads later, in 724 B.C., a second foot race was added, the 400-meter diaulos—a sprint down the length of the track, around a turning post, and back. It was not until 708 B.C. that a nonrunning competition—wrestling—was officially included. By the late seventh century B.C., the Games at Olympia had evolved to include the classical roster of events, including foot races, discus and javelin throws, long jump, wrestling, boxing, chariot races, bareback horse races, and the pankration—a fierce, no-holds-barred combination of boxing and wrestling that mimicked man to man combat on the field of battle.*

Photos: Above © George Ortiz Collection, Patrick Goetelen, Geneva; Below © Hermitage Museum, Saint Petersburg.

The heat, the crowds, the dust, and the flies could be so aggravating that, according to one story, a disobedient slave was threatened by his master with a visit to Olympia as punishment. According to Epictetus, "some unpleasant and hard things happen in life. And do they not happen at Olympia? Do you not swelter? Are you not cramped and crowded? Do you not bathe with discomfort? Are you not drenched whenever it rains? Do you not have your fill of tumult and shouting and other annoyances? But I fancy that you hear and endure all this by balancing it off against the memorable character of the spectacle."

The spectacle, however, was an exclusively male affair: no women were permitted, with the exception of the priestess of Demeter; and, according to the laws of Elis, any female who attempted to violate this taboo would be hurled to her certain death from a high, rocky cliff called the Tympaion. Fortunately, no female interlopers were ever caught—except for Kallipateira, who disguised herself as a male trainer to watch her son, Peisirodos, compete. When Peisirodos won his event, she jumped over a fence, uncovering her fraud in her excitement. Because Kallipateira's father, brothers, and son were all Olympic champions, her life was spared. But Olympic law was thereafter changed to require that all trainers, like athletes at the Games, had to enter the arena without clothing.

## THE DISCUS

*The metal discuses used at Olympia weighed up to 14 1/2 pounds. Competitors hurled them with a throwing technique similar to that used by athletes today.*

Photos: Above and right, Archives, Olympic Museum Lausanne.

On opening day, the excitement at Olympia began with the arrival of the athletes, preceded by trumpeters and heralds, purple-robed Hellenodikai, priests, and delegations of officials. After making sacrifices, the procession wound its way to the council hall (*bouleterion*) with its great statue of Zeus of Oaths clutching thunderbolts in his powerful hands. Here, the athletes, their fathers and brothers, and their trainers swore over a dismembered boar to abide by all the Olympic rules. The athletes vowed that they had been in full training for ten months, and the judges pledged that they would rigidly uphold the rules and punish all offenders.

Athletes who dishonored the Games by bribery or committing other crimes were banished from Olympia or compelled to pay fines. The money collected from them paid for dozens of statues of Zeus inscribed with cautionary words such as "You win with the speed of your feet and the strength in your body, and not with money."

After the first day of oaths and celebrations, the athletic competitions commenced. In the early fifth century, when the Games assumed their classical, five-day schedule, the very first event was the two-wheeled chariot race, held in the rectangular, open-air hippodrome. This immensely popular contest was one of very few in which competitors were clothed—and in which a woman could win the crown of olive, since victory went to the wealthy owner of the winning chariot and horses, and not to the anonymous driver.

During this heart-stopping event, as many as forty chariots, each driven by a team of four horses, hurtled back and forth down a 400-meter track as they attempted to complete twelve double laps, totaling nearly nine miles. Inevitably, chariots crashed and horses panicked in the dust and commotion as they careened wildly around the single turning post at each end of the narrow, undivided race course. In one race, celebrated by Pindar, only a single charioteer out of forty competitors made it to the finish line.

## THE PAIDOTRIBAI

*In the* gymnasia—*sports complexes which were central to the cultural life of every Greek city*—*athletes were rigorously drilled by whip-wielding trainers called* paidotribai.

*Photo: Archives, Olympic Museum Lausanne.*

After the chariot races, equestrian events continued with Olympic horse racing. Riders galloped, without saddles or stirrups, up and down the race course of the hippodrome, on turf that had been torn up by the teams of hard-charging chariots. As in the previous event, the crown of olive was awarded to the owner of the winning steed rather than to the jockey. On one occasion, the wreath was given to the owner of a mare named Breeze, who made it first to the finish line without the rider who had fallen off at the starting gate.

The second day's competitions ended with the pentathlon events—long jump, javelin and discus throwing, running, and wrestling—most of which were held in the Olympic stadium. The victor was the athlete who finished first in three of the five competitions. For the long jump, competitors carried semicircular weights, called *halteres,* which they swung forward on takeoff and backward upon landing. Made of stone or metal, the four- to nine-pound weights were used to extend the length of the jump and help the athlete land steadily on his feet. In the javelin contest, athletes hurled a blunt-tipped wooden spear, competing for the greatest distance. To help guide the javelin, competitors wrapped the shaft tightly with a leather thong, leaving a loop at one end through which they slipped one or two fingers. After a running start, the athlete hurled the javelin, which spun as the leather strap unwound. Five throws were permitted, and only the best performance counted. Similarly, pentathletes were scored on the best of five throws of the discus. Made of metal, the discuses at Olympia varied in size and heft, weighing up to 14 1/2-pounds, and were thrown using a technique similar to that employed today.

The pentathlon foot race was a 200-meter sprint down the length of the stadium, on a course of sand laid over a surface of clay. At the start of the race, the barefoot runners pushed off with their back feet from marble starting slabs, called *balbides,* which are still visible at Olympia. Finally, at the end of the second day, spectators crowded to watch the wrestling, the last event of the pentathlon. Matches were fought standing up, and victory went to the athlete who forced his opponent to the ground three times.

The morning of the third day was devoted entirely to religious processions and spectacles—culminating in the blood-soaked slaughter of a hundred oxen before the towering altar of Zeus, an enormous mound of ash rising

### THE STRIGIL

*To protect their skin, athletes rubbed their bodies with olive oil and covered themselves with dust. After training or competition, and before bathing, they scraped the oil and dirt from their bodies with a curved implement called a* strigil.

Photos: Below © Hermitage Museum, Saint Petersburg;
Bottom, Archives, Olympic Museum Lausanne.

## HORSE RACING

*Equestrian contests provided some of the most exciting moments of the ancient Olympic Games. During the horse racing event, riders galloped bareback up and down the 400-meter race track in the hippodrome. In the two-wheeled chariot race, one of the most dramatic competitions, dozens of four-horse teams charged twelve times up and down the undivided track, careening around a single turning post at each end of the course.*

Photos: Right © George Ortiz Collection, Patrick Goetelen, Geneva; Below, Archives, Olympic Museum Lausanne.

twenty-two feet high. The thighs of the slaughtered creatures were burned on a fire of white poplar at the top of the ash mound; the remains were reserved for feasting at the conclusion of the Games. Competition then resumed in the afternoon, when youths aged twelve through seventeen matched their speed and strength in sprints, wrestling, and boxing events.

The fourth day at Olympia was the very last day of competition. In the stadium, four to eight runners at a time competed in foot races—the 200-meter *stade* sprint, the 400-meter *diaulos* race, and the 4,800-meter *dolichos* long-distance event. An athlete who won all three races earned the title *Triastes*, a rare honor conferred four times on one champion, Leonidas of Rhodes.

The day ended with the hugely popular body-contact sports: wrestling, boxing, and the ferocious *pankration.* There were no weight classes or time limits for any of these brutal sports. Wrestlers, their thickly muscled bodies rubbed with oil and sand to toughen and protect their skin, gripped each other on a platform in the center of the stadium and struggled to force each other to the ground. Milo of Kroton, a champion with legendary strength who won the wrestling at Olympia six times, reportedly trained for this grueling event by ingesting a daily diet of twenty pounds each of bread and wheat and eighteen pints of wine.

### THE BALBIDES

*At the beginning of each foot race, runners positioned their bare feet against grooved marble starting slabs, called* balbides, *which were sectioned off to accommodate up to twenty competitors. A horizontal bar in front of the racers served as a starting gate. When the bar was dropped, the race began.*

Photo: Archives, Olympic Museum Lausanne.

### THE WREATH OF OLIVE

*Winning was everything to Olympic competitors; no second- or third-place prizes were awarded. Victors were crowned with a wreath of wild olive from a sacred grove at Olympia. On their return home, Olympic champions were welcomed as heroes. Statues were erected in their honor, and many were rewarded with cash as well as pledges of free food and lodging for life.*

Photo: Archives, Olympic Museum Lausanne.

Even more popular with the spectators was boxing, the bloodiest of all the Olympic combat sports. Boxers wrapped their fists tightly with narrow strips of leather and pummeled each other brutally until one was knocked unconscious or gave up by raising his right hand. Over time, leather thongs were replaced by fist coverings weighted or spiked with metal, and boxers were often beaten beyond recognition. One man named Olympikos, wrote Lucillius in the first century A.D., "used to have nose, chin, forehead, ears, and eyelids. But then he enrolled in the guild of boxing...."

The most demanding and highly regarded body-contact sport was the *pankration,* a combination of wrestling and boxing in which nearly every imaginable move was permitted, from kicking and trampling to punching and strangling. Only biting and eye gouging were forbidden. One pankratist, nicknamed "Mr. Fingertips," would bend his opponent's fingertips back and not let go until the victim gave up in agony. Another pankratist, overcome during a match by pain from a broken toe, tapped his opponent's shoulder in surrender—only to discover that he had already strangled his adversary to death. The judges awarded the wreath of olive to the corpse.

The final, somewhat comic, event of the Olympic Games was the race in armor—a 400-meter foot race in which contestants ran up and down the length of the stadium clad only in helmets, shields, and leg armor. The festival concluded on the evening of the fifth day with the reading of the list of winners and the crowning of the champions with the garlands of wild olive.

Olympic victory was considered so glorious that in A.D. 67—more than two hundred years after Greece had became a Roman province—the Emperor Nero made special arrangements to compete in the Olympic Games, proclaiming himself winner in six events. Under the emperor's absurd orders, the festival included musical and poetic competitions—unheard of at Olympia—and a ten-horse chariot race in which Nero had himself declared the victor even after he had ridiculously fallen out of his chariot. These Games were later expunged from the Olympic record.

By A.D. 324, however, when Christianity became the state religion of the Roman Empire, the influence and integrity of the Olympic Games had seriously degenerated. Professional athletes performed at Olympia, and the Games, which had become rife with bribery, resembled more of a circus rather than a sacred festival. In A.D. 394, the Games were banned as a pagan rite by Emperor Theodosius I. The temples and altars were tumbled and the statues melted down. The next year, the Goths, led by Alaric, swept through Olympia, and its ruin was completed by devastating earthquakes in A.D. 522 and 551. Eventually, nearly all traces of the sanctuary were erased by the river Kladeus, which changed its course and buried Olympia under twenty feet of earth and rubble. It was more than fourteen hundred years before the German archaeologist Ernst Curtius began to clear away the debris and bring the lost ruins and spirit of Olympia to light.

## THE HALTERES

*Long jumpers at Olympia used stone or metal weights, called* halteres, *to extend their leaps. Jumpers swung the four- to nine-pound weights forward to shoulder height on takeoff and backwards, to the knees, on landing.*

Photos: Below © George Ortiz Collection, Yoram Lehmann, Jerusalem; Opposite, Archives, Olympic Museum Lausanne.

# THE GAMES OF SUMMER

After racing for hours over twenty-five miles of rugged ravines and twisting mountain paths, Spiridon Loues pounded exhaustedly into the white marble Panathenean Stadium in Athens. Alone, with the closest runner a full seven minutes behind him, he was suddenly swept up by the thunderous cheers of 140,000 spectators who packed

**FROM ATHENS TO ATLANTA**
the stadium to the rims, swarmed over the surrounding hills, and showered the field around him with hats and flowers.

On that April day a century ago, Loues—a twenty-five-year-old Greek shepherd—carried some of Olympia's ancient magic into the modern world. He was the first Olympic champion from Greece in nearly fifteen centuries—the winner of the first marathon in the very first of the modern Olympic Games, held in Athens in 1896. He had raced along the route taken in 490 B.C., according to legend, by the Olympian Pheidippides, who died after running from Marathon to Athens with news of Greek victory in battle. But Loues, flanked in his exultant last lap by two princes of Greece, claimed a victory rich in history for himself and for his country, the birthplace of the ancient Games.

Loues wasn't the first winner of those first modern Olympics. That place in history belongs to American James Connolly—an undergraduate who had dropped out of Harvard to compete, paid his own travel expenses to the Games, and captured the first Olympic title in the triple jump. But when Loues won the marathon for Greece on the fifth day and was crowned with a wreath of wild olive leaves from Olympia, it was a moment that profoundly fused past and present, 1,500 years of history,

*1992 BARCELONA*

**CARL LEWIS, USA**

*At the Los Angeles Summer Games in 1984, American track phenomenon Carl Lewis became the first Olympic athlete to duplicate Jesse Owens's golds in four events. Lewis earned two more golds in 1988 and two again in 1992.*

Photos: Above © Duomo, Steven E. Sutton; Below, Archives, Olympic Museum Lausanne; Opposite © Duomo, David Madison.

with the sweaty, cheering, raucous reality of modern life. The Olympics were reborn—and from that day on they belonged not just to the Greek world but to the whole world.

To be sure, the Athens Games were in many ways a rough revival of the Olympic spirit. Most of the world knew or cared little about these Games. Although 311 athletes from thirteen nations competed in nine sports, three-quarters of the competitors were Greek. America's patched-together team was made up largely of college students who had mistakenly arrived just a day before the Games began—forgetting that there was a twelve-day difference between the Greek and American calendars. Great Britain's squad included two employees from its embassy in Athens, as well as a tourist named John Boland, who signed up for the tennis tournaments and won.

Germany's athletes were strong contenders in gymnastics and clinched the wrestling title, while France's Paul Masson pedaled to victory in three cycling events. America's squad of athletic club recruits managed to thoroughly dominate the track and field events. In one distressing upset for the Greeks, Robert Garrett, a shot-putter from Princeton, outhurled a popular Greek champion in the discus throw, even though Garrett had never seen a discus before setting foot in Greece. U.S. swimmer Gardner Williams, however, didn't have quite as much success adapting to Greek sport. Olympic swimming races were held in the choppy Bay of Zea, where the waters had cooled to an icy 55 degrees Fahrenheit. Used to the warmer temperatures of indoor pools, Williams plunged in, announced he was "freezing," and quit the competition.

Overall, the first Olympic Games were a roaring success, and Greece lobbied hard to remain the exclusive host of all subsequent Games. But Baron Pierre de Coubertin opposed the idea and succeeded in moving the second Olympiad to Paris in 1900. The Paris plans, however, were a disaster from the beginning. That year, the French capital was also hosting the enormous Universal Exposition. The Olympic Games were tacked onto the event as an afterthought and were for the most part ill-organized,

**1896 ATHENS**

**SPIRIDON LOUES, GRE**

*In the first of the modern Olympic Games, Spiridon Loues, a twenty-five-year-old Greek shepherd from the village of Amaroussion, won the 25-mile marathon race with a seven-minute lead. He was joined in his victory lap around the stadium by the royal princes of Greece and was offered rewards of free food, lodging, shaves, and hats.*

Photos: Left and above, Archives, Olympic Museum Lausanne.

**1896 ATHENS**

**PANAGIOTIS PARASKEVOPOLOUS, GRE**

*The discus event in Athens was a major upset for the Greeks, whose champion, Panagiotis Paraskevopolous, was beaten by American Robert Garrett—a Princeton student who had never seen a discus before he arrived in Athens for the Games.*

Photo: Archives, Olympic Museum Lausanne.

unpromoted, and ignored. The word "Olympics" never even appeared in the official program, which billed the competition as an "International Championship." Fewer than a thousand spectators attended, and some competitors had no idea that they were participating in the Olympic Games. The athletic spectacle itself had all the glamour of a brewery picnic. Events were held over five months and were staged in various parts of the city, many of them much more suitable for Sunday strolls than for track and field events. Jumpers had to dig their own landing pits with the spikes of their shoes, and hammer and discus throwers ended up hurling shots into the trees.

Despite the innumerable problems, teams from twenty-two countries entered the Paris Games, with France sponsoring the largest contingent. Thirteen new sports were added, including golf, rowing, and water polo, and women were allowed to compete in Olympic events for the first time, though solely in lawn tennis and golf. Champions included U.S. standing-jump champion Ray Ewry— the "Rubber Man"—who collected three gold medals in Paris and went on to win another seven in 1904, 1906, and 1908. Ewry's gold-medal harvest in Paris was topped by U.S. track star Alvin Kraenzlein, who introduced the technique of hurdling with one leg extended and swept four individual golds in track and field events.

Although the Paris Olympics were an admitted flop, the next Olympiad did nothing to improve the fortunes or the image of the Games. The 1904 Olympics were originally destined for Chicago, but President Theodore Roosevelt urged that they be held in St. Louis,

1904 ST. LOUIS

**ETIENNE DESMARTEAU, CAN**

*Etienne Desmarteau, a Montreal policeman, was fired for leaving work to compete in the Olympics. He was welcomed back on the job, however, after he beat a New York City policeman to win the gold in the 56-pound weight throw.*

Photo: Archives, Olympic Museum Lausanne / NOC / CAN.

Missouri, in conjunction with the Louisiana Purchase Exhibition. Once again, the thunder of the Games was stolen by massive civic entertainment. The event was billed as "a fair where there are also sports." And this time, because the Olympics were located so far from Europe, only twelve nations took part. Even Coubertin declined to make the trip. The carnival-like atmosphere sank to grotesque lows during a two-day Olympic "Anthropological Days" demonstration, in which African

Pygmies, Patagonians, and Philippine Igorots and Moros were recruited from sideshows at the World's Fair to compete in mud fights, pole climbing, and other "native games."

Official Olympic sports had their troubles, too. At least partly because of their overwhelming numbers, American athletes grabbed 238 out of 284 Olympic medals. And a wretchedly organized marathon test- ed athletes' endurance beyond ordinary limits. The race was staged in scorching heat, and runners had to gasp and dodge their way through the constant, dust-kicking traffic of bicycles, horses, and automobiles that clung to them along the route. One competitor, a Zulu tribesman named Lentauw, was forced to take a sudden detour when two large dogs chased him through a cornfield. The race was ultimately won by a Boston brass worker named Thomas Hicks, who swallowed small doses of strychnine along the way to numb the pain of running and had to be revived by four doctors after crossing the finish line.

To recover from the dismal experiences of Paris and St. Louis, Coubertin sanctioned the first— and only—interim Olympic Games, held in Athens in April 1906. Greeks enthusiastically welcomed the Games back, even during an unofficial Olympic year, and managed the event with energetic efficiency. Spectators packed the Panathenean Stadium, and twenty countries competed, including the first official American Olympic team. Although the

1904 ST. LOUIS

### WOMEN'S BOXING

*Boxing debuted at the 1904 Olympic Games, and women's boxing was a demonstration sport.*

Photo: Archives, Olympic Museum
Lausanne / AIO Athens.

1904 ST. LOUIS

### THE "NATIVE GAMES"

*In a demeaning sideshow event called "Anthropological Days," Pygmies, Patagonians, Kaffirs, and other "savages" were called on by Olympic organizers in St. Louis to participate in "native" contests such as archery, pole climbing, and mud fights.*

Photos: Above and left, Archives, Olympic Museum Lausanne;
Below, Archives, Olympic Museum Lausanne / AIO Athens.

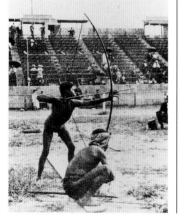

1904 ST. LOUIS

## RALPH ROSE, USA

*A 6-foot, 6-inch Californian, Ralph Rose won the shot put and took silver in the discus in 1904. He went on to win two more shot put golds in 1908 and 1912.*

Photo: Archives, Olympic Museum Lausanne.

1904 ST. LOUIS

## RAY EWRY, USA

*Ray Ewry spent his childhood partly paralyzed by polio and confined to a wheelchair. Determined to overcome his handicap, he exercised to strengthen his legs and amazingly won ten gold medals in Olympic jumping events from 1900 through 1908, including three-gold sweeps in both 1900 and 1904.*

Photo: Archives, Olympic Museum Lausanne.

1908 LONDON

**3,000-METER STEEPLECHASE**

*Runners splashed through a water jump in the chilly 1908 Olympic Games in London (opposite). The steeplechase event, which included seven water jumps and twenty-eight solid hurdles, was won by Arthur Russell of Great Britain.*

Photo: Archives, Olympic Museum Lausanne.

results of these interim Games are not counted in the Olympic record, they succeeded in reviving the flagging Olympic spirit and reassured organizers that the modern Games did, in fact, have a future.

Buoyed by success in Athens, the regular Olympic schedule picked up again in London in July 1908, after Rome declined to host the Games for financial reasons. Many modern Olympic traditions originated in this fourth Olympiad. For the first time, only nations, not individuals, were permitted to enter, and athletes representing twenty-three countries paraded behind their flags during the opening ceremonies. Beginning with the London Games, medals were awarded for third-place finishers, and women's participation was expanded to archery and gymnastics demonstrations.

Throughout the Games, however, the weather was miserably wet and cold, and there were fractious disputes among teams, including accusations of bad sportsmanship and chauvinism—particularly since all the judges were British. British spectators, by the same token, were aghast at the enthusiastic rooting of Americans, who cheered victory by tooting kazoos and singing "There'll be a Hot Time in the Old Town Tonight." In a legendary marathon incident that nearly strained international relations between America and Britain, the first runner to stagger into Shepherd's Bush Stadium, Dorando Pietri—a candymaker from Capri—collapsed on the track and was dragged over the finish line by overexcited English officials. After screams of unfair officiating, America's Johnny Hayes—the first to cross the tape under his own leg power—was finally awarded the gold medal. In another strange footnote to the marathon, Princess Mary requested that the race begin beneath the royal nursery windows at Windsor—a move that permanently lengthened the official international marathon distance from about twenty-five miles to twenty-six miles, 385 yards.

1912 STOCKHOLM

**PATRICK MCDONALD, USA**

*At 6-feet, 4-inches and 350 pounds, Pat McDonald made his presence felt at the 1912 Olympic Games, where he beat out Ralph Rose for a shot put gold. McDonald made his living as a New York City policeman, directing traffic in Times Square.*

Photo: Archives, Olympic Museum Lausanne.

Throughout the events, Great Britain captured the greatest number of medals, although the United States again dominated track and field. In the 110-meter hurdles, American Forrest Smithson shattered the world's record while, according to some accounts, clutching a Bible in his hand to protest the scheduling of the race on Sunday, and U.S. swimmer Charles Daniels earned his fourth individual Olympic gold in the 100-meter freestyle, adding to the three he had previously collected in 1904 and 1906.

After the poisonous squabbling and alleged jingoism of the London Games, many skeptics concluded that the Olympics did more to cause international strife than to encourage world peace. But the well-organized 1912 Olympics in Stockholm restored some of the luster to the Games. At Coubertin's urging, the number of sports was trimmed back from twenty-one to fourteen. Public address systems and electric timing systems were introduced, and there was high-profile press coverage of the athletic spectacle. Women competed in swimming, and the 100-meter freestyle was snared by Australia's Fanny Durack, who hauled through the water wearing a bulky woolen bathing suit. Boxing, however, was stricken from the program for the first and only time in Olympic history, since the sport was banned in Sweden.

1912 STOCKHOLM

**KENNETH MCARTHUR, SAF**

*Victorious Kenneth McArthur, a thirty-year-old South African policeman, was carried off the field by his proud countrymen after winning the marathon, held in brutally hot weather. Francisco Lazaro, a Portuguese runner, collapsed during the race and died in the hospital the next day.*

Photos: Below and right Archives, Olympic Museum Lausanne.

The most impressive marathons took place not on the road but in the wrestling arena. The final bout of the light-heavyweight event went on for a grueling nine hours, and Finnish and Russian middleweights grappled for nearly twelve hours under a brutal sun. In men's swimming events, America's Duke Kahanamoku—who introduced the flutter kick and Hawaiian crawl in international competition—sprinted to a gold medal in the 100-meter freestyle race. George Patton, future World War II general—then a lieutenant at West Point—ranked fifth in a new event, the modern pentathlon. And there were astonishing performances in track and field. Hannes Kolehmainen, a vegetarian bricklayer, became the first of the famous "Flying Finns" when he flashed to gold medals in three cross-country races.

### 1912 STOCKHOLM

## JIM THORPE. USA

*One of the greatest Olympians of all time was the astonishing Jim Thorpe. Part Irish, part French, and part Native American, Thorpe easily swept gold medals in the grueling pentathlon and decathlon events. Sweden's King Gustav V declared him "the greatest athlete in the world." Six months later, however, a newspaper reported that Thorpe had accepted $25 a week for playing minor-league baseball, and he was stripped of all his Olympic medals. His record was not reinstated until 1982, nearly thirty years after his death.*

Photo: Archives, Olympic Museum Lausanne.

### 1924 PARIS

## ERIC LIDDELL. GBR

*Celebrated in the movie Chariots of Fire, Eric Liddell was a Scottish divinity student who flashed past his rivals to take gold in the 400 meters. "I do not like to be beaten," he was often heard to say.*

Photo: Archives, Olympic Museum Lausanne.

### 1912 STOCKHOLM

## JOHAN "HANNES" KOLEHMAINEN. FIN

*When "Hannes the Mighty" Kolehmainen raced to victory in Stockholm in the 5,000-, 8,000-, and 10,000-meter races, Finland pulled ahead of the pack as a world power in distance running. Kolehmainen went on to triumph in the marathon in the 1920 games.*

Photo: Archives, Olympic Museum Lausanne.

But dwarfing all other competitors was U.S. collegiate track and football star Jim Thorpe. Part Sac and Fox Indian, Thorpe—whose tribal name was Wa-Tho-Huck or Bright Path— had never thrown a javelin until two months before the Games. But he easily mastered both the decathlon and pentathlon in an unmatched display of all-around athletic prowess. Sweden's King Gustav V declared the Oklahoman "the greatest athlete in the world." Six months later, however, a Boston newspaper reported that Thorpe had been paid $25 a week for playing minor-league base- ball in Rocky Mount, North Carolina, and Thorpe was heartbreakingly stripped of all his medals. It wasn't until 1982—nearly thirty years after his death—that Thorpe's record was officially reinstated by the International Olympic Committe (IOC).

The cataclysmic upheaval of World War I postponed the next Olympic Games until 1920, when they were held in the war-ravaged city of Antwerp, Belgium. Despite persistent rain, the economic toll of war, and the exclusion of Germany, Austria, Hungary, Bulgaria, and Turkey, the Antwerp Games managed to revive the Olympics after a savage eight-year interruption. This time America's domination of track and field was challenged by the fleet-footed Finns. But French military veteran Joseph Guillemot—who had been badly gassed in combat during World War I—edged past Paavo Nurmi, Finland's "mechanical Frankenstein," in the 5,000-meter run. Another war veteran, Great Britain's Albert Hill, scored golds in the 800- and 1,500-meter races, while the silver in the 1,500 was clinched by teammate Philip Baker, who went on to receive the Nobel Peace Prize in 1959. In the pool, Duke Kahanamoku splashed to a second freestyle gold, and Ethelda Bleibtry, who had suffered from childhood polio, swam to two individual gold medals in world-record times.

Paris was given a second chance to host the Olympics in 1924. Eager to repair their city's Olympic image, the French hosts took pains to prepare carefully for the event. Again, Germany was encouraged to stay home, but athletes from forty-four other nations converged on the French capital, and more than 600,000 spectators jammed the Games. The home- town team took honors in cycling and fencing, and Great Britain's Eric Liddell and Harold Abrahams—later mythologized in the movie *Chariots of Fire*—paced to golds in the 400- and 100-meter races. In his second Olympic appearance, the "Flying Finn," Paavo Nurmi—who had drilled

1924 PARIS

JOHNNY WEISSMULLER, USA

*Born in Romania, Johnny Weissmuller was four when his family emigrated to the U.S. At age twenty, he swam off with three gold medals in the 1924 Olympics and took two more Olympic pool titles in 1928. Weissmuller's greatest fame came after 1932, when he starred in* Tarzan the Ape Man, *the first of his eighteen* Tarzan *movie roles.*

Photo: Archives, Olympic Museum Lausanne.

himself by outracing the mail train at home in Turku, Finland—stunned spectators by taking five gold medals in track and field events, even though he had injured his legs during training. In brutally hot weather, Nurmi trotted coolly over stony, thistle-choked paths to the finish in the 10,000-meter cross-country, while twenty-four of his thirty-eight rivals collapsed in exhaustion along the route. U.S. sharpshooter Carl Osburn raised his Olympic medal total to eleven, including five golds. A member of the winning U.S. rowing team was a 6-foot, 4-inch Ivy League sculler named Benjamin Spock, and Tarzan-to-be Johnny Weissmuller, winner of sixty-seven world records, streaked to three golds in freestyle swimming.

Germany finally rejoined the Olympic Games in Amsterdam in 1928, where, for the first time, the Olympic flame burned throughout the competitions. Nurmi and Weissmuller each added another gold to their collections, but the Games were generally disappointing for the U.S., whose historic preeminence in track and field continued to decline. India, on the other hand, began its brilliant domination of field hockey, which lasted until 1960. And Uruguay scored its second gold in soccer, an immensely popular event mobbed by more than 200,000 fans. It was a landmark Olympics for women, too, who for the first time were allowed to compete in gymnastics and five track and field events. In swimming, Germany's Hilde Schrader breaststroked so quickly past her rivals on her way to gold and a new world record that she ripped the straps of her bathing suit in the process. "I would have gone even faster," she confided, "if I had not been so embarrassed."

1928 AMSTERDAM

## PERCY WILLIAMS, CAN

*A former waiter from Vancouver, Percy Williams, 20, took home golds for Canada in both the 100- and 200-meter sprints. "That boy doesn't run—he flies," declared U.S. competitor Charley Paddock.*

Photo: Archives, Olympic Museum Lausanne.

1928 AMSTERDAM

## PAAVO NURMI, FIN

*"Flying Finn" Paavo Nurmi captured the 10,000-meter gold in 1928 by six-tenths of a second—bringing his Olympic gold medal total to nine. The nearly invincible Nurmi had raced off with three golds in the 1920 Games and scored five more in 1924 in Paris.*

Photo: Archives, Olympic Museum Lausanne.

### JUAN CARLOS ZABALA, ARG

*Twenty-year-old Juan Carlos Zabala of Argentina collapsed after crossing the finish line first in the 1932 Olympic marathon. He had a 19-second lead over his nearest competitor, Sam Ferris of Great Britain.*

Photo: Archives, Olympic Museum Lausanne /
International News Photos.

### JAPANESE SWIM TEAM

*Seizing the spotlight in Los Angeles was an astonishingly young team of Japanese swimmers, who captured four pool titles. The 100-meter freestyle winner, Yasuji Miyazaki, was just seventeen years old. Teammate Masaji Kiyokawa, who nailed the 100-meter backstroke, was sixteen, and Kusuo Kitamura, the 1,500-meter freestyle champ, was only fourteen years of age.*

Photo: Archives, Olympic Museum Lausanne.

Just three years after the New York stock market crash, in the midst of global economic depression, Los Angeles successfully secured the 1932 Olympic Games. The city had overcome the less-than-happy legacy of the previous American Olympics in St. Louis by promising bountiful financial and organizational resources. Because of the expense of traveling to Los Angeles from Europe, however, only thirty-seven nations participated, compared to forty-six in Amsterdam. But crowds were enormous, the weather was warm, and local authorities even winked at Prohibition laws by allowing French athletes to bring in their own wine.

The hands-down queen of the Los Angeles Olympic Games was Mildred "Babe" Didrikson, who personally embodied the Olympic motto "Faster, Higher, Stronger" by sweeping gold medals in both hurdles and the javelin and scoring silver in the high jump. Under special Olympic rules for women, these were the only three events she was permitted to enter, even though she had qualified for five. Didrickson—who apparently earned her nickname because she could slug a baseball like Babe Ruth—later launched a phenomenally successful career as a professional golfer, winning the world championship four times under her married name, Babe Zaharias. Another superwoman, Ohio resident Stella Walsh, competed for her native country of Poland and ran off with the gold in the 100-meter race. Walsh stunned the public again, forty-eight years later, when an autopsy revealed that she was, in actuality, a man.

The International Amateur Athletic Foundation barred Finland's phenomenal Nurmi from the Los Angeles Games, accusing him of professionalism. But there was no lack of excitement when Swedish strongmen muscled six gold medals in wrestling, and Japanese swimmers made a splash by sweeping up four individual golds. Italy brought home two gold medals in cycling—including one claimed by Attilio Pavesi, who kept himself fueled on the individual road race, according to one report, by wearing a bib packed with spaghetti, sweet rolls, bananas, and cheese sandwiches.

Standing firm against a firestorm of controversy and the threat by many countries to boycott the event, the IOC insisted on holding the 1936 Games in Berlin

1932 LOS ANGELES

## BABE DIDRIKSON, USA

*Mildred "Babe" Didrikson took gold medals in the hurdles and the javelin and a silver in the high jump—the only three events she was permitted to enter under special rules for women. Asked by a reporter if there was anything she didn't play, Didrikson responded dryly, "Yeah. Dolls."*

Photo: Archives, Olympic Museum Lausanne.

1932 LOS ANGELES

## LOS ANGELES COLISEUM

*In the middle of the Great Depression, the Los Angeles Olympics opened glamorously under sunny July skies in the specially refurbished Coliseum. Four thousand doves were released, and nearly 100,000 people attended the majestic opening ceremonies. "It was like a fantasyland," remembered Evelyne Hall, a hurdler from Chicago. "Nobody thought about their problems."*

Photo: Archives, Olympic Museum Lausanne.

under the ominous aegis of Hitler's Nazi Party. For the Nazi organizers, these Games became a virtual festival of propaganda—spectacular in presentation and chilling in their political overtones. The *Hindenburg* airship hovered over the massive new stadium, which had seating for 110,000 people, as athletes marched to music composed by Richard Strauss and the throng sang "Deutschland über alles." Reichsführer Adolf Hitler, dressed in a brown uniform, conspicuously attended nearly every event, and anti-Semitic signs that had been displayed around the city were temporarily removed during the Games—convincing credulous Olympic officials that their decision to trust Nazi goodwill had been correct. Taking a thoroughly rose-colored view of the monumental political event, Avery Brundage, then president of the American Olympic Committee, proclaimed, "No nation since ancient Greece has captured the true Olympic spirit as has Germany."

It was the athletes, through the sheer power of their physical performance, who subverted the Nazis' desire to present the Games as a symbol of Aryan supremacy. The ten African American stars of the U.S. track and field team—considered subhuman by Nazi organizers—outscored all their competitors. And more than any other athlete, Jesse Owens, the black American track phenomenon, dominated the Berlin Olympics. Owens, the grandson of slaves, seized four gold medals and set records in the 200-meter dash, broad jump, and 400-meter relay. In another blow to Nazi racial theories, Germany's only Jewish competitor, fencer Helène Mayer—who had been promised complete "Aryan" status if she returned from the U.S. to compete for Germany—was beaten to the gold by another Jewish swordswoman, Hungary's Ilona Elek.

Following behind the once-again dominant Americans in track and field were the Finns, who swept the 5,000 and 10,000 meters and the steeplechase. New Zealand's Jack Lovelock set a new world record in the 1,500-meter run, while

---

**1936 BERLIN**

**JESSE OWENS, USA**

*The son of an Alabama cotton picker, Jesse Owens, 22, infuriated the Nazi organizers of the 1936 Berlin Games with his superb track and field performance. Flying in the face of Nazi claims that blacks were inferior to Aryan supermen, Owens outshone every other athlete at the Games, winning four gold medals in ten days in the 100 meters, 200 meters, broad jump, and 400-meter relay.*

Photos: Archives, Olympic Museum Lausanne.

---

**1936 BERLIN**

**THE BERLIN OLYMPICS**

*In the first torch ceremony of the Olympic Games, a runner triumphantly carried the Olympic flame into the center of Berlin to light the brazier in the Reichssportfeld during the 1936 Opening Ceremonies. The lavish spectacle, attended by Hitler, Göring, and Goebbels, featured music by Richard Strauss, the release of 20,000 doves, and the hovering presence of the airship* Hindenburg, *which suspended the Olympic flag over the massive stadium.*

Photo: Archives, Olympic Museum Lausanne.

**FANNY BLANKERS-KOEN, HOL**

*Holland's "Magnificent Mama"*
*Fanny Blankers-Koen flashed*
*through track and field events in*
*London's postwar "austerity*
*Olympics." Blankers-Koen, thirty*
*years old and the mother of two,*
*bolted to four gold medals in the*
*100 meters, the 80-meter*
*hurdles, the 200 meters, and the*
*400-meter relay.*

Photo: Archives, Olympic Museum Lausanne / O.P.A.

France's Robert Charpentier dominated cycling, winning three gold medals. The Dutch eclipsed other competitors in women's swimming events, but the springboard diving gold was won by a thirteen-year-old child wonder, America's Marjorie Gestring.

World War II obliterated any chance of holding Olympic Games as originally planned in Tokyo in 1940 or London in 1944. In 1948, however, despite endless rain, food rationing, housing shortages, and the damage wreaked by Hitler's bombs, London managed to stage a postwar "austerity Olympics." For the first time, athletes from communist countries were included in the list of fifty-nine participating nations.

The wonder woman at the London Games was Holland's "Magnificent Mama," Francina "Fanny" Blankers-Koen. The thirty-year-old mother of two dashed to four golds on the soggy track in the 100- and 200-meter races, the 80-meter hurdles, and the 400-meter team relay. Seventeen-year-old American decathlete Bob Mathias, a future congressman, became the youngest male athlete to win an individual gold medal—despite the fact that he had never even attempted two of his events, the javelin and pole vault, until four months before the Games.

Finland, a country with a tradition of legendary athletes, hosted its first Olympic Games in 1952 in its capital, Helsinki. Allied fighter bombers were pounding communist forces in Korea in a hot war, and Cold War politics added treacherous new rivalries to the Games. After an absence of forty years, Russian athletes under the flag of the Soviet Union took part for the first time, but they and other Eastern Bloc competitors kept to themselves in a separate Olympic village, surrounded by barbed wire and draped with mammoth images of Stalin. Adding to nationalist tensions, Taiwan boycotted the Games because mainland Chinese athletes were competing.

For athletes and spectators, however, the Games had rich moments. In his second Olympics, the teeth-gnashing, arm-waving Czech Army captain Emil Zatopek—nicknamed "the Beast of Prague"—zoomed past rivals to win three golds in the 5,000 and 10,000 meters and the marathon. "He runs," an observer said, "like a man who has just been stabbed in the heart." Zatopek, who spoke five languages, was known for

**BOB MATHIAS, USA**

*Only seventeen years old, Bob*
*Mathias clinched the 1948*
*Olympic decathlon—despite*
*the fact that, until a few*
*months before the Games, he*
*had never thrown a javelin,*
*pole vaulted, or run a 1,500-*
*meter race, and he had hardly*
*ever broad jumped or raced*
*400 meters. He took the*
*Olympic decathlon title*
*again in 1952.*

Photo: Archives, Olympic Museum
Lausanne / Olympia-Kuva.

## 1952 HELSINKI

### EMIL ZATOPEK, CZE

*Emil Zatopek (below), "the Beast of Prague," left rivals in the dust, streaking to gold medals in the 5,000 meters, the 10,000 meters, and the marathon. Zatopek, a captain in the Czech Army, was known for his grimacing, grunting racing style. "He runs," an observer said, "like a man who has just been stabbed in the heart."*

Photo: Archives, Olympic Museum Lausanne.

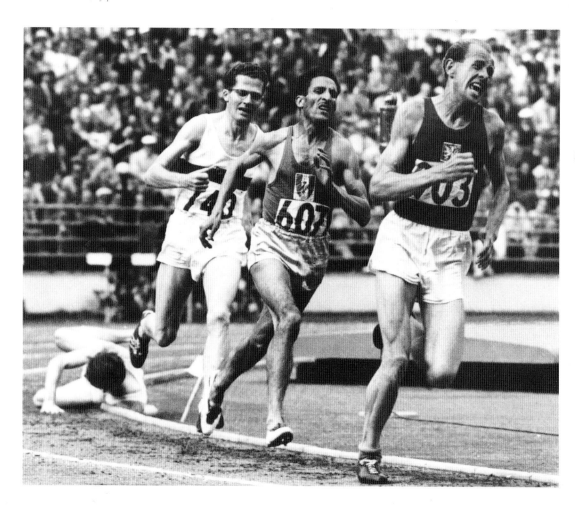

1952 HELSINKI

**A. FERREIRA DA SILVA, BRA**

*In Helsinki, Adhemar Ferreira da Silva (opposite)—a Brazilian world-record-holding leaper who spoke seven languages fluently— scored a gold medal and new world record in the triple jump. In six jumps during the event, da Silva smashed his own world record four times. He repeated his win in 1956.*

Photo: Archives, Olympic Museum Lausanne / Olympia-Kuva.

running ten to twenty-five miles a day, frequently in bulky army boots. Minutes after he won the 5,000, his wife, Dana, scored the gold in the javelin. Another unforgettable family moment occurred when, overcome by emotion, the father of a French freestyle winner leaped into the pool completely clothed, still wearing his beret.

Australia's Marjorie Jackson bolted to world records in the 100 and 200 meters, and Bob Mathias owned the decathlon for a second consecutive time. In the shooting events, Hungary's resourceful Károly Takács bagged his second gold in the rapid-fire pistol. The formerly right-handed marksman had lost his pistol hand in 1938 in a grenade accident; he scored his two Olympic golds after teaching himself to fire with his left.

In 1956, when the Games were held in Melbourne, Australia, more than a shift in seasons threw Olympic plans off-kilter. The wet-weather Games were held in November and December to coincide with summer in the Southern Hemisphere, and because of Australia's strict animal quarantine laws, the equestrian events had to be held in Stockholm. More calamitous, however, were the escalating military conflicts around the world. Brutal shooting wars, including the Suez crisis and the Soviet invasion of Hungary, eroded most semblance of international goodwill and led to a bitter Olympic boycott by Spain, Switzerland, the Netherlands, Egypt, Iraq, and Lebanon. And this time the communist Chinese refused to compete when nationalist China was invited.

1956 MELBOURNE

**HAMIT KAPLAN, TUR**

*Super heavyweight Hamit Kaplan of Anatolia muscled a gold medal in freestyle wrestling at the Melbourne Games, breaking Russia's winning streak. Kaplan went on to take a silver in 1960 and a bronze in 1964.*

Photo: Archives, Olympic Museum Lausanne.

Political snarling spilled over into a vicious water polo semifinal between the Soviet Union and Hungary, which turned into a bloody "boxing match under water." For at least one couple, however, love conquered Cold War jitters. Soon after the Games, American Harold Connolly, Melbourne's gold-medalist in the hammer throw, wed the Czech Olympic women's discus champion, Olga Fikotova, with Emil Zatopek standing by as best man.

Australia's powerful swimmers stormed the pool in Melbourne, racking up eight golds. On the track, sprinters Betty Cuthbert from Australia and Bobby Joe Morrow from the U.S. each picked up three gold medals, and Ukrainian Vladimir

1960 ROME

### ABEBE BIKILA, ETH

*A member of Emperor Haile Selassie's Palace Guard, Abebe Bikila of Ethiopia first raced barefoot for twenty-six miles, 385 yards to victory in the Olympic marathon in Rome. He repeated his performance— with shoes on—in Tokyo in 1964 (below).*

Photo: Archives, Olympic Museum Lausanne.

1960 ROME

### WILMA RUDOLPH, USA

*The nineteen-year-old sprinter Wilma Rudolph overcame enormous odds just to reach the 1960 Olympic Games in Rome. Due to polio and other crippling diseases, Rudolph could not walk without a leg brace until she was eleven. Despite these overwhelming challenges, Rudolph effortlessly captured gold medals in three events in Rome, including the prestigious 100-meter dash.*

Photo: Archives, Olympic Museum Lausanne.

1960 ROME

### RAFER JOHNSON, USA

*In the decathlon in the 1960 Games, Rafer Johnson waged a titanic battle in the ten events against his rival and former UCLA teammate, Yang Chuan-Kwang, who was competing for Taiwan. Johnson took home the gold and the title as the best overall athlete in the world.*

Photo: Archives, Olympic Museum Lausanne.

Kuts flashed to the USSR's first two titles in men's track and field events. America's legendary discus star Al Oerter threw for his first of four consecutive wins, Soviet gymnast Larisa Latynina snatched four titles, and USSR wrestlers took five Greco-Roman golds.

After the political powder keg of Melbourne, the Olympics moved relatively peacefully to Rome in 1960. Television cameras beamed the competitions around the world, and Olympic performances peaked. Like the racers of ancient Greece, Ethiopia's Abebe Bikila sprinted barefoot down the Appian Way to the finish line in the torch-lit moonlight marathon, capturing the gold in record time. Bikila, one of Emperor Haile Selassie's palace guards, was unwilted by the twenty-six-mile slog: "I could have gone around the course again without any difficulty," he declared.

In their second Olympic appearance, Soviet athletes came on strong. Boris Shakhlin took four golds in the gymnastic events, and the Soviet women's massive sweep of track and field golds, led by sisters Tamara and Irina Press, was only stopped by American racing legend Wilma Rudolph. One of twenty-two children in her family, the amazing Rudolph—known as "Skeeter" to her friends—had suffered from a crippling string of childhood ailments, including malnutrition, polio, double pneumonia, and scarlet fever, and wore a leg brace from the age of six. But Rudolph kicked off her orthopedic shoes at age eleven, and after training and competing relentlessly in high school and college, she exploded on the track at Rome, claiming triple golds in the 100- and 200-meter sprints and the 400-meter relay. But the athlete who attracted the most attention at the Games was a charismatic eighteen-year-old boxer named Cassius Marcellus Clay, who later changed his name to Muhammad Ali. After the light heavyweight slugged his way to the championship title, he wore his beloved Olympic medal so much that the gold finish started wearing off.

In an exhausting battle of near-equals, America's Rafer Johnson edged to decathlon gold over his UCLA teammate, Yang Chuan-Kwang, who was competing for Taiwan. And in one of the first signs of emerging Olympic dope scandals, Danish cyclist Knut Jensen died of a drug overdose after a grueling 100-kilometer road race.

In 1964, the Olympic Games traveled to Tokyo, the first Asian city to host the Games. Largely recovered from the devastation of World War II, the city managed the event with skill and precision despite continuing

### 1960 ROME

**CASSIUS CLAY, USA**

*At age eighteen, boxer Cassius Marcellus Clay—who later changed his name to Muhammad Ali—charmed his fellow athletes in Rome and pummeled Poland's Zbigniew Pietrzykowski to claim the light heavyweight Olympic gold. Clay wore his prized gold medal so frequently that the gold finish started wearing off.*

Photos: Above, Archives, Olympic Museum Lausanne; Below © Allsport / Archives, Olympic Museum Lausanne.

political storms. South Africa was excluded from the Games because of its apartheid policies, Indonesia was barred for having hosted the unsanctioned Games of the New Emergent Forces in 1962, and North Korea withdrew its team in protest. But, once again, the heroics of the athletes claimed center stage. U.S. boxer Joe Frazier battled his German opponent Hans Huber with a broken right hand to take heavyweight gold. Abebe Bikila, this time wearing shoes, swept his second marathon title—only forty days after he'd had an appendectomy. Australia's swimming sensation Dawn Fraser seized her third consecutive gold in the 100-meter freestyle, despite neck injuries she had suffered in a serious car crash. And incredibly, Al Oerter, in terrible pain from torn cartilage in his ribs, a slipped cervical disk, and internal hemorrhaging, braced himself with bandages to hurl the discus for a third gold medal.

Controversy clung to the Mexico City Games in 1968, the first Olympics to be staged in Latin America. Many athletes worried about the high altitude of the city—7,573 feet above sea level—and in fact there were cases of severe exhaustion among Olympians who had trained for endurance events near sea level. Others fretted about drug tests that were administered for the first time. Despite the balloons and cheerful mariachi bands celebrating Mexico's "Peace Olympics," serious political problems again shadowed the Games. The Soviets had invaded Czechoslovakia two months earlier. Ten days before the Games, massive student riots at the University of Mexico had been brutally suppressed by government troops, resulting in hundreds of deaths and injuries. And two American track medalists—Tommie Smith and John Carlos—were suspended after stepping shoeless onto the medal stand, as a symbol of black poverty in the U.S., and raising black-gloved fists in a black power salute when the American anthem was played.

But for many, the most astounding moments of the Games took place in competition. American long jumper Bob Beamon left spectators speechless when he flew an incredible 29 feet, 2 1/2 inches—outdistancing the world record by nearly two feet and setting a new record that remained unbroken for twenty-three years. Beamon's gold-winning teammate Dick Fosbury also took track and field performance to new levels with his groundbreaking running high-jump technique, the

**1968 MEXICO CITY**

**BOB BEAMON, USA**

*In the high-altitude Mexico City Games, Bob Beamon, a twenty-two-year-old long jumper from New York City, soared nearly two feet past the world record. His leap of 29-feet, 2 1/2-inches set a staggering new record that remained unbroken for twenty-three years.*

*Photos: Above © Allsport; Right, Archives, Olympic Museum Lausanne.*

## 1972 MUNICH

### OLGA KORBUT, SOV

*Tiny, 85-pound Olga Korbut finished seventh in Munich in the women's all-around gymnastics competition. But she stole spectators' hearts, won golds in the floor exercises and the balance beam—on which she introduced the back flip—and set a new, diminutive size standard in women's gymnastics.*

Photo: Archives, Olympic Museum Lausanne.

## 1972 MUNICH

### VASSILY ALEXEYEV, SOV

*Super-strongman Vassily Alexeyev—a 337-pound mining engineer who was seen breakfasting on a steak and twenty-six fried eggs—snatched Olympic gold with feats that included heaving a 562-pound barbell. Alexeyev, who set eighty world records from 1970 to 1977, repeated his Olympic win in 1976.*

Photo: Archives, Olympic Museum Lausanne.

backward "Fosbury Flop." Meanwhile, U.S. boxer George Foreman took the super heavyweight championship, Czech gymnast Vera Cáslavská swept four golds, and discus star Al Oerter slipped and tore a thigh muscle on the rain-soaked field, and then hurled his way to a fourth consecutive Olympic title. In his first Olympic appearance, eighteen-year-old Mark Spitz won two relay golds. And Kenya's Kipchoge Keino, a Nandi tribesman who raced in Mexico City with a raging gall bladder infection, blasted across the tape in the 1,500-meter race—after first jogging a mile to the stadium to escape a traffic jam.

Political turmoil took a hideous turn four years later, when a terrorist massacre bloodily eclipsed the 1972 Olympic Games in Munich. On September 5, with a worldwide audience of a billion people focused on the Games, eight Palestinian guerrillas from the Black September group invaded the quarters of the Israeli team in the Olympic village, murdering two Israelis immediately and taking nine others hostage. The terrorists made their way to the airport, where all the Israeli captives and three of the terrorists were killed during a failed rescue attempt; the other Palestinians were captured.

### 1972 MUNICH

### MARK SPITZ, USA

*Mark Spitz splashed to Olympic history and worldwide celebrity in 1972, when he captured an incredible seven gold medals—the most that had ever been won by any athlete in a single Olympics. Spitz's phenomenal performance in Munich brought his gold medal collection to nine, including the two golds he won in the Mexico City Games.*

Photo: Below © Duomo; Right, Archives, Olympic Museum Lausanne.

To many, it seemed impossible that the Olympics could go on, that the gaze of the world could turn from the bloody murder of the athletes to the entertaining spectacle of sport. But the Games did go on, with the consent of the Israelis, the very next day, after a morning memorial service attended by 80,000 people in Munich's main stadium. *New York Times* sportswriter Red Smith reflected the anguished sentiments of many when he commented that Olympic organizers had "ruled that a little blood must not be allowed to interrupt play."

The Munich Games were forever scarred in the world's memory, however, despite the determination of the West Germans to stage a cheerful, relaxed gala and the superb performances of Olympic athletes. In the first week of the Games, Mark Spitz set seven world records and swept seven Olympic golds—the most ever won by an individual in a single Games. Fifteen-year-old Shane Gould grabbed three glittering swimming golds for Australia. And Soviet sprite Olga Korbut—4-feet, 11-inches and 85 pounds—stole the gymnastics show, scoring gold in two events and shifting the sport's spotlight from balletic women to daring, agile waifs. Aleksandr Medved, the 231-pound Minsk muscleman, held his own

1976 MONTREAL

**NADIA COMANECI, ROM**

*With peerless grace and
courage, Romanian gymnast
Nadia Comaneci, 14,
captivated spectators and
judges in the Montreal
Olympics—scoring
an unheard-of seven perfect
10s, three golds, a silver,
and a bronze.*

Photo: © Duomo, Steven E. Sutton.

against 412-pound opponent, America's Chris Taylor, to take his third consecutive

**"SUGAR" RAY LEONARD, USA**

*Named after the celebrated singer Ray Charles, Maryland-born "Sugar" Ray Leonard rose to stardom himself after he outpunched Cuba's Andrés Aldama for the light welterweight gold in Montreal.*

Photo: © Duomo.

freestyle wrestling gold. Kip Keino added a gold in the 3,000-meter steeplechase. And the Soviet basketball team elbowed aside the Americans to win the Olympic title 51–50, ending America's thirty-six-year winning streak.

Four years later, with the help of $100 million worth of security forces, the physical safety of the athletes was ensured at the 1976 Olympic Games in Montreal. These were, however, the most expensive Olympics ever held, and among the most contentious. The Taiwanese boycotted because Canada would not recognize their country as the Republic of China. And immediately before the Games, twenty nations, mainly from Africa, withdrew from competition, refusing to share the Olympic stage with New Zealand because its rugby team had toured South Africa.

But once again, athletic performances were brilliant. Although Czech cyclists suffered a setback when their wheels and spare tires were mistakenly collected as garbage and crushed in a compactor, team champion Anton Tkac went on to pedal to the gold in the 100-meter sprint. The West Germans—who had filled their tires with helium—flew past rivals to capture the 4000-meter team pursuit title. American boxers—including "Sugar" Ray Leonard and the Spinks brothers, Michael and Leon—outpounded the competition. Bruce Jenner blasted through ten events to claim the decathlon title, Edwin Moses surged to the gold in the 400-meter hurdles, and Cuba's "El Caballo," Alberto Juantorena, swept the 400- and 800-meter dashes. The U.S. took back the basketball title, while East Germany's Kornelia Ender and America's John Naber each lapped up four swimming golds.

**COE, WELLS, AND OVETT, GBR**

*Great Britain stormed to triple golds in track and field at the 1980 Games. Allan Wells, a Scottish marine engineer, was the first runner from Great Britain to win the 100 meters since Harold Abrahams dashed to the title in 1924. And arch racing rivals Steven Ovett and Sebastian Coe each took home a gold—Ovett in the 800 meters and Coe in the 1,500 meters. Coe repeated his 1,500-meter win in 1984.*

Photo: © Duomo.

With fearless, flawless grace, fourteen-year-old Romanian gymnast Nadia Comaneci performed the never-before-imagined, winning seven scores of perfect 10s and three Olympic golds. In another astonishing display, Japanese gymnast Shun Fujimoto heroically ignored his fractured right leg, encased in a hip-to-ankle cast, and helped his team score a gold in the combined exercises after flying off the rings in a triple somersault and landing, bravely, in excruciating pain. The Soviet Union's Nikolai Andrianov gathered up the most medals of the Games, including four gymnastics golds.

Since its reentry into competition in 1952, the USSR had emerged as an immense Olympic power, and it planned to celebrate its place in Olympic history by hosting spectacular Games in Moscow in 1980. Although eighty-one countries participated in what turned out to be an orderly, high-security event, the United States and dozens of other non-communist nations—including Japan and the Federal Republic of Germany—shunned the Games to protest the USSR's invasion of Afghanistan in December 1979. With about half the expected athletes competing, the Moscow Games turned into a virtual tug-of-war between the Eastern Bloc powerhouses—the USSR and East Germany—which together took 50 percent of all the medals.

East German swimmers—led by freestyler Barbara Krause, a state police official—churned through the pool to claim twenty-six medals, and the USSR's Aleksandr Ditiatin—the only male Olympic gymnast to score a perfect 10—surpassed Mark Spitz's bounty by collecting eight gymnastics medals, including three golds. Nadia Comaneci, however—no longer an urchin at eighteen—tumbled off the parallel bars and her gymnastics throne, surpassed by 70-pound Soviet star Yelena Davydova. Cuba's Teofilo Stevenson took his third consecutive boxing title. And Great Britain raised its Olympic profile when Sebastian Coe stormed first to the finish in the 1,500 meters, Steve Ovett claimed gold in the 800-meter race, Allan Wells won the first 100-meter dash for Great Britain since 1924, and Daley Thompson scored gold in the decathlon.

### 1980 MOSCOW

### ALEKSANDR DITIATIN, SOV

*When he captured three golds, four silvers, and a bronze in 1980, Soviet gymnast Aleksandr Ditiatin made history for the home team, winning the most medals of any athlete in a single Olympics.*

Photo: ©Allsport, Tony Duffy.

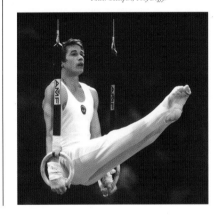

At the next Olympiad, the Soviets, along with sixteen of their allied nations, turned the tables on the U.S. by boycotting the 1984 Games in Los Angeles. Libya also dropped out of competition after two Libyan journalists were barred from entering the United States. But athletes from 140 other nations competed in a pageant marked by high Hollywood production values, copious commercial sponsorship, and a touch of scandal when eleven Olympic athletes flunked their drug tests.

The first gold medal of the Games went to communist China's pistol champion—a fertilizer salesman and slingshot whiz named Xu Haifeng. America's Joan Benoit paced easily to a win in the first Olympic women's marathon. And there was melodrama in the women's 3,000-meter race, when U.S. favorite Mary Decker and Great Britain's barefoot front-runner Zola Budd collided painfully on the track, allowing Romania's Maricica Puica to breeze by them to the gold. Italy's crack cycling team sped past rivals on aerodynamic, spokeless disk wheels to win the road race in record time, even after stopping to change a wheel. U.S. track phenomenon Carl Lewis matched Jesse Owens's four-gold sweep and screeched to the finish line in the 100 meters a full eight feet ahead of his nearest rival. U.S. hurdler Edwin Moses nailed his second Olympic gold, and Portugal's Carlos Lopes left marathon rivals in the dust, easily clinching the gold medal despite the fact that he had been struck by a car while training only fifteen days before.

Gymnast Mary Lou Retton, under 4-feet, 9-inches tall, turned in a towering performance. Retton captured the coveted all-around gymnastics crown, squeaking by Romania's balletic Ecaterina Szabo, who had taken three gold medals. Peerless diver Greg Louganis soared past his competitors for gold in both the platform and springboard competitions. American cyclists, who had come home empty-handed from the Games since 1912, zoomed to four golds. U.S. biking champs included Connie Carpenter-Phinney, winner of the first Olympic women's road race, who had competed as a speed skater in Sapporo. And super heavyweight Jeff Blatnick struggled back from cancer surgery to win the first U.S. gold in Greco-Roman wrestling.

---

### 1984 LOS ANGELES

**LI NING, CHN**

*Powerful Li Ning, 21, led China's high-flying gymnastics team in 1984. Li, who as a child practiced handsprings all the way to school, struck gold in the pommel horse, rings, and floor exercise events. "I didn't come all this way," Li said, "to fail."*

Photo: © Duomo, Steven E. Sutton.

---

### 1984 LOS ANGELES

**MARY DECKER AND ZOLA BUDD**

*Just after Great Britain's favorite, Zola Budd, passed America's Mary Decker in the 3,000 meters in Los Angeles, the two accidentally collided, sending Decker sprawling across the track with a pulled hip muscle and dashed Olympic hopes. Although Budd stayed on her bare feet, she was beaten to the finish line by Romania's Maricica Puica.*

Photo: © Duomo, David Madison.

*Following spread: 1984 Olympics, Los Angeles Coliseum.*

Photo: © Duomo, Steven E. Sutton.

## 1984 LOS ANGELES

### DALEY THOMPSON, USA

*In Los Angeles, Great Britain's Francis "Daley" Thompson clung onto the Olympic decathlon title he had first captured in 1980. It was the third Olympics for the half-Scottish, half-Nigerian super-athlete, who outscored German rival Jürgen Hingsen for the gold.*

Photo: © Allsport, Steve Powell.

## 1984 LOS ANGELES

### JOAN BENOIT, USA

*Waving her white painter's cap, America's Joan Benoit paced easily to victory in the marathon with a 400-meter edge over her closest competitor, Norway's Grete Waitz. Benoit had pulled well ahead of her rivals after only fourteen minutes, and the Maine native never let up, keeping her commanding lead for the next two hours and ten minutes.*

Photo: © Duomo, David Madison.

## 1984 LOS ANGELES

### EDWIN MOSES, USA

*Super-hurdler Edwin Moses had scored gold in the 1976 Olympics, and by the time the 1984 Games rolled around he had won an astonishing 102 consecutive races. He added to his streak in Los Angeles, capturing his second gold in the 400-meter hurdles. Moses, who had studied physics on an academic scholarship at Morehouse College, started hurdling as a hobby and honed an unstoppable, thirteen-step pace between hurdles. His streak finally came to an end in 1987, after 107 wins.*

Photo: © Duomo, Steven E. Sutton.

## 1984 LOS ANGELES

### GABRIELE ANDERSEN-SCHEISS, SWI

*In a harrowing moment of the 1984 Olympic marathon, Switzerland's Gaby Andersen-Scheiss, who worked as a ski instructor in Idaho, stumbled into the stadium, overcome by heat prostration. Nevertheless, she refused medical attention and staggered to the finish line in thirty-seventh place. Within two hours, she had fully recovered from her ordeal.*

Photo: © Duomo, David Madison.

*Following spread: Australian cycling team, 1984.*

Photo: © Duomo.

1988 SEOUL

**JACKIE JOYNER KERSEE. USA**

*Regarded as the world's greatest female athlete, Jackie Joyner Kersee dominated the heptathlon and long jump competitions in Seoul, striking gold in both events. She powered to gold in the heptathlon again in Barcelona in 1992.*

Photo: © Duomo, Steven E. Sutton.

The 1988 Games moved to the bustling megalopolis of Seoul, South Korea. These magnificently organized Games were the first in twelve years in which both Americans and Soviets competed, but North Korea—joined by a number of hard-line allies including Cuba, Albania, and Ethiopia—turned its back on the Games, claiming that it had the right to host half of the events. And Olympic competitions were marred by ugly boxing disputes and continuing drug controversies. In one ringside disaster, a New Zealand referee, Keith Walker, was physically attacked by South Korean boxing officials and security guards who were incensed over what they believed to be biased  judging. And Canada's Olympic hopes soared, and then crashed, with the fortunes of sprinter Ben Johnson. In the 100 meters, the Jamaican-born runner flashed past his racing rival, Carl Lewis, to take the gold. But three days later, Johnson was forced to forfeit his medal after testing positive for steroids. Four other medalists—two Bulgarian weightlifters, a Hungarian lifter, and a British judo expert—were also caught in the drug-testing web.

Churning up the track in Seoul was Florence Griffith Joyner, as famous for her running as for the racing outfits she designed herself. "Flo-Jo"—bank teller, beautician, and wife of 1984 Olympic triple-jump champion Al Joyner—galloped across the finish line to three gold medals, while her fleet-footed sister-in-law, Jackie Joyner Kersee, triumphed in the heptathlon and long jump. Family feats were shared by Soviet husband and wife Viktor and Olga Bryzgin, who each breezed to a gold medal on the track.

Once again, Soviet hoopsters spiked the U.S. and Yugoslavia to take the title, but U.S. women scored their own basketball gold. In the water, East German pool shark Kristin Otto stroked to six gold medals. America's "big fish," 6-foot, 7-inch Matt Biondi, reeled in five, ranking him second only to Mark Spitz.

## MATT BIONDI, USA

*The "big fish" at the Seoul
Games was American
swimmer Matt Biondi. His
haul included five golds,
ranking him second only to
Mark Spitz, who swam away
with seven gold medals in
1972. At the Barcelona
Games in 1992, Biondi added
a sixth gold in the 400–
meter freestyle relay.*

Photo: © Duomo.

## 1992 BARCELONA

### THE DREAM TEAM. USA

In Barcelona, for the first time, Olympic basketball was open to professional players—and the U.S. assembled the most magnificent team ever, with a roster of hoop idols including "Magic" Johnson (below), Michael Jordan (right), Larry Bird, Patrick Ewing, and Charles Barkley. Not surprisingly, the "Dream Team" outscored all rivals and claimed Olympic gold.

*Photo: Below © Duomo, Mitchell Layton; Right © Duomo, Al Tielemans.*

Tennis returned to the Games after a sixty-four-year absence, featuring a lineup of high-paid pros, and the new Olympic sport of table tennis was aced by the Chinese and Koreans. Greg Louganis—who only months before had been diagnosed HIV-positive—reprised his platform and springboard golds despite a fever, an injured hand, and four stitches in his head from hitting the board during a dive.

In 1992, the world's best athletes came together again, beneath blue skies and a blazing Mediterranean sun, at the Olympic Games in Barcelona, Spain. With no boycotts or Cold War skirmishes marring the event for the first time in twenty years, a record 12,000 athletes from 172 nations took part, and South Africa was welcomed back after twenty-eight years of Olympic exile. The opening ceremonies threw a spotlight on the world's newly fractured political fault lines. Twelve former Soviet republics paraded together under separate flags and the rubric Unified Team, while Latvia, Estonia, and Lithuania entered as independent nations. Yugoslavia had been torn apart, and its athletes competed as Croats or Independent Olympic Participants. The shifting kaleidoscope of nations included new Olympic members such as the Himalayan nation of Bhutan, whose archers had never before traveled on a plane or seen the sea.

Now politically independent—but athletically dominant as ever—the Unified Team swept forty-five Olympic golds. The hometown Spanish squad clinched an amazing thirteen gold medals—after capturing a total of four in the entire history of the Games. Paraskevi Patoulidou leaped to the gold in the women's 100-meter hurdles, becoming Greece's first track medalist since 1896. Hungarian swimmers triumphed, too—Tamas Darnyi stroked to double golds in the men's races, and Krisztina Egerszegi tripled in the women's. Russia's 6-foot, 6-inch Aleksandr Popov splashed past Matt Biondi to take two freestyle titles.

For U.S. diver Mark Lenzi—who took up his sport after watching Greg Louganis's 1984 Olympic performance on television—the Barcelona Games turned to gold when he inherited his idol's springboard title. Competing in a wicked wind, Carl Lewis claimed his third gold medal in the long jump—surpassing Mike Powell, who had broken Bob Beamon's super jump record in 1991. Hurdler Kevin Young achieved his dream of breaking Edwin Moses's nine-year-old world record,

1992 BARCELONA

TATIANA GUTSU, EUN

*Despite a tumble from the balance beam, the Unified Team's Tatiana Gutsu, 15, substituted for injured teammate Roza Galieva in the all-around women's gymnastics competition and scored Barcelona gold.*

Photo: © Allsport, Tony Duffy.

and Jackie Joyner Kersee whipped through the heptathlon—holding tight to her title as the greatest female athlete in the world.

But towering above all the other champions was smiling, 6-foot, 9-inch Earvin "Magic" Johnson—former star point guard of the Los Angeles Lakers—who led America's basketball "Dream Team" to the hoop of gold in Barcelona. For the first time, Olympic basketball competition permitted the participation of professional players. And Johnson had persuaded a host of fellow NBA superstars—including Michael Jordan, Larry Bird, Patrick Ewing, and Charles Barkley—to join him on the Olympic courts. A year before, Johnson stunned the world by announcing that he had tested positive for HIV. Now he was shooting for Olympic gold, and thousands of fans were pressing to touch him, screaming "Ma-jeek" everywhere he went in Barcelona. To no one's surprise, Johnson and the "Dream Team" crushed all comers and went home with gold around their necks. For Johnson—who was named the NBA's Most Valuable Player three times—it was, he confided, a magnificent moment. "It's sort of hard to put into words what [winning the Olympics] means….I've won every championship there is to win. You can throw them all in a hat, and it'll never compare to this."

1992 BARCELONA

**FERMIN CACHO RUIZ, SPA**

*Spain's Fermin Cacho Ruiz sprinted to the finish in the 1,500 meters and joyfully captured the gold medal for the home team.*

Photo: © Duomo, Steven E. Sutton.

1992 BARCELONA

**PETER FARKAS, HUN**

*Hungary's Peter Farkas powered to gold in the Greco-Roman wrestling 181-pound class. His countryman, Tibor Komáromi, had silvered in the event in 1988.*

Photo: © Allsport, G. Vandystadt.

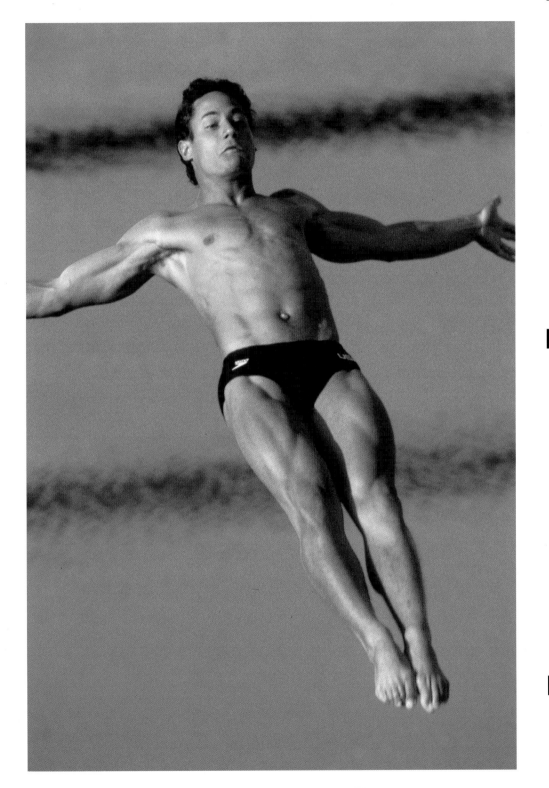

### 1988 SEOUL

## GREG LOUGANIS, USA

*After gashing his head on the
diving board during the
preliminaries in Seoul,
unstoppable Greg Louganis (left)
went on to win the springboard
and platform titles. It was the
second set of diving golds for
Louganis, who had mastered the
two events in Los Angeles.*

### 1992 BARCELONA

## MANUEL ESTIARTE, SPA

*Led by high-powered offensive
player Manuel Estiarte (opposite),
the highest goal scorer in the Los
Angeles and Seoul Olympics—
Spain's water polo team was
favored to win, but was forced to
settle for silver after being edged
out by the Italian squad.*

### 1992 BARCELONA

## SOCCER

*Following spread: The Spanish
home team swept past Poland in
the gold-medal soccer match in
Barcelona, taking Spain's first-
ever Olympic title in the event.*

## 1896 - 1992

*Blending Olympic symbolism with the spirit of the host cities, the posters of the Summer Olympic Games are*

# THE SUMMER OLYMPIC POSTERS

*part of the "National Art Exhibitions" called for by the Olympic charter. One of the posters—announcing the 1912 Olympic Games in Stockholm—was considered so daring that it was not distributed in a number of countries. The poster created for the 1952 Helsinki Games features the image of the great Finnish runner Paavo Nurmi, winner of nine Olympic gold medals. The Olympic symbol of five intertwining rings, featured on all of the posters after 1928, was taken from an altar at the ancient Greek city of Delphi and symbolizes the brotherhood of nations.*

Photos: Archives, Olympic Museum Lausanne.

*Athens 1896*

*Paris 1900*

*Paris 1924*

*Amsterdam 1928*

*Melbourne 1956*

*Rome 1960*

*Moscow 1980*

*Los Angeles 1984*

*St. Louis 1904*

*London 1908*

*Stockholm 1912*

*Antwerp 1920*

*Los Angeles 1932*

*Berlin 1936*

*London 1948*

*Helsinki 1952*

*Tokyo 1964*

*Mexico City 1968*

*Munich 1972*

*Montreal 1976*

# THE GAMES OF WINTER

Mix the power and skill of Olympic sport with the slick speed of ice and snow. Add the unpredictability of weather and the vertical velocity of mountain slopes, and you have the Winter Games—the ultimate test of world-class athletes and the elements.

The Winter Olympics are younger than their sister Games of Summer.

## FROM CHAMONIX TO LILLEHAMMER

There were, of course, no snowbound sports played on the sweltering fields of Olympia in Greece. Perhaps because there was neither mythology nor classical tradition to shape them, the Winter Games have typically been more informal and convivial than the warm-weather Olympiads. A smaller corps of athletes, many of whom know each other well, compete in Winter Olympic sports, and small nations like Norway are regularly big winners. But despite the cozy, winter-carnival intimacy of these Games, they are heightened by an extra element of danger. When speeds are magnified by gravity and ice, when control is routinely traded for acceleration, risk is a cold companion that haunts the most seasoned competitors.

Initially, Pierre de Coubertin, the founder of the modern Games, had no interest in adding winter competitions to the Olympic program. But the growing cadre of snow-sport enthusiasts clamored for the inclusion of cold-weather events, and in 1924 the Winter Olympic Games—initially titled "International Sports Week"—debuted in the little Alpine resort of Chamonix in France.

The opening of those first Winter Olympics, like many since, was hair-raising due to freakish swings in weather. A month before the Games, there was no snow at all in Chamonix. Then, overnight, there was

## 1976 INNSBRUCK

### FRANZ KLAMMER, AUT

*On the treacherous Patscherkofel downhill course in Innsbruck, Austria, hometown hero Franz Klammer, 22, flew to the finish line at speeds up to eighty miles per hour—edging Switzerland's Bernhard Russi for the Olympic gold by four-tenths of a second.*

Photos: Above © Duomo, William R. Sallaz; Below, Archives, Olympic Museum Lausanne; Opposite © Duomo.

so much snow that it buried the skating rink, which had to be excavated by hand. A few weeks later, torrential rains transformed the ice stadium into a lake, but a freeze followed, and the Games began.

As they would in many subsequent Winter Olympics, Scandinavians dominated the sixteen competitive events. Their edge in Nordic skiing, ski jumping, and skating had been finely honed in the Nordic Games, inaugurated in 1901, and in Norway's celebrated Holmenkollen, an annual week of ski jumping and cross-country competitions. To no one's surprise, Finland's champion speed skater, Clas Thunberg, hurtled away with three gold medals, while Norway's Thorleif Haug raced to three golds in Nordic skiing. Sweden's Gillis Grafström won his second gold medal in figure skating, which had first been unseasonably featured in the 1908 and 1920 Summer Olympic Games.

Canada, the country that invented ice hockey, captured the second of many wins in its national sport, which had been introduced in the 1920 Summer Olympics in Antwerp. The lone U.S. winner was Charles Jewtraw, who streaked to the gold—the first medal of the Games—in the 500-meter skating race. And, although she was unknown at the time, the most famous competitor at Chamonix was not a medalist at all. It was an eleven-year-old Norwegian named Sonja Henie, who finished at the bottom of the list in women's figure skating.

Henie had, amazingly, clinched the skating championship of Norway just a few weeks before the Games—defeating many older, much more seasoned competitors. Although she didn't distinguish herself in her first Olympic competition, it proved to be an experience that helped prepare her for one of the most successful skating careers of all time. By 1928, when the second Winter Games opened in St. Moritz, Switzerland, Henie had drilled herself in ballet as well as skating and, at the tender age of thirteen, had already captured the world championship. Henie never practiced more than three hours a day—"I'd simply go nuts," she said. But she still managed to transfix Olympic crowds in St. Moritz

## 1924 CHAMONIX

### CURLING

*The sport of curling, which originated in Scotland more than four centuries ago, was featured at the first Winter Olympic Games in 1924. Players slide 42-pound granite stones across the ice toward fixed targets, using brooms to smooth the ice and help direct the moving stones. Curling reappeared as an Olympic demonstration sport in 1988 in Calgary, and it will be reintroduced as an official Winter Olympic event at the 1998 Games in Nagano.*

Photo: © Presse Sport.

## 1924 CHAMONIX

### BOBSLEDDING

*The first official international bobsled race was held at the 1924 Winter Games. The Swiss team clinched the four-man event; two-man racing was introduced in 1932.*

Photos: Left © Presse Sport; Opposite, Archives, Olympic Museum Lausanne.

## 1924 CHAMONIX

### HERMA VON SZABO-PLANCK, AUT

*At the first Winter Games, Austria's Herma von Szabo-Planck skated off with the women's figure skating title. In last place was a Norwegian girl named Sonja Henie.*

Photo: Archives, Olympic Museum Lausanne.

## SONJA HENIE, NOR

*One of the greatest figure skaters ever was Norway's ice queen, Sonja Henie. Henie was just eleven years old and already Norway's national skating champion when she entered the first Winter Olympic Games in 1924. Although she didn't do well in Chamonix, she went on to gold-medaling performances in 1928, 1932, and 1936. After she retired from competition following the 1936 Games, Henie bewitched movie audiences in a new Hollywood career.*

Photo: © Presse Sport.

with her near-perfect figures and imaginative "Dying Swan" routine, which shattered tradition by incorporating the fluid movements of ballet. Henie skated off with the gold—a feat she repeated at the next two Winter Games. In 1936 she retired from competition—after amassing nearly 1,500 trophies, cups, and medals—and launched a new, smashingly successful career as a Hollywood movie star.

Things didn't go quite so smoothly for all the other athletes at St. Moritz. Weird weather again bedeviled the Games: first a warm spell and no snow, and then heavy rain, forced the cancellation of some bobsled and speed skating events. On one day, the thermometer bounced between 0 and 77 degrees Fahrenheit, confounding cross-country athletes dependent on temperature-sensitive ski waxes. And once again, Gillis Grafström won the men's figure skating gold, Canada easily dispatched its rivals in ice hockey, and the Scandinavians, particularly the Norwegians, went home clutching most of the medals. The U.S., however, began its two-decades-long domination of the bobsled run, and brothers Jennison and John Heaton from New Haven, Connecticut, hurtled head-first to gold and silver wins on a heavy sled, the skeleton toboggan, in a rare event called the Cresta Run, held only in St. Moritz.

Americans did better in the 1932 Winter Games, held for the first time on home turf at the Adirondack resort of Lake Placid, New York. Franklin Roosevelt, then New York's governor, opened the Olympics, and his wife, Eleanor, gamely rattled down the bob run. But right on cue, weather again menaced the events. Tons of snow had to be trucked down from Canada, and due to rain, several ski jumpers splashed down in an unexpected pond. Because of the distance from Europe, only seventeen nations competed, compared to twenty-five in St. Moritz. But the masses of spectators—more than 78,000—made up for the

1948 ST. MORITZ

**REIDAR LIAKLEV, NOR**

*Norwegian racers dashed off with three out of four speed skating golds in St. Moritz. Reidar Liaklev snatched the title in the 5,000 meters. His Swedish rival Åke Seyffarth ran into trouble when he collided with an overeager photographer on the ice.*

Photos: Above and below, Archives, Olympic Museum Lausanne.

1948 ST. MORITZ

**BARBARA ANN SCOTT, CAN**

*Nineteen-year-old Barbara Ann Scott, the reigning world champion, captured the women's figure skating gold for Canada in 1948. To prove to Olympic officials that she hadn't turned professional, the Ottawa native returned a canary-yellow car that had been presented to her by hometown officials.*

Photo: Archives, Olympic Museum Lausanne.

lack of international competitors. They mobbed the figure skating events, which Henie won again, and

1948 ST. MORITZ

**DICK BUTTON, USA**

*With his perfectly executed double axel jump—a move he had mastered only two days before—Dick Button, eighteen, wowed judges and won the men's figure skating gold in the St. Moritz Winter Games.*

Photo: Archives, Olympic Museum Lausanne.

the U.S.-dominated bobsled runs. One of the winning U.S. bobbers was Eddie Eagan, a gold-medal-winning light heavyweight boxer in the 1920 Summer Games who landed another gold by switching Olympic sports and seasons. The Canadians scored another win in ice hockey, and the Scandinavians wrapped up the skiing competitions. Sparking controversy, American and Canadian speed skaters dominated their events due to the imposition of North American Rules, which called for rough-and-tumble mass starts instead of skaters racing in pairs against the clock.

Traditional speed skating rules, favoring the Europeans, were reinstated when the Winter Games crossed the Atlantic again in 1936. This time the host was Germany, which had fallen under Adolf Hitler's domination in 1933. The Führer himself, his mustache white with snowflakes, opened the Games attended by his propaganda minister, Joseph Goebbels, and his aviation minister, Hermann Göring. Despite the grim presence of Nazi troops and heavy rain, the events—held in the twin Bavarian villages of Garmisch and Partenkirchen—were a popular success, drawing half a million spectators and athletes from twenty-eight countries. The undisputed king of the ice was Norwegian speed skater Ivar Ballangrud, who streaked away with three gold medals. The ice queen, once again, was Sonja Henie, who ended her amateur career with a third figure skating gold—this time edging out a fifteen-year-old British skater named Cecilia Colledge.

The biggest surprise of the Games was the trouncing of Canada's champion ice hockey team by the British, whose lineup on the ice mainly consisted of British-born Canadians. Despite Hitler's racist policies, Germany's ice hockey team included star player Rudi Ball—a Jewish

1952 OSLO

**HALLGEIR BRENDEN, NOR**

*In Oslo, the 15-kilometer Nordic skiing title was claimed by the host country's national steeplechase champion, Hallgeir Brenden—a lumberjack and farmer who repeated his gold-medaling performance in 1956.*

Photo: Archives, Olympic Museum Lausanne.

## TONI SAILER, AUT

*Austria's Anton "Toni"
Sailer, the Kitzbühel
cannonball, dominated the
1956 Winter Games,
capturing the downhill triple
crown with huge leads over
his competitors.*

Photo: Archives, Olympic Museum Lausanne.

### 1952 OSLO

## STEIN ERIKSEN, NOR

*Norwegian heartthrob Stein
Eriksen zigzagged to victory in
the 1952 Olympic giant slalom.
In 1954, after winning the
world combined alpine
championship title, he launched
a career as a sought-after ski
instructor in the U.S., where he
was known for his debonair style
on and off the slopes.*

Photo: Archives, Olympic Museum Lausanne.

1960 SQUAW VALLEY

**CAROL HEISS, USA**

*In her second Olympic*
*appearance, America's Carol*
*Heiss, 20, easily skated away*
*with the women's figure skating*
*title at the Squaw Valley*
*Games. Her future brother-in-*
*law, David Jenkins, captured*
*the men's figure skating gold—a*
*title previously held by his*
*brother and Heiss's soon-to-be*
*husband, Hayes Alan Jenkins,*
*who gold-medaled in 1956.*

Photos: Below and right, Archives,
Olympic Museum Lausanne.

athlete who, after fleeing to France to escape Nazi anti-Semitism, was recruited to play for the Fatherland. Scandinavians again clinched the Nordic skiing competitions, and Norwegian ski jumper Birger Ruud, who had won in 1932, scored his second gold in the event. Later, during World War II, Ruud and his two brothers were imprisoned in a concentration camp for refusing to assist the Nazis.

With the world gripped by war and its terrible aftermath for much of the next decade, the Winter Games did not resume until 1948, when they returned to the neutral Swiss mountain resort of St. Moritz. Notably absent from the Games were teams from defeated Germany and Japan, but athletes from twenty-eight other nations competed—including, for the first time, teams from Denmark, Chile, Iceland Lebanon, and Korea. The war might have been over, but there was plenty of squabbling around the snow-packed Alpine town. American bobsledders claimed that their equipment had been sabotaged, and a hockey game between Sweden and Canada ended in a raging fist-fight. Major disputes broke out when the U.S. entered two rival ice hockey teams—one by the Amateur Hockey Association and another by the American Olympic Committee.

On more amicable notes, Alpine (downhill) skiing events, which had first been introduced in 1936, drew nearly twice as many competing teams as the Nordic (cross-country) skiing races. France's Henri Oreiller hurtled to two golds in the downhill events, and America's pigtailed Gretchen Fraser snatched a surprise gold in the women's slalom. U.S. figure skater Dick Button, an eighteen-year-old Harvard freshman, made his Olympic debut at St. Moritz, where his athletic style and powerful double axel jump—a move he'd mastered only two days before—landed him the gold. And Canada's favorite, Barbara Ann Scott, captured the women's figure skating gold after agreeing to return a canary-yellow car—a gift from the City of Ottawa—to put to rest accusations of professionalism.

Germany and Japan were invited back to the Winter Games in 1952, hosted by Oslo. Good weather and good spirits prevailed, and the Games were an indisputable victory party for the Norwegians. Their teams swept up seven golds, including three won by speed skating truck driver Hjalmar Anderson. Next best, surprisingly, was the U.S., whose four-gold record was led by nineteen-year-old downhiller Andrea Mead Lawrence. The young Vermonter beat out Europe's fastest skiers for gold medals in both the slalom and giant slalom, and Dick

Button nailed his second gold in figure skating with a jaw-dropping triple-loop jump. The Germans set a record of sorts, too. Giving new meaning to the term "heavy sledding," their bobsled team thundered to two gold medals—partly because their two-man crew weighed in at more than five hundred and twenty pounds, and their hefty four-man team tipped the scales at well over one thousand pounds. After the Games, Olympic officials announced new weight limits of two hundred and twenty pounds per man. "It's diet or quit," lamented one of the record-busting bobbers.

In 1956, for the first time, there was a massive global audience for the Winter Games, as television beamed images of Olympic skiers and skaters around the world. Although the balmy-weather Games were held in the slush-filled Italian ski resort of Cortina d' Ampezzo, they were owned, hands down, by skier Toni Sailer—Austria's Kitzbühel cannonball. The twenty-year-old plumber and future movie star *wedeled* to victory in all three Alpine events, outracing the other skiers by huge margins. The Soviets had a lot to celebrate, too. At Cortina, their very first Winter Olympics, they claimed sixteen medals—the most of any country—and took golds in

ice hockey and speed skating. The pairs skating event, however, was most notable for its surly spectators. Unhappy with the judging, the crowd took to hurling oranges at the officials, forcing crews to clear smashed fruit from the rink three times before skating could resume. American wins were limited to the figure skating singles golds, won by Hayes Jenkins and Tenley Albright. Although stoic Albright had fallen less than two weeks before the Games, slashing her right ankle to the bone with her skate blade, her father, a Boston surgeon, had flown to Cortina to stitch her up so she wouldn't miss the competition. Albright became a surgeon herself after ending her skating career.

The decision by the International Olympic Committee to hold the 1960 Winter Games at Squaw Valley, California, ignited a storm of controversy. The remote site, forty miles from Reno in the Sierra Nevada Mountains, had absolutely no facilities—everything, from skating rinks to ski runs, lifts, and lodging, had to be built from scratch. The organizers also decided to strike bobsled races from the Games, on the grounds that the small number

1968 GRENOBLE

**JEAN-CLAUDE KILLY, FRA**

*France's skiing superstar Jean-Claude Killy repeated Toni Sailer's remarkable triple-gold sweep in 1968. With his glamorous style, breakneck speed, and technical virtuosity, Killy dominated the 1968 Grenoble Games.*

Photos: Left and below, Archives, Olympic Museum Lausanne.

of teams competing didn't justify the steep cost of constructing a bob run. But despite disputes, heavy snow, and the heating up of the Cold War, the Games proceeded smoothly in an informal and remarkably congenial setting. Walt Disney staged opening ceremonies filled with school bands and balloons and presided over by Vice President Richard Nixon. And, a year before the Berlin Wall went up, the East and West German athletes competed as one team, using Beethoven's Ninth Symphony in their victory ceremonies, rather than their respective national anthems.

Soviet schoolteacher Lydia Skoblikova clinched two of the women's speed skating races—the first ever held in the Olympics. Scandinavians dominated Nordic skiing, Canadian downhiller Anne Heggtveit nailed the slalom, and Americans—this time, David Jenkins and Carol Heiss—again took the figure skating honors. By far the biggest surprise of the Games was America's shocking capture of the Olympic hockey title. Riding an amazing lucky streak, the underdog U.S. "Team of Destiny"—a patchwork crew that included a fireman, two carpenters, a couple of insurance agents, and an ad salesman—came out of nowhere to sweep past traditional hockey powers, including Czechoslovakia, Canada, and the Soviets, to score the winning gold.

Luck, however, at first seemed to turn against the next Winter Olympic Games, held in Innsbruck, Austria, in 1964. Two athletes, an Australian skier and a Polish-born British luger, were killed in training accidents. And a mere week before the opening ceremonies, the slopes were still agonizingly bare of snow. Fortunately, 3,000 Austrian troops accomplished what the weather wouldn't, hauling 40,000 cubic meters of snow to Olympic ski runs and carting 20,000 bricks of ice from Alpine peaks to line the luge and bobsled runs.

The events themselves were a triumph, once again, for Soviet athletes. Lydia Skoblikova bettered her 1960 wins, picking off all four speed skating golds, and teammate Claudia Boyarskikh took three golds in Nordic skiing. The Soviets also reclaimed the ice hockey championship, and the passionate pairs skaters, Ludmilla Belousova and Oleg Protopopov—known for their legendary "death spiral"—captured their first figure skating gold. The unofficial hero of the Games, however, was Italy's world champion bobsledder, Eugenio Monti. When the British bob team sheared a bolt on their sled, Monti—who had just come down the run—pulled a bolt out of his own so that his competitors could race. The British shot down the chute to win the gold.

1968 GRENOBLE

**NANCY GREENE, CAN**

*In her third Olympics, Canada's Nancy Greene charged down the slopes to score gold in the women's giant slalom. Greene, from Rossland, British Columbia, won Canada's first women's alpine gold since Anne Heggtveit raced to victory in the slalom in the 1960 Winter Games.*

Photos: Below and right, Archives, Olympic Museum Lausanne.

## YUKIO KASAYA, JPN

*In Sapporo, ski jumper Yukio Kasaya, a local champion from the island of Hokkaido, won the second Winter Games medal ever for Japan when he soared to the gold in the normal hill competition. Teammates Akitsugu Konno and Seiji Aochi made it a clean sweep for Japan when they captured the silver and bronze in the event.*

Photo: Archives, Olympic Museum Lausanne.

1972 SAPPORO

## ERHARD KELLER, GER

*After racing to the speed skating gold in the 500 meters at Grenoble in 1968, West Germany's Erhard Keller held onto his Olympic title in 1972. In the 500, Keller outpaced the Netherlands's Ard Schenk who won every other men's speed skating event at the Sapporo Games.*

Photo: Archives, Olympic Museum Lausanne.

1976 INNSBRUCK

## KARL SCHNABL, AUT

*Following spread: Austria claimed its first gold medal in ski jumping when Karl Schnabl took first place on Innsbruck's 90-meter hill. Fellow Austrian Ernst Vettori duplicated Schnabl's feat in Albertville in 1992.*

Photo: © Duomo.

Monti finally got his own gold medals at the Grenoble Winter Games in 1968. But virtually all the athletes competing in the French Alps were overshadowed by "Le Superman," French ski god Jean-Claude Killy. Combining precision and explosive speed, Killy zipped off with all three gold medals in the Alpine—matching Toni Sailer's 1956 feat—despite record-setting winds, thick fog, and a haze of controversy surrounding the giant slalom race. The arguments arose after Austria's Karl Schranz had cut short his second run, having missed two gates. Officials allowed him to ski the course again after he claimed that he had been distracted by a shadowy figure, possibly a course policeman, who had mysteriously crossed the track. Schranz's time for the last run would have earned him the gold, but the French protested. After deliberating for hours, the Olympic jury determined that Schranz had missed a gate before the distraction occurred. They awarded the gold medal to Killy, giving him the third jewel in his triple crown.

1976 INNSBRUCK

**DOROTHY HAMILL, USA**

*With her fluid skating style and signature wedge haircut, America's Dorothy Hamill glided to the women's figure skating gold in 1976.*

Photos: Below and right, Archives, Olympic Museum Lausanne.

1980 LAKE PLACID

**ICE HOCKEY**

*In a stunning upset for the Soviet Union, which had dominated Olympic ice hockey since 1956, an upstart U.S. team scored Olympic gold— jubilantly duplicating America's unexpected "miracle on ice" win over the Soviet champions in 1960.*

Photo: © Duomo, Paul J. Sutton.

There were other controversies, too, at the Grenoble Games. Female athletes were required to undergo gender tests for the first time. The East German women were disqualified from the luge event for heating the runners of their sled, prompting their officials to complain of a "capitalist revanchist plot." And the International Olympic Committee clashed with top downhill skiers, insisting that they remove their brand-name-adorned equipment before posing for news and television cameras. But the quarrels didn't tarnish the bright spots of the Games. Canada's Nancy Greene zigzagged through the gates to claim the giant slalom gold, and for the first time a non-Scandinavian, Italy's Franco Nones, captured an individual Nordic skiing title. Figure skater Peggy Fleming, battling the flu and wearing a costume stitched together by her mother, won America's only gold medal. And British speed skater David Bodington earned top points in sportsmanship when he voluntarily dived onto the ice and out of competition to avoid injuring a rival who'd fallen in his lane.

Unfortunately, however, the fog of controversy that had shrouded Grenoble continued to hover over the 1972 Winter Olympics at Sapporo, the first ever held in Asia. The IOC threw Karl Schranz, Austria's ski hero, out of the Games, choosing to make an example of him for appearing in commercial advertising. Furious, the Austrian team pulled out altogether, then reentered at Schranz's urging. The Canadians joined the near-frenzied debate over amateurism, boycotting the ice hockey competition to protest state sponsorship of Eastern European teams.

But the Games, held in the pristine shadow of Mount Eniwa, ended happily for the Japanese, whose home team amazingly swept three medals in ski-jumping events. The men's speed skating races were wrapped up by the flying Dutchman, Ard Schenk, who glided off with three gold medals, and the women's races were dominated by two Americans from Northbrook, Illinois, Anne Henning and Dianne Holum. Another U.S. competitor, Barbara Cochran, edged her rivals by a sheer two-hundredths of a second to take gold in the slalom.

Denver, Colorado, was tapped to host the 1976 Winter Olympics, but voters got cold feet and vetoed financing for the event. So the Games went to Innsbruck for a second time. Local ski hero Franz Klammer schussed off with the gold medal for Austria in the downhill, and West Germany's Rosi Mittermaier starred in the women's slalom and downhill. The Soviets dominated speed and pairs skating, ice dancing made its Olympic debut, and America's Dorothy Hamill—as famous for her signature haircut as for her seamless style on ice—won the figure skating gold.

Four years later, in 1980, the Winter Games returned to Lake Placid, New York, but there was little that was placid about these Games. Billed as "An Olympics in Perspective," they were the first Winter Games attended by a team from the People's Republic of China.

**1980 LAKE PLACID**

**ERIC HEIDEN, USA**

*Super–speed skater Eric Heiden from West Allis, Wisconsin, swept gold medals in all five men's events at Lake Placid, dominating both the short sprints and the long-distance endurance races.*

Photo: © Duomo, Steven E. Sutton.

**1984 SARAJEVO**

**KATARINA WITT, GDR**

*East Germany's brilliant Katarina Witt dramatically captured gold in women's figure skating in 1984 (opposite) and decisively repeated her triumph in 1988 (below)—becoming the first since Sonja Henie to take the Olympic title in two consecutive Winter Games.*

Photos: Below and right © Duomo, Paul J. Sutton.

**1984 SARAJEVO**

**TORVILL & DEAN, GBR**

*The British ice-dancing duo of
Jayne Torvill and Christopher
Dean captivated spectators in
Sarajevo, winning twelve
perfect scores and dancing off
with the gold medal to the music
of Ravel's* Bolero.

Photo: © Duomo.

Transportation was frozen by a bus system strike that left irate Olympic spectators stranded in frigid cold and prompted the governor of New York to declare a limited state of emergency. Bad luck also hit U.S. pairs skaters Randy Gardner and Tai Babilonia, who were forced to leave the ice after Gardner, suffering from a groin injury, fell four times in warm-ups. But nothing—not even the major concussion he'd suffered five months earlier—could stop Sweden's Arctic skiing phenomenon, Ingemar Stenmark, who rocketed to golds in both the slalom and giant slalom on mountain courses packed with man-made snow. And nobody has ever matched the spectacular winning streak of U.S. speed skater Eric Heiden, who shut out competitors by sweeping five individual gold medals, the most of any Winter Olympian in a single year. In a stupefying climax to the Games, an inexperienced U.S. hockey team somehow managed a repeat performance of the American team's stunning 1960 "miracle on ice," boosting the country's bruised national pride and breaking the Soviets' sixteen-year-long streak of wins.

Surrounded by the pine-forested Dinaric Mountains, Sarajevo, Yugoslavia, was chosen to host the Winter Games in 1984. Until then, the city had been most famous as the place where the Archduke Ferdinand of Austria had been assassinated, igniting World War I. The beginning of the Winter Games, unfortunately, was not a great deal more auspicious. Flags flew at half-mast to mark the death of Soviet premier Yuri Andropov, and Sarajevo was at first buried by snow, then blinded by fog, and blasted by 120-mile-per-hour gusts that shredded the Alpine schedule. But when the cold white curtain parted, the focus turned to spectacular performances. West Germany careened to a win in the two-man luge event, propelled by 244-pound slider Hans Stangassinger. Bill Johnson captured America's first downhill gold, while teammate Phil Mahre won the slalom, trailed by his silver-medaling twin brother, Steve.

But the biggest stars at Sarajevo were on skates. East German women swept the speed skating events, and Canada's Gaetan Boucher took two golds in the men's races. Most of the media

## 1988 CALGARY

### MICHAEL EDWARDS, GBR

*The most dazzling Olympic ski-jumping performance in Calgary belonged to Finland's Matti "Nuke-'em" Nykänen, who scored triple golds in the event. But folk-hero status was awarded to Great Britain's sole entrant, Michael "Eddie the Eagle" Edwards. The twenty-four-year-old plasterer from Cheltenham, England, had started jumping only two years earlier and collected the lowest scores of any Olympic ski jumper, alarming spectators along the course with his frighteningly shaky landings.*

Photos: Left, Archives, Olympic Museum Lausanne;
Below © Duomo.

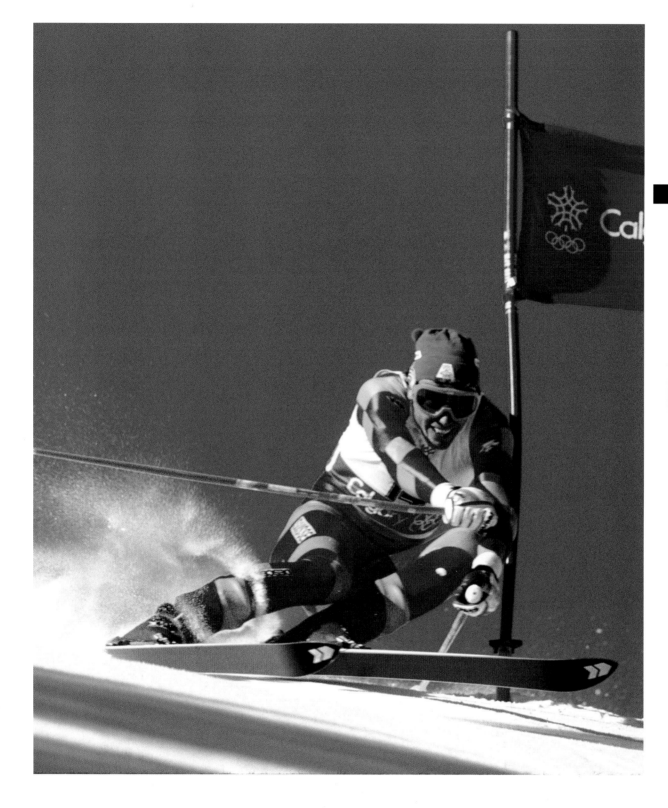

## PIRMIN ZURBRIGGEN, SWI

*Swiss skier Pirmin Zurbriggen was favored to take gold in all five Olympic Alpine events in Calgary, but he went home to the Valais Alps with only one gold medal in the downhill, having narrowly edged teammate Peter Müller.*

Photo: © Duomo, Steven E. Sutton.

1988 CALGARY

**BONNIE BLAIR, USA**

*America's enduring Bonnie "the Blur" Blair—a speed skating powerhouse from Champagne, Illinois—flashed to her first 500-meter gold medal in Calgary, then went on to collect four more Olympic gold medals in the 500- and 1,000-meter races in the Albertville and Lillehammer Games.*

Photo: © Duomo, David Madison.

1988 CALGARY

**ALBERTO TOMBA, ITA**

*Alberto Tomba, Italy's skiing superstar, thrilled fans by streaking to double golds in both the slalom and giant slalom in Calgary. "La Bomba" returned to the Games for a second giant slalom win in Albertville in 1992.*

Photo: © Duomo, William R. Sallaz.

*Following spread:*

*U.S. luger Erica Terwilliger competing in Albertville in 1992.*

Photo: © Duomo, Paul J. Sutton.

attention focused on the brilliant, dramatic Katarina Witt, East Germany's figure skating prima donna, and the astonishing performance of Great Britain's ice-dancing royal couple, Jayne Torvill and Christopher Dean. Nottingham's "T & D" miraculously skated off with twelve perfect scores, while America's Scott Hamilton squeaked by Canada's Brian Orser for the men's figure skating title.

On his home turf at the windy Calgary Winter Games in 1988, Orser had a second chance to duel for the figure skating gold—this time against his good friend America's Brian Boitano in a matchup that was billed as the "Battle of the Brians." Though Boitano edged Orser for the title, Canada got in its licks when Elizabeth Manley beat out America's Debi Thomas for the women's silver. Skating seductively to Bizet's *Carmen*, Katarina Witt dazzled spectators for her second gold in the event, ranking her as the first woman since Henie to take the figure skating title in two consecutive Games.

On the slick downhill slopes, blasted by howling chinook gales, Italian heartthrob Alberto Tomba raced to victory in the slalom and giant slalom, while France's Franck Piccard took the gold in the new super giant slalom—scoring the first downhill victory for France since Killy's golds in 1968. Despite the wicked winds, Finland's irascible ski jumper Matti "Nuke-'em" Nykänen soared to two gold-medal distances and a third team jumping gold. Jamaica's first-ever bobsled team—including a reggae singer and a helicopter pilot—rumbled down the chute, and America's Bonnie "the Blur" Blair outpaced her rivals to the gold in women's speed skating. But favored U.S. skater Dan Jansen tragically slipped and fell in the 500-meter race just hours after learning that his twenty-seven-year-old sister, Jane, had lost her life to leukemia. Four days later, while competing in the 1,000-meter speed skating event, Jansen, hobbled by grief, caught an edge and agonizingly crashed to the ice again.

### 1992 ALBERTVILLE

#### VEGARD ULVANG, NOR

*Vegard "the Viking" Ulvang, Norway's adventurer-hero from the Arctic Circle, raced to three Nordic skiing golds in Albertville. In his spare time, Ulvang has ridden across Outer Mongolia on horseback, skied across Greenland, and climbed the highest mountain peaks in North America, South America, and Africa.*

Photo: © Duomo, Paul J. Sutton.

### 1992 ALBERTVILLE

#### JAMAICAN BOBSLED TEAM

*Driven to compete, the Jamaican bobsled team made its second Olympic appearance at the Winter Games in Albertville. The team, which attracted worldwide attention in Calgary in 1988, originally gained its bobbing skills by practicing on pushcarts in the snowless Blue Mountains of Jamaica. At the 1994 Lillehammer Games, the Jamaican four-man team finished in fourteenth place, beating the U.S.*

Photos: Above, Archives, Olympic Museum Lausanne; Opposite © Duomo, David Madison.

## KRISTI YAMAGUCHI, USA

*Kristi Yamaguchi, 20, gracefully twirled and jumped to America's first gold in women's figure skating since Dorothy Hamill won the Olympic title in 1976. Born with clubfeet—an impairment that was corrected— Yamaguchi grew up in Fremont, California, playing with a Dorothy Hamill doll.*

Photo: © Duomo, David Madison.

## BIATHLON

*The demanding biathlon event, which combines Nordic skiing and riflery, was introduced as a Winter Olympic sport in 1960. Biathletes must demonstrate enormous physical control by skiing vigorously, then shooting at targets fifty meters away. Moldova's Gherhi Vasilii competed in the 1994 Olympic men's biathlon, which was dominated by the Russians.*

Photo: © Duomo, David Madison.

Blair and Jansen had a second shot at gold medals four years later at the 1992 Winter Olympics in Albertville, France. Again, Blair flashed past her competitors, this time snaring two golds. And again, Jansen crumbled. This time it was sheer lack of speed that tripped him up—he finished fourth in the 500-meter and twenty-sixth in the 1,000-meter race. But despite the speed skating reprise, winds of change whipped through other Olympic event sites, scattered across 620 square miles of sun-glazed Alpine peaks. Athletes from the now-bloodied country that was Yugoslavia took part  under the emblems of Yugoslavia, Croatia, and Slovenia. Most Olympians from the former Soviet republics competed as the Unified Team—without an anthem or a superpower budget but with enough talent to muscle golds in ice hockey, men's figure skating, pairs skating, ice dancing, and five Nordic events, including the first-ever women's ski-and-shoot biathlon.

The bone-quaking sport of freestyle mogul skiing debuted as an Olympic medal event, won by America's Donna Weinbrecht and France's Edgar Grospiron. In the ice rink, America's Kristi Yamaguchi—who had grown up playing with a Dorothy Hamill doll—calmly outperformed four top-ranked rivals to win the first U.S. women's figure skating gold since 1976. And up on the sun-splashed Savoie slopes, it was total Tomba-mania as frenzied Italians roared for their Alpine idol, "La Bomba." Not one to disappoint, Alberto Tomba zipped through the gates to a gold in the giant slalom—and a record as the first Olympic downhiller to take two consecutive golds in the same event. His teammate, Deborah Compagnoni, sped off with another gold for Italy in the super giant slalom.

Two years later in Lillehammer, Norway—the first Games on a new Olympic schedule that alternates summer and winter events every two years—Compagnoni did it again, this time in the giant slalom. America's Diann Roffe-Steinrotter swooped down Kvitfjell Mountain for a gold in the Super G, and the downhill belonged to her ballistic teammate Tommy Moe. There was no question, though, that the Games themselves belonged to the Norwegians, who swept twenty-six medals—including ten

1994 LILLEHAMMER

**CATHY TURNER, USA**

*At Lillehammer, Cathy Turner—a part-time singer and songwriter—clinched her second gold medal in 500-meter short-track speed skating. The collision-prone, pack-skating event debuted at the 1992 Winter Games in Albertville, where Turner took the title.*

Photos: Left, Archives, Olympic Museum Lausanne; Below © Duomo, William R. Sallaz.

*Following spread: Tommy Moe speeds to gold in Lillehammer in 1994.*

Photo: © Duomo, Al Tielemans.

1994 LILLEHAMMER

**BRIAN BOITANO, USA**

*U.S. Olympic figure skating
champion Brian Boitano—who
had edged his good friend,
Canadian favorite Brian Orser,
for the gold medal in the 1988
Calgary Games—returned to
the Olympics in 1994. This
time, however, Boitano went
home empty-handed after
taking a spill during his triple
axel combination.*

Photo: © Duomo, Paul J. Sutton.

golds, the most of any nation. While the off-rink melodrama of U.S. figure skaters Tonya Harding and Nancy Kerrigan enthralled much of the media, Oksana Baiul, a Ukrainian teenager, shimmered on the ice and upstaged her competitors for the gold— even while skating with three stitches in her leg and a bruised spine from a tumble she had taken in practice.

Under the vast arched timbers of the Vikingskipet skating hall, Norway's speed skating sensation, Johann Olav Koss, scored triple golds in the 1,500-, 5,000-, and 10,000-meter races. America's Bonnie Blair retired—declining to compete in the 1998 Games in Nagano, Japan—after bolting to her fifth Olympic gold in the 1,000-meter sprint. And in the best Cinderella story of these—or perhaps

1994 LILLEHAMMER

**OKSANA BAIUL, UKR**

*Braving painful leg injuries,
Ukrainian figure skating star
Oksana Baiul, 16, enchanted
judges with a flawlessly
expressive routine and
upstaged American favorite
Nancy Kerrigan for the
Olympic gold.*

Photo: © Duomo, Al Tielemans.

any—Olympic Games, star-crossed skater Dan Jansen, beaten in his best event, the 500-meters, finally glided to a gold medal and a new world record in the 1,000—his very last Olympic race. As the hearts of millions went out in happiness to Jansen, the lights went out inside the Viking ship, and he skated a breathtaking victory lap alone with his baby daughter, Jane, cradled in his arms. The rapture of that moment wasn't about medal counts or winning or national Olympic pride. As a Japanese coach had mused earlier, touching his hand to his chest and pondering Jansen's anguishing Olympic journey, "The gold medal is, maybe, in the heart."

## DAN JANSEN, USA

*Victory was sweet for star-crossed U.S. speed skater Dan Jansen (opposite), who finally claimed gold in Lillehammer in the 1,000 meters—his very last Olympic race—after failing to medal at the Calgary and Albertville Winter Games.*

Photo: © Duomo, Al Tielemans.

## SKI JUMPING

*German and Norwegian ski jumpers glided to gold medals in 1994. The Germans, led by Jens Weissflog, dominated the team jumping and large hill competitions, while Espen Bredesen took the title in the normal hill jump, clinching Norway's first gold in ski jumping since 1964.*

Photo: © Duomo, William Sallaz.

## JOHANN OLAV KOSS, NOR

*Local hero Johann Olav Koss stormed to triple golds for Norway in three speed skating events—the 1,500-, 5,000-, and 10,000-meter races. Koss clinched his first Olympic gold at Albertville in the 1,500 meters.*

Photo: © Duomo, Steven E. Sutton.

*Since the very first Winter Olympics*

*at Chamonix, France, in 1924, the*

## THE WINTER OLYMPIC POSTERS

*intimate, snow-swept spirit of the Games*

*has been conveyed in posters produced by*

*Olympic host towns in Europe, North*

*America, and Asia. The first Winter*

*Games poster was created by the Paris-*

*Lyon-Méditerranée railway, which*

*subsidized construction of the skating rink*

*and other facilities in Chamonix.*

*Chamonix 1924*

*St. Moritz 1928*

*Cortina d'Ampezzo 1956*

*Squaw Valley 1960*

*Lake Placid 1980*

*Sarajevo 1984*

*Lake Placid 1932*

*Garmisch–Partenkirchen 1936*

*St. Moritz 1948*

*Oslo 1952*

*Innsbruck 1964*

*Grenoble 1968*

*Sapporo 1972*

*Innsbruck 1976*

# ARTS AND
# THE ATHLETES

Linked with the grueling effort and exhilaration of Olympic sport is the spellbinding beauty of performance. The sinewed bodies of the athletes, pushing with profound grace the limits of the elements and human will, have fascinated artists since ancient times. Olympic champions have inspired lasting ideals of physical beauty and, in

THE CULTURAL OLYMPIAD

art and architecture, moving collective expressions of human aspiration. Today, with television broadcasts of Olympic pageantry, triumphs, and failures reaching virtually every corner of the planet, the Olympic Games are also an awesome dramatic spectacle—in effect, world theater played out before an audience of half the human race.

In ancient Greece, where the Olympic Games were born more than twenty-seven centuries ago, art and physical performance were intertwined. Both the artist and the athlete were inspired by the goal of striving, as much as humanly possible, for godlike perfection. Athletes oiled their muscles and trained rigorously to the music of flutes in wrestling, discus, running, and other disciplines. While they practiced, artists watched, carefully observing the beauty of anatomy in motion and using that knowledge to create some of the world's greatest examples of figurative sculpture.

Art in Greece was intended for public display, and Olympia, where the ancient Games were played, was crammed with sculpture immortalizing the athletes, mythological heroes, and the gods to whom the Games were consecrated. The aesthetic setting of the Games was

## ANATOMY IN MOTION

*In ancient Greece, the physical beauty of Olympic athletes— exemplified in recent times by the muscular grace of diver Greg Louganis (opposite), and pole vaulter Sergei Bubka (below)—inspired some of the world's greatest achievements in figurative art.*

*Photos: Above, Archives, Olympic Museum Lausanne; Below and right © Duomo, Steven E. Sutton.*

OLYMPIC INSPIRATION

*Since the founding of the
modern Games in 1896,
painting, sculpture, and other
visual and performance arts
have been an integral part of
the Olympic experience.*

*Above: Lithograph by
Venezuelan optic artist Carlos
Cruz Díez. "Suite Olympic
Centennial," Olympic Museum,
Lausanne, Switzerland. Below:
Jesse Owens, 1942, modeled
from life by Joseph Brown.
Ohio State University,
Columbus, Ohio.*

enhanced by monumental architecture, particularly the towering Temple of Zeus, constructed in the mid-fifth century B.C. Behind its soaring columns and sculpted pediments loomed the colossal seated statue of the god Zeus, one of the Seven Wonders of the World. Now perished, the statue was created of wood overlain with gold and ivory by the famed sculptor Phidias, who kept his workshop at Olympia. The influence of the Olympic Games on Hellenic art was so strong that, according to one scholar, Greece's greatest aesthetic achievements would never have been possible if the Games had not existed.

When Pierre de Coubertin revived the Olympics in 1894, his goal was not simply to reestablish what he saw as the classical link between physical training, competition, and national leadership. He also sought to rekindle the Greek spiritual connection between art and sport. The universal messages of the Games, Coubertin saw, needed to be communicated through artistic symbols and ceremony, such as the dramatic flight of doves that opened the very first of the modern Games in Athens in 1896. In that spirit, other icons and rituals followed. The Olympic flag, with its design of five interlacing rings representing the five participating continents, was raised for the first time at the 1920 Olympics in Antwerp, and the Olympic oath was first movingly pronounced there by the Belgian fencer Victor Boin. The Olympic flame first blazed at the 1928 Games in Amsterdam, and in 1936, at the Berlin Olympics, it was first carried hand to hand from Olympia in Greece in a fiery relay that recalled the ceremonial torch races of ancient Hellas.

For Coubertin, however, the relationship of art and Olympic sport was more fundamental than these symbolic gestures. Reflecting this conviction, he added a clause to the Olympic charter stating that cultural events "of an equal standard" should be organized in conjunction with the Games. In 1906, he convened a conference in Paris to explore the connection of art, literature, and sport and the ways in which they might be formally combined in celebration of the revived Olympic Games. The conference recommended that, in addition to athletic contests, the Olympics should include official competitions in five aesthetic areas: architecture, sculpture, painting, music, and literature. Quadrennial prizes would be awarded for the best new works that found their inspiration in sport.

These artistic competitions were officially included in the 1912 Olympics in

Stockholm, and they were part of every Olympic program over the next three decades. After the 1948 Games in London, however, they were abandoned. The mediocre quality of many of the entries was one reason. It was also plain that the majority of spectators were interested chiefly, if not exclusively, in Olympic sports events. Although Olympiads after 1948 jettisoned the artistic competitions, they continued to celebrate the link between sport and art in exhibitions, performances, dramatic ceremonial displays, and often spectacular works of architectural design.

In Mexico City in 1968, the Games were coupled with a year-long Cultural Olympiad that drew painters, poets, sculptors, musicians, and performers from five continents and featured a  massive exposition of children's art. Spectators at the Munich Olympics in 1972 passed under a colossal sky sculpture by Otto Piene called *Olympic Rainbow*— an inflated, two-thousand-foot-long arch, made up of five colored, helium-filled tubes. And the 1992 Games in Barcelona took place surrounded by installations of more than fifty new commissioned works of urban sculpture created by artists such as Richard Serra, Ellsworth Kelly, Roy Lichtenstein, and Antoni Tàpies.

Perhaps the ultimate Olympic art celebration took place in Los Angeles in 1984. The city's 10-week Olympic Arts Festival, planned in conjunction with the twenty-third Olympiad, brought together nearly a hundred exhibits and performances from more than twenty countries. Fusing traditional and avant-garde artistic currents from Asia and the West, the Festival attracted artists ranging from the Korean National Dance Company and the Royal Opera of Covent Garden to Australia's free-form Circus Oz, the provocative Pina Bausch Wuppertaler Tanztheater from the Federal Republic of Germany, and China's traditional Central Ensemble of National Music.

Inspiring and often technically daring works of architecture have also conveyed the artistic energy of numerous Olympiads since 1948. For many cities, the prospect of hosting the Olympic Games sparked a renaissance and redesign of urban spaces, led by the construction of new stadiums, swimming pools, and other sports facilities. Beginning with the Helsinki Games in 1952, however, Olympic architecture broke out of its largely functional tradition with spirited, modern structures of unified design. Eight years later, the drama of the Olympic Games in Rome was staged in daringly engineered, domed sports palaces designed by Pier Luigi Nervi—as well as in the

### DRAMA AND SPECTACLE

*At the 1984 Summer Olympic Games, the Los Angeles Coliseum was packed with 93,000 spectators for the $6 million Opening Ceremonies spectacular. The extravaganza featured 10,000 performers, flags, and pageantry, including a choir of 960 voices and 84 baby grand pianos (below).*

*Following spread: 1984 Opening Ceremonies in Sarajevo.*

Photos: Below and following spread
© Duomo, Steven E. Sutton.

spectacular environs of the city's ancient architectural masterpieces. Gymnasts performed in the elaborately arched Baths of Caracalla, while wrestlers grappled in the colossal Basilica of Maxentius, and marathoners paced to the finish line beneath the soaring span of the Arch of Constantine.

In Munich in 1972, a boldly designed, curving lattice of steel cables and acrylic glass towered over the Olympic stadiums and titanic swimming pool, which had sufficient seating to accommodate 10,000 spectators. Munich's "Olympiaplatz," a vast sports park built for the Games, remains one of the city's most frequently recreational areas. By contrast, the 1984 Olympics in Los Angeles produced no new architectural landmarks. Existing civic and university buildings were used as settings for the Games; however, their exteriors were temporarily transformed by the illusions of bold color, three-dimensional graphics, scaffolding, tents, fabric, paper, and mylar. Like a stage set, the dazzling façade came down when the Games left town.

For Seoul, South Korea, hosting the 1988 Olympics was a catalyst for reimagining the city center and experimenting with inventive architectural design. The city's gymnastic and fencing stadiums were capped by revolutionary fabric roofs supported by radiating webs of tension cables. These groundbreaking "tensegrity" domes, based on the theoretical work of the pioneering architect and engineer R. Buckminster Fuller, were the first such structures ever built. New architectural technology and forms also created a striking setting for the 1994 Winter Olympic Games in Lillehammer, Norway. Designed to resemble the capsized hull of a Viking ship, the roof of the Olympic skating rink in Hamar, south of Lillehammer, was supported by the longest expanse of wooden beams of any structure in the world. Architectural and geological engineering records were also broken in the construction of the Gjøvik Olympic Cavern Arena, a 6,000-seat underground hockey rink hewn out of the red rock side of Hovdetoppen mountain.

Architecture and design set the stage on which the Olympic drama is played out. But the beauty of the human form and the struggle and

grace of competition form the emotional heart of the art of the Games. Modern Olympic moments frozen in figurative images, such as Joseph Brown's bronze statue of track paragon Jesse Owens pounding to the finish line, capture the drama of athletes pushing themselves beyond the limits of ordinary humans. In cinema, as well, artists have attempted to frame riveting Olympic images. The most masterly example ever produced is German filmmaker Leni Riefenstahl's documentary *Olympia* (1938). Despite her uncritical admiration for Adolf Hitler, Riefenstahl's four-hour film of the lavish, propagandist 1936 Berlin Games is a romantic, moving tribute to Olympic sport. In contrast to Riefenstahl's mythic glorification of the Games, another masterpiece—Kon Ichikawa's intimate film *Tokyo Olympiad*, produced in 1964—documents instead the lonely anxiety of the athletes as they struggle to excel.

The twin emotions of agony and rapture that drive Olympic athletes to compete also compel us to watch, transfixed, as whole lifetimes of effort climax in a single Olympic moment. It is a melodrama as cathartic as any scripted piece of theater. For a few weeks every four years, the athletes wear our nation's colors on their sleeves and carry our hopes with them into competition. Perhaps nowhere is this collective aspiration—for success and peace and the ideal of fair play—more potently expressed than in the spectacle of the Opening Ceremonies.

It is mesmerizing theater, amplified by Olympic pageants that stretch the limits of the imagination. In Moscow in 1980, 16,000 performers filled the stadium during a four-hour opening spectacle. Four years later, in Los Angeles, the Games opened with the release of millions of white and gold balloons and a cinematic evocation of American history and culture by 10,000 performers, including more than eighty pianists. In 1988, the Seoul Opening Ceremonies awed 70,000 spectators and a television audience of nearly three billion, as a cast of nearly 14,000 performed Koreran rituals and dances. Children rolled metaphorical hoops of hope, and *tae kwon do* experts split pieces of wood as a symbol of shattering barriers among the people of the world. At the

## A PAGEANT OF PEOPLE

*In Seoul, South Korea (below and following spread), the field of the Olympic Stadium was filled with 13,625 men, women, and children who performed Korean dances, rituals, and martial arts displays during the Opening Ceremonies.*

Photos: Below © Duomo, Paul J. Sutton;
Following spread © Duomo, Steven E. Sutton.

## CULTURAL DISPLAYS

*During Opening Ceremonies in Calgary (opposite) and Seoul (below), millions of people watched the parade of athletes and costumed performers.*

Photos: Oppposite © Duomo, Paul J. Sutton;
Below © Duomo, Steven E. Sutton.

*Performers dressed as trolls and elves surround a glowing image of the earth during the Opening Ceremonies of the 1994 Winter Olympic Games in Lillehammer (opposite). The avant-garde Opening Ceremonies of the 1992 Albertville Winter Games (below) featured stiltwalkers, bungee jumpers, and women bedecked in transparent plastic bubbles.*

Photos: Opposite © Duomo, David Madison; Below © Duomo, Steven E. Sutton.

climax of the spectacle, a high school student, university student, and teacher were raised to the top of a 95-foot column called the World Tree to kindle the Olympic flame.

The magic was unbroken by Barcelona in 1992, where the Games opened with a $28 million allegorical confection of robots, fighter jets, sea monsters, Spanish dancers, and operatic tenors.

The opening of the Winter Games that year in Albertville, France, was equally spectacular and exuberantly avant-garde. Eight stunt planes streamed rainbows of colored smoke, and sixty-four rollerbladers—one for each participating nation—carried emblems of the Olympic teams. The athletes themselves were led into the stadium by women costumed in transparent plastic bubbles filled with simulated snowflakes. Stilt walkers, dancers, jugglers, and acrobats spilled out of three fifteen-foot-high cornucopias, bungee jumpers ricocheted off the ground, and gigantic, inflated, neon green and yellow worms wiggled in the Alpine night. Olympic fantasy opened the 1994 Lillehammer Winter Games as well. Trolls, elves, and other creatures from Norse myths teemed around a giant egg-shaped globe that rose into the sky, surrounded by a silent flock of doves.

These spectacles echo the real, electrifying moments of competition, but the most gripping beauty and drama of the Games takes place in the stadiums and pools and on the tracks and icy slopes. Artists mirror the hope and emotional spirit of these instants. To paraphrase the critic George Jean Nathan, art is a tangible dream—and Olympic art, from figurative images to fantastic pageantry, gives moving form to the dream of Olympic glory.

*In the most dramatic moment of the 1992 Opening Ceremonies in Barcelona, Antonio Rebollo—a polio-stricken archer from Madrid—fired a flaming arrow through the night sky to set ablaze the Olympic cauldron.*

Photo: © Duomo, David Madison.

LAUSANNE

## THE OLYMPIC MUSEUM

*Opened in 1993 in Lausanne, Switzerland, the Olympic Museum celebrates the tradition of the Games with extensive exhibitions of Olympic artwork, memorabilia, and historical artifacts. Designed by Pedro Ramirez Vásquez of Mexico City and Jean-Pierre Cahen of Lausanne, the new museum, located on the shore of Lake Geneva, contains five stories of collections ranging from Greek antiquities to specimens of all the Olympic torches carried since 1936. Works by artists* such as Auguste Rodin and Antoni Tàpies, along with exhibitions of Olympic stamps, coins, pins, and medals; Olympic equipment; and a vast library of books, photographs, film, and *video all document the history and culture of the Olympic Games.*

*Photos: Above, Archives, Olympic Museum Lausanne, Donatsch / Prahn; Far right, Archives, Olympic Museum Lausanne, Donatsch; Left and right, Archives, Olympic Museum Lausanne.*

*Athens 1896*

*Athens 1896*

*Paris 1900*

*St. Louis 1904*

*London 1908*

*London 1908*

*Stockholm 1912*

*Stockholm 1912*

*Stockholm 1912*

*Antwerp 1920*

*Paris 1924*

*Paris 1924*

*Amsterdam 1928*

*Amsterdam 1928*

*Los Angeles 1932*

*Berlin 1936*

*Berlin 1936*

*Berlin 1936*

*Berlin 1936*

*Melbourne 1956*

*Rome 1960*

*Rome 1960*

*Rome 1960*

*Tokyo 1964*

*Mexico City 1968*

*Munich 1972*

*Montreal 1976*

*Moscow 1980*

*Moscow 1980*

*Los Angeles 1984*

*Los Angeles 1984*

*Los Angeles 1984*

*Seoul 1988*

*Barcelona 1992*

*Barcelona 1992*

One of the most popular side events at the Olympic Games is the sport of pin trading. The history of Olympic pins goes back to the beginning of the

## OLYMPIC PINS

modern Games in 1896. The first pins were distributed at the inaugural Olympic Games in Athens as identification badges for athletes, judges, and officials. At the 1912 Olympics in Stockholm, pins were advertised and offered for sale to spectators for the first time in an effort to raise money for the Games. Pin trading began to flourish at the 1924 Summer Games in Paris, and, after five decades of increasing popularity, it became a genuine craze at the Lake Placid Winter Games in 1980. By the 1984 Summer Olympics, 20,000 "pinheads" a day were swarming parking lot trading tents in Los Angeles, and at the Winter Games in 1988, the University of Calgary sponsored a symposium on the fine art of Olympic pin trading and negotiating. Pin fever continued unabated in Seoul, Barcelona, Albertville, and Lillehammer.

Athens 1896

Paris 1900

St. Louis 1904

*Two types of medals are awarded at the Olympic Games: gold, silver, and bronze victory medals, which are*

## THE COMMEMORATIVE MEDALS

Los Angeles 1932

Berlin 1936

London 1948

*presented to the winners, and Olympic commemorative medals (right), which are awarded, along with diplomas, to all competitors and Olympic and team officials participating in the Games. In addition, special medals have also been produced during certain Olympiads, such as the Olympic Medal of King Gustav V, which was distributed to members of the Swedish royal family, dignitaries, and Swedish medalists during the 1912 Olympics. A similar royal medal, bearing the likeness of Belgium's King Albert, was minted for the Antwerp Olympic Games in 1920.*

Munich 1972

Montreal 1976

Moscow 1980

Photos: Archives, Olympic Museum Lausanne.

Chamonix 1924

St. Moritz 1928

Lake Placid 1932

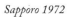

Innsbruck 1964

Grenoble 1968

Sapporo 1972

Innsbruck 1976

*London 1908*

*Stockholm 1912*

*Antwerp 1920*

*Paris 1924*

*Amsterdam 1928*

*Helsinki 1952*

*Melbourne 1956*

*Rome 1960*

*Tokyo 1964*

*Mexico City 1968*

*Los Angeles 1984*

*Seoul 1988*

*Barcelona 1992*

*Garmisch–Partenkirchen 1936*

*St. Moritz 1948*

*Oslo 1952*

*Cortina d'Ampezzo 1956*

*Squaw Valley 1960*

*Lake Placid 1980*

*Sarajevo 1984*

*Calgary 1988*

*Albertville 1992*

*Lillehammer 1994*

# TRAINING AND TECHNOLOGY

Luge is a sport for speed demons. Flat on their backs, free-falling down serpentine ice chutes at screamingly fast speeds up to seventy-five miles per hour, lugers abandon themselves like human bullets to the power of velocity. Sliding is all about big speed, big adrenaline rushes, and big risks. Winning an Olympic medal in luge, however, is an altogether

different matter. What separates a gold medalist from an also-ran is not a huge margin of daring and speed, but a hairsbreadth of an advantage—hundredths, sometimes thousandths, of a second. For sliders, gaining that edge can come down to a tough choice between raising their heads for an instant to see where in the world they're going, thereby risking a millisecond of air drag, and keeping their bodies as unwaveringly flat and aerodynamic as a rocket—and possibly risking a bone-jarring crash into the side of the chute.

Helping athletes achieve that sometimes decisive extra measure of performance is the mission of sports science and technology. It's a discipline that first took off in the 1950s, when Eastern European nations seized the lead in developing scientifically based methods for training their athletes. As a result of their sophisticated approaches, the USSR and the German Democratic Republic swept many of the medals at the 1976 Olympic Games in Montreal—provoking the western nations to scurry to launch sports science programs of their own. As a result, biomechanists, physiologists, engineers, computer scientists, and psychologists have been pooling their scientific expertise to give elite athletes the

## THE LUGE START

*The most critical moment of the luge run is the start, when athletes paddle across the ice before plunging down the chute. By shaving a tenth of a second off the start with faster, more efficient moves, sliders can cut three-tenths of a second off their finishing times.*

Photos: Above © Duomo, David Madison; Below © Duomo, Steven E. Sutton.

MEASURING PERFORMANCE

*At the U.S. Olympic Training Center in Colorado Springs, sports scientists gauge athletes' physiological responses to the stress of exercise. Swimmers (opposite) are tested for the efficiency of their oxygen intake in a 50,000-gallon flume tank, in which they swim against an artificial current. Cyclists' heart rates and oxygen intake are tested on stationary equipment (below) in the sports phsyiology lab.*

*Photos: Opposite © Duomo, David Madison; Below © Duomo.*

benefit of every advance in training, equipment, technique, and mental preparation—details that can lead to a hair-splitting advantage in Olympic competition.

For American lugers—upstarts in a sport dominated for decades by the Germans, the Austrians, and the Italians—the focus of research is the start, the most pivotal moment in the race. Before they plunge down the chute, sliders sit on their sleds and push off from stationary handles, then accelerate by paddling across the ice with metal-spiked gloves before positioning themselves flat on their backs. A mere tenth of a second saved during the luge start can shave three-tenths of a second off a competitor's finishing time.

In Lake Placid, New York, biomechanists are working to boost the efficiency of every aspect of the sliders' starting motions and techniques. High-speed video cameras record athletes' balance and timing, while strain gauges on the start handles and accelerometers attached to the sled measure horizontal and vertical forces, paddling symmetry, and velocity as sliders hurtle across the ice. Telemetry systems are being designed that will instantaneously transmit the data to a computer, so that lugers will receive immediate feedback on the speed and effectiveness of their starts. The goal of all the scientific data is to fine-tune athletes' individual training programs and techniques—helping them approach, and possibly achieve, ideal levels of performance.

In boating sports such as rowing, canoeing, and kayaking, real-time biomechanical information is already being gathered and relayed to coaches and athletes for instant analysis. With this data, athletes can work to maximize the propulsion power of their oar

strokes and minimize the drag created by air and water as their boats speed over 500- to 2,000-meter courses.

*Cross-country ski boot*

SKATES

*Over the years, ice skates have been uniquely modified for speed, maneuverability, and precision. Speed skates, for example, have no toe pick—a design feature that is essential for athletes executing the sudden stops and jumps required in figure skating routines.*

*Photos: All footwear, Archives, Olympic Museum Lausanne, J. Donatsch.*

*Figure skate, late 1800s*

*Speed skate, 1900–1920*

*Short-track speed skate, 1988*

*Figure skate, about 1956*

*Figure skate, 1993*

Improving on the early lead of East German scientists, who developed an effective but ungainly 100-pound assemblage of onboard scientific instruments, American engineers have outfitted a two-person rowing shell with a featherweight, pound and a half of sensitive equipment that measures the force and angle of the oars, the speed of the boat, and acceleration. Additional instruments will also gauge boat dynamics, as well as the oarsman's heart rate and body position. Data is transmitted real-time, by radio telemetry, to a computer carried on the coach's boat, so that training instructions can be refined, minute by minute, to maximize performance.

In addition to instrumentation, biomechanists rely on the visual impact of video enhanced by computer software. Sports scientists have long been using high-speed film and video to capture detailed views of athletes in action. Over the last few years, however, biomechanists have paired video cameras with computerized digital technology to create three-dimensional, stick-figure-like graphics of an athlete's every move. During the 1992 Olympics in Barcelona, for example, high-speed video cameras recorded a wide range of competitions, including pole vaulting, javelin throwing, ring gymnastics, and the men's 100-meter freestyle swimming event. The video images were then digitized and studied to understand the motions used by the best-performing athletes.

In figure skating, biomechanists have created three-dimensional graphics of every move that skaters use in the difficult, three-and-a-half revolution, triple axel jump—a maneuver mastered by Canadian champion Brian Orser and American gold medalist Brian Boitano in the 1988 Calgary Winter Games. Sports scientists are also using digitized images to give Olympic weight lifters a vivid, visual description of their positioning and the crucial symmetry of their lifting motions.

The quicker an athlete receives performance feedback, the more useful it is in training. Video digitizing, however, can be a very time-consuming process, so scientists are turning to other forms of computer-enhanced imaging to give athletes and coaches faster input. Within an hour, for example, decathletes can view a still video image of their shot-put throw, overlaid by computer-generated graphics that point out the height, angle, and velocity of their release. In ice dancing, a sport with an important aesthetic component, partners can study similar images, produced minutes after they leave the ice, that visually quantify key elements of their performance, such as their alignment and angle of lean.

## 3·D GRAPHICS

*Biomechanists are harnessing computer technology to analyze the performance of elite athletes. The three-dimensional chart below graphs the progression of movements made by a skater while performing the difficult triple axel jump. The graphic can be rotated on the computer screen to display the maneuver from a variety of angles.*

Photo: © U.S. Olympic Training Center.

*Boxing shoe*

## DIGITIZED IMAGES

*Using high-speed video cameras and computerized digital technology, biomechanists are able to create stick-figure-like images of every motion used by top-performing athletes in the long jump, figure skating triple axel, pole vault, javelin throw, and a wide range of other elite competitions. Athletes and their coaches study the images to learn the most effective motions and positioning.*

Photos: Above left © Duomo, Steven E. Sutton;
Above right © Paul J. Sutton;
Below © U.S. Olympic Training Center.

Thanks to a device called the "Leaper Beeper," developed by Florida State University sports scientist John Shea, divers can also get immediate feedback during training sessions. Electronic sensors, connected to a laptop computer, instantly gather information on the height of each dive and the force of the diver's impact on the board. Coded beeps emitted by the system give athletes information about their dives before they even hit the water.

Sports scientists have also exploited laser technology to improve training techniques. Olympic shooters, for example, now practice using a rifle or pistol mounted with a finger-sized laser that projects a light beam onto the target. The beam, recorded on video, tracks shooters' aim and the steadiness of their hold before firing. The system is now also being adapted to help archers perfect their aim.

While new training technology is enabling athletes to coax extra power and control out of their muscles, improvements in equipment are also helping Olympic-caliber competitors achieve faster, higher, and stronger performances than ever thought possible. Over the past forty years, record after record has been shattered, partly as the result of stronger, lighter, and more accurate athletic gear. To be sure, natural factors have also contributed to competitive success. With the tripling of the world's population since 1900, there are probably more talented athletes in the world today than there were a century ago. Better nutrition and medicine in many countries have also enhanced sports performance.

But scientific innovations in equipment design may play the single biggest role in helping athletes accomplish the incredible. The sport of pole vaulting is a good example. In the 1960s, the bamboo pole traditionally used in the event was replaced by a fiberglass version, borrowed from a deep-sea fishing-rod design. After elite athletes switched to the new poles—and, more recently, to poles made of carbon composite materials—they vaulted 30 percent higher than ever before, raising the world record from fifteen feet to more than twenty feet.

Records also fell fast—frighteningly so—after the javelin was redesigned. In the 1950s, an American engineer, Dick Held, constructed a streamlined aluminum javelin for his brother

*Cross-country ski boot*

*Hockey skate*

Bud, a college athlete, because traditional wooden javelins often broke and were expensive to replace. With the new, aerodynamic javelin, Bud Held was able to reach astonishing distances, shattering the previous world record by more than twenty feet. By the early 1980s, engineers had refined Held's original design so much that the newest javelins traveled even farther. In fact, they were quite capable of sailing out of the field and into the bleachers, imperiling spectators and unsuspecting athletes. Alarmed, the sport's rules committee decided to restrain scientific progress in the name of safety and, in 1986, banished these aerodynamically advanced models. As a result, the world record in the javelin throw has since plunged by thirty feet.

A more successful outcome has resulted from improvements in archery equipment. Olympic-caliber archers are amazingly accurate, able to cluster most of their arrows within the top-scoring center circle of the target. But recent innovations in bow and arrow design have made the best archers even better. Instead of using traditional wooden bows, which can be affected by fatigue, moisture, and temperature changes, tournament archers now use more stable, lighter-weight bows made of fiberglass and carbon fibers sandwiched around a core of glass beads and foam. Linen bowstrings have been replaced by polyethylene strings that fire arrows at greater speeds. And the arrows themselves—once made of wood with eagle- and turkey-feather fletches—are now highly engineered projectiles fashioned out of ultrathin, carbon-wrapped aluminum with plastic stabilizers at their tails. As a result of these

### STRAIGHT ARROWS

*New ultrathin aluminum arrows stabilized with plastic fletches, fired from polyethylene bowstrings, are more consistent projectiles than the old-fashioned wood-and-feather arrows, which were propelled by bowstrings made of linen.*

*Photo: © Duomo.*

changes in technology, winning archery scores in top competition rounds have shot up from the 1,100s in the 1960s—out of a perfect score of 1,440—to the mid-1,300s today.

U.S. Olympic rifle and pistol shooters have benefited from a big improvement in the .22-caliber ammunition that they use. For years, the U.S. team purchased their ammunition from European manufacturers, who were widely recognized as producing the best-quality .22-caliber bullets. U.S. shooters remained at a disadvantage, however, because the top-of-the-line bullets were usually reserved for the European shooting teams. To level the playing field, U.S. Olympic Committee (USOC)

### HIGH-TECH BOWS

*Archers' scores are benefiting from new lightweight fiberglass bows, which are less sensitive to temperature and moisture than traditional wooden bows. Laser aim-tracking devices, used by Olympic shooters, are being adapted to help archers improve their accuracy.*

*Photo: © Duomo, Steven E. Sutton.*

sports scientists analyzed the characteristics of the best-performing, straightest-flying bullets. They then teamed up with a U.S. manufacturer to produce new ammunition called UltraMatch, which is made to exacting specifications with highly refined gunpowder. Armed with UltraMatch, U.S. shooters improved their standing and scored medals in Barcelona—Launi Meili's gold in the women's three-position rifle competition, the first for an American woman, and Bob Foth's silver in the men's.

### A BETTER BULLET

*U.S. sports scientists analyzed the qualities of the world's best .22-caliber bullets, then teamed with a manufacturer to produce super-high-quality UltraMatch ammunition. The new bullets helped U.S. shooters successfully target Olympic medals in Barcelona.*

Photo: © Allsport, Powell.

Changes in equipment have also helped speed skaters smash racing records. In February 1962, Canadian skater Paul Enoch astonished spectators at an international racing meet in Hamar, Norway—not just by his performance, which beat the world record by three seconds—but also by his unusual attire. At a time when speed skaters still wore flapping woolen clothing, Enoch sped around the rink dressed in a pair of his wife's skintight nylon stockings. His eyebrow-raising, aerodynamic outfit reduced air drag, propelling him to a record-breaking performance and setting a new standard for speed skating apparel. A year later, the first nylon racing suit was on the market, which evolved into the head-to-toe-sheathing racing skins worn by Olympic speed skaters today. In the near future, racers may be further aided by the new Norwegian "superskate," which has not yet been worn in Olympic competition. The completely redesigned carbon-fiber and steel skate weighs 30 percent less than traditional models and has an aerodynamic covering that encases the boot and blade almost to the ice. Its designers claim that, for every one hundred meters skated, it can increase a racer's speed by a full tenth of a second.

In some instances, it is technique rather than technology that breaks performance barriers. When U.S. Olympic high jumper Dick Fosbury introduced the revolutionary "Fosbury Flop" by hurling himself backward over the bar at the Mexico City Games in 1968, he beat the previous Olympic record by two and a half inches, took home the gold, and created a new, dominant style of jumping. And in the Winter Olympic sport of ski jumping, today's jumps far outstrip those of the 1960s, thanks to the innovative technique pioneered by Swedish jumper Jan Boklov. Instead of keeping his skis close together and parallel in the air—the usual jumping position—Boklov spread his ski tips far apart in an unconventional V-shaped formation. In this position, Boklov was able to sail enormous distances. Eventually, his

*Weightlifting shoe*

*Ski jumping boot*

controversial V-jump became a standard among ski jumpers, leading to jump distances that have increased nearly 50 percent in the last twenty-five years.

Mental preparedness can be every bit as important as athletic form. In fact, for Olympic athletes, the greatest challenge may not be the physically demanding schedule of practices and competition, but the intense psychological pressure that comes from competing in the world's most intensely watched arena. To help athletes bear up—and even more importantly, muster the mental control they need to win—sports psychologists coach competitors in breathing control, relaxation, and visualization methods. These techniques can have a powerful impact on performance.

Before the 1984 Games in Los Angeles, for example, gold-medal-winning U.S. gymnast Peter Vidmar and his teammates would, right before they ended practice every day, imagine that they were tied with the People's Republic of China in the last event of the Olympic men's team finals. Vidmar would close his eyes and picture himself standing in front of 10,000 people, fantasizing that millions more were watching him on television and that his performance would determine whether his team won or lost. Worked up by the imaginary intensity of competition, his heart would begin to pound as he began his last routine of the day. "Of course," Vidmar later recalled, "it was just practice, and we never really thought we would have to confront such a situation in the Olympics."

## THE FOSBURY FLOP

*At the Mexico City Games in 1968, U.S. high jumper Dick Fosbury revolutionized the sport with his backward "Fosbury Flop" over the bar. With his new jumping technique, Fosbury hurled himself two and a half inches past the previous Olympic record.*

Photo: Allsport / MSI

But as it turned out, they did. Going into the last event of the 1984 Games, the U.S. and Chinese scores were very close, and Vidmar was one of two final competitors on the horizontal bar. Just before his turn, he realized how well prepared he was for the enormous pressure of that moment—because he had already lived it dozens of times in his imagination. Vidmar's mental preparation worked. Feeling relaxed and comfortable, he scored a near-perfect 9.95 on his routine, and his team brought home the Olympic gold.

*Track shoe*

Every one of these performance-enhancing factors—scientific training, state-of-the-art equipment, and mental preparation—are being marshalled to help the U.S. cycling team gear up for the 1996 Games in Atlanta. The multidisciplinary effort, known as Project '96, involves an innovative, intense collaboration among the U.S. Cycling Federation, USOC sports scientists, and commercial sponsors including GT Bicycles, Mavic (a manufacturer of bicycle components), EDS computer technology, and Pearl Izumi (a bike-racing-wear designer).

To make sure that U.S. cyclists are at peak conditioning for the Games, scientists are monitoring each athlete's pedaling mechanics, aerodynamic positioning, power output, speed, and heart rate, as well as lactic acid measurements (high levels of lactic acid can signal that muscles are being overworked). With the data in hand, coaches are able to design highly individualized training regimens. Groundbreaking equipment will help reduce wind resistance, which can account for more than 90 percent of the forces that slow down a rider and bicycle at speeds of more than thirty miles per hour.

One of the main weapons against aerodynamic drag will be the GT Superbike—a new, wafer-thin, aluminum-frame bicycle that weighs in at less than seventeen pounds. The ultrastreamlined Superbike features a rear disk wheel, an aerodynamically spoked front wheel, a smooth profile with no protruding bolts or cables, and custom-designed aero handlebars. Positioned far over the front wheel, aero-bars force riders into the low-slung tuck position that helped U.S. cyclist Greg LeMond snatch victory in the 1989 Tour de France. In addition, bell-shaped helmets and one-piece, drag-resistant racing suits—tested, with the other equipment, in the General Motors wind tunnel—will make U.S. cyclists as "slippery" as possible in the road races and the velodrome.

Every millisecond gained could make a difference. In a recent match, the world champion U.S. pursuit cycling team beat the defending Australians by less than three-hundredths of a second—well within the speed advantage made possible by advances in training and aerodynamic equipment. In cycling, as in virtually every speed sport, the focus of technique, training, and science is to bridge the often infinitesimal gap between fast and fastest, between the effort and the gold.

### COMPUTERS SCORE PUNCHES

*Science and technology are also having an impact on the Olympic judging process. A new computerized scoring system in boxing instantly tallies results and maintains databases that, for the first time, keep tabs on judges' scoring patterns. The system is designed to detect any potential inconsistencies or bias—a new, technological solution to a problem that's as old as sport.*

*Photo: © Duomo.*

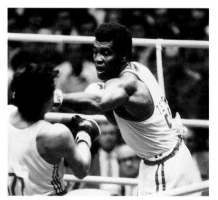

### WIND TUNNEL TESTS

*Wind resistance is a key factor in speed sports such as cycling. To help U.S. cyclists hone their edge for the 1996 Atlanta Games, the aerodynamics of their racing gear have been tested in the General Motors wind tunnel.*

*Photo: © U.S. Olympic Training Center.*

*Improvements in equipment engineering have led to big leaps in athletic performance. Back in the 1920s, for example, bike racers couldn't cover forty-five kilometers in one hour on their wood-and-steel, fixed-speed*

## ADVANCES IN EQUIPMENT

*bikes, and it wasn't until 1935 that this barrier fell. Even on modern racing bikes in the 1970s, cyclists couldn't break fifty kilometers in an hour. Then, riding bikes with aerodynamic disk wheels, Italy's Francesco Moser bolted more than fifty-one kilometers in an hour in 1984 and Swiss cyclist Tony Rominger topped fifty-five kilometers in 1994. Changing racket technology is also putting new spins on the sport of tennis. Until the late 1960s, all rackets were made of wood. Today, they are constructed of kevlar, graphite, and other lightweight materials. And the new wide-body rackets, stiffer and with heads almost twice as wide as traditional models, put much more speed and power in the ball. Opposite: Bobsled technology, too, has come a long way since the sport debuted in Switzerland in the late 1880s. Since the 1980s, mathematical simulations, wind-tunnel testing, computer modeling, and aerodynamic designs have helped boost Olympic bobsled speeds to new levels.*

Photos: Archives, Olympic Museum Lausanne, J. Donatsch;
1996 bicycle © GT Bicycles.

1896

1937

1984

1996

1992

1890

1910

1930

1976

1992

1904

1910

1920

1952

1984

# FASTER, HIGHER, STRONGER

Records fall, and the greatest athletic achievements are eventually eclipsed. But, for an Olympic champion, the moment of victory is etched in the world's memory. The virtuosity and courage that drives Olympic winners to the gold earns them a place in our modern pantheon of heroes. In a contest of giants, they are the best of the best.

## THE OLYMPIC CHAMPIONS

The listing of Olympic champions that follows is limited to gold-medal winners in both Summer and Winter events. Their winning scores are listed in times, distances, or points, and nationalities are indicated by country codes that have been adopted by the International Olympic Committee.

### KEY

| | | | | |
|---|---|---|---|---|
| AFG Afghanistan | | ISR Israel | PHI Philippines | TUN Tunisia |
| ALG Algeria | Armenia, Azerbaijan, Belarus, | ITA Italy | POL Poland | TUR Turkey |
| ARG Argentina | Georgia, Kyrghyzstan, | IVC Ivory Coast | POR Portugal | UAR United Arab Republic (Egypt |
| AUS Australia | Kazakhstan, Moldova, Russia, | JAM Jamaica | PRK North Korea (People's | and Syria) |
| AUT Austria | Tadjikistan, Turkmenistan, | JPN Japan | Republic of Korea) | UGA Uganda |
| BAH Bahamas | Ukraine, and Uzbekistan in | KAZ Kazakhstan | PUR Puerto Rico | UKR Ukraine (1994) |
| BEL Belgium | 1992) | KEN Kenya | ROM Romania | URU Uruguay |
| BER Bermuda | FIN Finland | KOR South Korea | RUS Russia (1908-1912, and 1994) | UZB Uzbekistan |
| BOH Bohemia | FRA France | KUW Kuwait | SAA Saar | USA United States of America |
| BRA Brazil | GBR Great Britain and Northern | LAT Latvia | SAF South Africa | VEN Venezuela |
| BUL Bulgaria | Ireland | LEB Lebanon | SEN Senegal | VIR U.S. Virgin Islands |
| BWI British West Indies (Jamaica | GDR East Germany (German | LIE Liechtenstein | SIN Singapore | YUG Yugoslavia |
| and Trinidad) | Democratic Republic, 1956- | LIT Lithuania | SLE Sierra Leone | ZAM Zambia |
| CAM Cameroon | 1988) | LUX Luxembourg | SMR San Marino | ZIM Zimbabwe |
| CAN Canada | GER Germany (1896-1936), West | MAD Madagascar | SOV Soviet Union | |
| CHI Chile | Germany (Federal Republic | MAL Malaysia | SPA Spain | TERMS: |
| CHN China | of Germany, 1952-1988) | MEX Mexico | SRL Sri Lanka (Ceylon) | |
| COL Colombia | GHA Ghana | MLW Malawi | SUD Sudan | |
| CON Congo | GRE Greece | MON Mongolia | SUR Surinam | |
| CRC Costa Rica | GUA Guatemala | MOR Morocco | SWE Sweden | |
| CUB Cuba | GUY Guyana | MYA Myanmar (Burma) | SWI Switzerland | |
| CZE Czechoslovakia | HAI Haiti | NGR Nigeria | SYR Syria | |
| DEN Denmark | HOL Holland (Netherlands) | NIG Niger | TAI Taiwan | |
| DJI Djibouti | HUN Hungary | NLA Netherland Antilles | TAN Tanzania | |
| DOM Dominican Republic | ICE Iceland | NOR Norway | TCH Czech and Slovak | |
| EGY Egypt | INA Indonesia | NZE New Zealand | Federative Republic | |
| EST Estonia | IND India | OMA Oman | THA Thailand | |
| ETH Ethiopia | INT International Team | PAK Pakistan | TOG Togo | |
| EUN Unified Team (represented | IRL Ireland (Eire) | PAN Panama | TON Tonga | |
| the former Soviet republics of | IRN Iran | PER Peru | TRI Trinidad and Tobago | |
| | IRQ Iraq | | | |

**TERMS:**

| | | | |
|---|---|---|---|
| * | variations in types of matches or distances | EOR | Equaled Olympic Record |
| | | EWR | Equaled World Record |
| + | one-hand lift | ICt | Indoor court |
| ++ | two-hand lift | OR | Olympic Record |
| ▲ | events held during Summer Olympic Games, prior to commencement of official Winter Olympics in 1924 | pts. | points |
| | | T | total |
| | | w | wind-aided |
| | | WB | World Best |
| | | WR | World Record |

**RECORD RESOURCE:**
*The Complete Book of the Olympics (David Wallechinsky, 1992 Edition.)*
Archery, Badminton, Baseball, Basketball, Canoeing, Cycling, Equestrian, Fencing, Field Hockey, Football (Soccer), Gymnastics, Handball, Judo, Modern Pentathlon, Rowing, Shooting, Swimming and Diving, Table Tennis, Tennis, Volleyball, Weightlifting, Wrestling, Yachting. All 1924-1988 Winter Olympic Champions and Records: Alpine Skiing, Bobsledding, Biathlon, Cross-Country Skiing- Men's and Women's, Figure Skating, Luge, Ski Jumping, Speed Skating, Short Track Speed Skating

*The World Almanac and Book of Facts 1994:*
Boxing, Track and Field - Men's and Women's, and all 1992 and 1994 Winter Olympic Records

*The U.S. Olympic Committee:*
All 1992 Summer Olympic Records
*Note:* Some country codes were changed in 1992 and are not reflected in this listing.

Discontinued events have not been inluded in this listing.

## CHAMPIONS OF THE SUMMER GAMES

### SUMMER GAMES SITES

| | |
|---|---|
| 1896 | Athens, Greece |
| 1900 | Paris, France |
| 1904 | St. Louis, USA |
| 1906 | Athens, Greece* |
| 1908 | London, Great Britain |
| 1912 | Stockholm, Sweden |
| 1920 | Antwerp, Belgium |
| 1924 | Paris, France |
| 1928 | Amsterdam, Holland |
| 1932 | Los Angeles, USA |
| 1936 | Berlin, Germany |
| 1948 | London, Great Britain |
| 1952 | Helsinki, Finland |
| 1956 | Melbourne, Australia |
| 1960 | Rome, Italy |
| 1964 | Tokyo, Japan |
| 1968 | Mexico City, Mexico |
| 1972 | Munich, Germany |
| 1976 | Montreal, Canada |
| 1980 | Moscow, USSR |
| 1984 | Los Angeles, USA |
| 1988 | Seoul, Korea |
| 1992 | Barcelona, Spain |
| 1996 | Atlanta, USA |
| 2000 | Sydney, Australia |

*Games not recognized by International Olympic Committee.

### ARCHERY

**MEN'S INDIVIDUAL**
*1896–1968 not held*
1972 John Williams, USA   WR
1976 Darrell Pace, USA   WR
1980 Tomi Poikolainen, FIN
1984 Darrell Pace, USA   OR
1988 Jay Barrs, USA
1992 Sebastian Flute, FRA
1996

**MEN'S TEAM**
*1896–1984 not held*
1988 KOR
1992 SPA
1996

**WOMEN'S INDIVIDUAL**
*1896–1968 not held*
1972 Doreen Wilber, USA   WR
1976 Luann Ryon, USA   WR
1980 Keto Lossaberidze, SOV
1984 Seo Hyang-soon, KOR   OR
1988 Kim Soo-nyung, KOR
1992 Cho Youn Jeong, KOR
1996

**WOMEN'S TEAM**
*1896–1984 not held*
1988 KOR
1992 KOR
1996

### BADMINTON

**MEN'S SINGLES**
*1896–1988 not held*
1992 Alan Budi Kushuma, INA
1996

**MEN'S DOUBLES**
*1896–1988 not held*
1992 Kim Moon-Soo, Park Joo-Bong, KOR
1996

**WOMEN'S SINGLES**
*1896–1988 not held*
1992 Susy Susanti, INA
1996

**WOMEN'S DOUBLES**
*1896–1988 not held*
1992 Hwang Hye Young, Chung So-Young, KOR
1996

### BASEBALL · BASKETBALL

**BASEBALL**
*Demonstration sport eight times previously.*
1992 CUB
1996

**MEN'S BASKETBALL**
*1896–1932 not held*
1936 USA
1948 USA
1952 USA
1956 USA
1960 USA
1964 USA
1968 USA
1972 SOV
1976 USA
1980 YUG
1984 USA
1988 SOV
1992 USA
1996

**WOMEN'S BASKETBALL**
*1896–1972 not held*
1976 SOV
1980 SOV
1984 USA
1988 USA
1992 EUN
1996

### BOXING

**LIGHT FLYWEIGHT**
*1896–1964 not held*
1968 Francisco Rodriguez, VEN
1972 György Gedó, HUN
1976 Jorge Hernandez, CUB
1980 Shamil Sabyrov, SOV
1984 Paul Gonzalez, USA
1988 Ivailo Hristov, BUL
1992 Rogelio Marcelo, CUB
1996

**FLYWEIGHT**
*1896–1900 not held*
1904 George Finnegan, USA
*1908–1912 not held*
1920 William De Genaro, USA
1924 Fidel LaBarba, USA
1928 Antal Kocsis, HUN
1932 István Énekes, HUN
1936 Willi Kaiser, GER
1948 Pascual Perez, ARG
1952 Nathan Brooks, USA
1956 Terence Spinks, GBR
1960 Gyula Török, HUN
1964 Fernando Atzori, ITA
1968 Ricardo Delgado, MEX
1972 Georgi Kostadinov, BUL
1976 Leo Randolph, USA
1980 Peter Lessov, BUL
1984 Steve McCrory, USA
1988 Kim Kwang-sun, KOR
1992 Su Choi Choi, PRK
1996

**BANTAMWEIGHT**
*1896–1900 not held*
1904 Oliver Kirk, USA
1908 A. Henry Thomas, GBR
*1912 not held*
1920 Clarence Walker, SAF
1924 William Smith, SAF
1928 Vittorio Tamagnini, ITA
1932 Horace Gwynne, CAN
1936 Ulderico Sergo, ITA
1948 Tibor Csik, HUN
1952 Pentti Hämäläinen, FIN
1956 Wolfgang Behrendt, GDR
1960 Oleg Grigoryev, SOV
1964 Takao Sakurai, JPN

1968 Valery Sokolov, SOV
1972 Orlando Martinez, CUB
1976 Gu Yong-Jo, PRK
1980 Juan Hernandez, CUB
1984 Maurizio Stecca, ITA
1988 Kennedy McKinney, USA
1992 Joel Casamayor, CUB
1996

**FEATHERWEIGHT**
*1896–1900 not held*
1904 Oliver Kirk, USA
1908 Richard Gunn, GBR
*1912 not held*
1920 Paul Fritsch, FRA
1924 John Fields, USA
1928 Lambertus van Klaveren, HOL
1932 Carmelo Robledo, ARG
1936 Oscar Casanovas, ARG
1948 Ernesto Formenti, ITA
1952 Jan Zachara, CZE
1956 Vladimir Safronov, SOV
1960 Francesco Musso, ITA
1964 Stanislav Stepashkin, SOV
1968 Antonio Roldan, MEX
1972 Boris Kousnetsov, SOV
1976 Angel Herrera, CUB
1980 Rudi Fink, GDR
1984 Meldrick Taylor, USA
1988 Giovanni Parisi, ITA
1992 Andreas Tews, GER
1996

**LIGHTWEIGHT**
*1896–1900 not held*
1904 Harry Spanger, USA
1908 Frederick Grace, GBR
*1912 not held*
1920 Samuel Mosberg, USA
1924 Hans Nielsen, DEN
1928 Carlo Orlandi, ITA
1932 Lawrence Stevens, SAF
1936 Imre Harangi, HUN
1948 Gerald Dreyer, SAF
1952 Aureliano Bolognesi, ITA
1956 Richard McTaggart, GBR
1960 Kazimierz Paździor, POL
1964 Józef Grudzień, POL

1968 Ronald Harris, USA
1972 Jan Szczepański, POL
1976 Howard Davis, USA
1980 Angel Herrera, CUB
1984 Pernell Whitaker, USA
1988 Andreas Zuelow, GDR
1992 Oscar De La Hoya, USA
1996

**LIGHT WELTERWEIGHT**
*1896–1948 not held*
1952 Charles Adkins, USA
1956 Vladimir Yengibaryan, SOV
1960 Bohumil Nemeček, CZE
1964 Jerzy Kulej, POL
1968 Jerzy Kulej, POL
1972 Ray Seales, USA
1976 Ray Leonard, USA
1980 Patrizio Oliva, ITA
1984 Jerry Page, USA
1988 Vyacheslav Yanovsky, SOV
1992 Hector Vinent, CUB
1996

**WELTERWEIGHT**
*1896–1900 not held*
1904 Albert Young, USA
*1908–1912 not held*
1920 Albert Schneider, CAN
1924 Jean Delarge, BEL
1928 Edward Morgan, NZE
1932 Edward Flynn, USA
1936 Sten Suvio, FIN
1948 Julius Torma, CZE
1952 Zygmunt Chychia, POL
1956 Nicolae Linca, ROM
1960 Giovanni Benvenuti, ITA
1964 Marian Kasprzyk, POL
1968 Manfred Wolke, GDR
1972 Emilio Correa, CUB
1976 Jochen Bachfeld, GDR
1980 Andrés Aldama, CUB
1984 Mark Breland, USA
1988 Robert Wangila, KEN
1992 Michael Carruth, IRL
1996

**LIGHT MIDDLEWEIGHT**
*1896–1948 not held*
1952 László Papp, HUN
1956 László Papp, HUN
1960 Wilbert McClure, USA
1964 Boris Lagutin, SOV
1968 Boris Lagutin, SOV
1972 Dieter Kottysch, GER
1976 Jerzy Rybicki, POL
1980 Armando Martinez, CUB
1984 Frank Tate, USA
1988 Park Si-hun, KOR
1992 Juan Lemus, CUB
1996

**MIDDLEWEIGHT**
*1896–1900 not held*
1904 Charles Mayer, USA
1908 John Douglas, GBR
*1912 not held*
1920 Harry Mallin, GBR
1924 Harry Mallin, GBR
1928 Piero Toscani, ITA
1932 Carmen Barth, USA
1936 Jean Despeaux, FRA
1948 László Papp, HUN
1952 Floyd Patterson, USA
1956 Gennady Schatkov, SOV
1960 Edward Crook, USA
1964 Valery Popenchenko, SOV
1968 Christopher Finnegan, GBR
1972 Vyacheslav Lemechev, SOV
1976 Michael Spinks, USA
1980 José Gomez, CUB
1984 Shin Joon-sup, KOR
1988 Henry Maske, GDR
1992 Ariel Hernandez, CUB
1996

**LIGHT HEAVYWEIGHT**
*1896–1912 not held*
1920 Edward Eagan, USA
1924 Harry Mitchell, GBR
1928 Victor Avendaño, ARG
1932 David Carstens, SAF
1936 Roger Michelot, FRA
1948 George Hunter, SAF

1952 Norvel Lee, USA
1956 James Boyd, USA
1960 Cassius Clay, USA
1964 Cosimo Pinto, ITA
1968 Dan Poznjak, SOV
1972 Mate Parlov, YUG
1976 Leon Spinks, USA
1980 Slobodan Kacar, YUG
1984 Anton Josipović, YUG
1988 Andrew Maynard, USA
1992 Torsten May, GER
1996

**HEAVYWEIGHT**
*1896–1980 not held*
1984 Henry Tillman, USA
1988 Ray Mercer, USA
1992 Felix Savon, CUB
1996

**SUPER HEAVYWEIGHT (UNLIMITED)**
*(known as heavyweight 1904–1980)*
1904 Samuel Berger, USA
1908 Albert Oldham, GBR
*1912 not held*
1920 Ronald Rawson, GBR
1924 Otto von Porat, NOR
1928 Arturo Rodriguez Jurado, ARG
1932 Santiago Lovell, ARG
1936 Herbert Runge, GER
1948 Rafael Inglesias, ARG
1952 H. Edward Sanders, USA
1956 T. Peter Rademacher, USA
1960 Franco De Piccoli, ITA
1964 Joe Frazier, USA
1968 George Foreman, USA
1972 Teofilo Stevenson, CUB
1976 Teofilo Stevenson, CUB
1980 Teofilo Stevenson, CUB
1984 Tyrell Biggs, USA
1988 Lennox Lewis, CAN
1992 Roberto Balado, CUB
1996

## CANOEING

### MEN'S KAYAK SINGLES 500 METERS
*1896-1972 not held*

| | | |
|---|---|---|
| 1976 | V. Diba, ROM | 1:46.41 |
| 1980 | V. Parfenovich, SOV | 1:43.43 |
| 1984 | I. Ferguson, NZE | 1:47.84 |
| 1988 | Z. Gyulay, HUN | 1:44.82 |
| 1992 | M. Yrjoe Kolehmainen, FIN | 1:40.34 |
| 1996 | | |

### MEN'S KAYAK SINGLES 1000 METERS
*1896-1932 not held*

| | | |
|---|---|---|
| 1936 | G. Hradetzky, AUT | 4:22.90 |
| 1948 | G. Fredriksson, SWE | 4:33.20 |
| 1952 | G. Fredriksson, SWE | 4:07.90 |
| 1956 | G Fredriksson, SWE | 4:12.80 |
| 1960 | E. Hansen, DEN | 3:53.00 |
| 1964 | R. Peterson, SWE | 3:57.13 |
| 1968 | M. Hesz, HUN | 4:02.63 |
| 1972 | A. Shaparenko, SOV | 3:48.06 |
| 1976 | R. Helm, GDR | 3:48.20 |
| 1980 | R. Helm, GDR | 3:48.77 |
| 1984 | A. Thompson, NZE | 3:45.73 |
| 1988 | G. Barton, USA | 3:55.27 |
| 1992 | C. Robinson, AUS | 3:37.26 |
| 1996 | | |

### MEN'S KAYAK PAIRS 500 METERS
*1896-1972 not held*

| | | |
|---|---|---|
| 1976 | J. Mattern, B. Olbricht, GDR | 1:35.87 |
| 1980 | V. Parfenovich, S. Chukhrai, SOV | 1:32.38 |
| 1984 | I. Ferguson, P. MacDonald, NZE | 1:34.21 |
| 1988 | I. Ferguson, P. MacDonald, NZE | 1:33.98 |
| 1992 | K. Bluhm, T. Gutsche, GER | 1:29.84 |
| 1996 | | |

### MEN'S KAYAK PAIRS 1000 METERS
*1896-1932 not held*

| | | |
|---|---|---|
| 1936 | A. Kainz, A. Dorfner, AUT | 4:03.80 |
| 1948 | H. Berglund, K. Klingström, SWE | 4:07.30 |
| 1952 | K. Wires, Y. Hietanen, FIN | 3:51.10 |
| 1956 | M. Scheuer, M. Miltenberger, GER | 3:49.60 |
| 1960 | G. Fredriksson, S. Sjödelius, SWE | 3:34.73 |
| 1964 | S. Sjödelius, N. Utterberg, SWE | 3:38.54 |
| 1968 | A. Shaparenko, V. Morozov, SOV | 3:37.54 |
| 1972 | N. Gorbachev, V. Kratassyuk, SOV | 3:31.23 |

| | | |
|---|---|---|
| 1976 | S. Nagorny, V. Romanovsky, SOV | 3:29.01 |
| 1980 | V. Parfenovich, S. Chukhrai, SOV | 3:26.72 |
| 1984 | H. Fisher, A. Morris, CAN | 3:24.22 |
| 1988 | G. Barton, N. Bellingham, USA | 3:32.42 |
| 1992 | K. Bluhm, T. Gutsche, GER | 3:16.10 |
| 1996 | | |

### MEN'S KAYAK FOURS 1000 METERS
*1896-1960 not held*

| | | |
|---|---|---|
| 1964 | SOV | 3:14.67 |
| 1968 | NOR | 3:14.38 |
| 1972 | SOV | 3:14.02 |
| 1976 | SOV | 3:08.69 |
| 1980 | GDR | 3:13.76 |
| 1984 | NZE | 3:02.28 |
| 1988 | HUN | 3:00.20 |
| 1992 | GER | 2:54.18 |
| 1996 | | |

### MEN'S CANADIAN SINGLES 500 METERS
*1896-1972 not held*

| | | |
|---|---|---|
| 1976 | A. Rogov, SOV | 1:59.23 |
| 1980 | S. Postrekhin, SOV | 1:53.37 |
| 1984 | L. Cain, CAN | 1:57.01 |
| 1988 | O. Heukrodt, GDR | 1:56.42 |
| 1992 | N. Boukhalov, BUL | 1:51.15 |
| 1996 | | |

### MEN'S CANADIAN SINGLES 1000 METERS
*1896-1932 not held*

| | | |
|---|---|---|
| 1936 | F. Amyot, CAN | 5:32.10 |
| 1948 | J. Holeček, CZE | 5:42.00 |
| 1952 | J. Holeček, CZE | 4:56.30 |
| 1956 | L. Rotman, ROM | 5:05.30 |
| 1960 | J. Parti, HUN | 4:33.93 |
| 1964 | J. Eschert, GDR | 4:35.14 |
| 1968 | T. Tatai, HUN | 4:36.14 |
| 1972 | I. Patzaichin, ROM | 4:08.94 |
| 1976 | M. Ljubek, YUG | 4:09.51 |
| 1980 | L. Lyubenov, BUL | 4:12.38 |
| 1984 | U. Eiche, GER | 4:06.32 |
| 1988 | I. Klementyev, SOV | 4:12.78 |
| 1992 | N. Boukhalov, BUL | 4:05.92 |
| 1996 | | |

### MEN'S CANADIAN PAIRS 500 METERS
*1896-1972 not held*

| | | |
|---|---|---|
| 1976 | S. Petrenko, A. Vinogradov, SOV | 1:45.81 |
| 1980 | L. Foltán, I. Vaskuti, HUN | 1:43.39 |
| 1984 | M. Ljubek, M. Nišović, YUG | 1:43.67 |
| 1988 | V. Reneisky, N. Zhuravsky, SOV | 1:41.77 |
| 1992 | A. Masseikov, D. Dovgalenok, EUN | 1:41.54 |
| 1996 | | |

### MEN'S CANADIAN PAIRS 1000 METERS
*1896-1932 not held*

| | | |
|---|---|---|
| 1936 | V. Syrovátka, J. Brzák-Felix, CZE | 4:50.10 |
| 1948 | J. Brzák-Felix, B. Kudrna, CZE | 5:07.10 |
| 1952 | B. Rasch, F. Haunstoft, DEN | 4:38.30 |
| 1956 | A. Dumitru, S. Ismailciuc, ROM | 4:47.40 |
| 1960 | L. Geischtor, S. Makarenko, SOV | 4:17.94 |
| 1964 | A. Khimich, S. Oschepkov, SOV | 4:04.64 |
| 1968 | I. Patzaichin, S. Covaliov, ROM | 4:07.18 |
| 1972 | V. Česiunas, Y. Lobanov, SOV | 3:52.60 |
| 1976 | S. Petrenko, A. Vinogradov, SOV | 3:52.76 |
| 1980 | I. Patzaichin, T. Simionov, ROM | 3:47.65 |
| 1984 | I. Patzaichin, T. Simionov, ROM | 3:40.60 |
| 1988 | V. Reneisky, N. Zhuravsky, SOV | 3:48.36 |
| 1992 | U. Papke, I. Spelly, GER | 3:37.42 |
| 1996 | | |

### MEN'S KAYAK SLALOM SINGLES
*1896-1968 not held*

| | | |
|---|---|---|
| 1972 | S. Horn, GDR | |

*1976-1988 not held*

| | | |
|---|---|---|
| 1992 | P. Ferrazzi, ITA | |
| 1996 | | |

### MEN'S CANADIAN SLALOM SINGLES
*1896-1968 not held*

| | | |
|---|---|---|
| 1972 | R. Eiben, GDR | |

*1976-1988 not held*

| | | |
|---|---|---|
| 1992 | L. Pollert, TCH | |
| 1996 | | |

### MEN'S DOUBLE CANOE SLALOM
*1896-1988 not held*

| | | |
|---|---|---|
| 1992 | J. Jacobi, S. Strausbaugh, USA | |
| 1996 | | |

### WOMEN'S KAYAK SINGLES 500 METERS
*1896-1936 not held*

| | | |
|---|---|---|
| 1948 | K. Hoff, DEN | 2:31.90 |
| 1952 | S. Saimo, FIN | 2:18.40 |
| 1956 | Y. Dementyeva, SOV | 2:18.90 |
| 1960 | A. Seredina, SOV | 2:08.08 |
| 1964 | L. Khvedosyuk, SOV | 2:12.87 |
| 1968 | L. Pinayeva (Khvedosyuk), SOV | 2:11.09 |
| 1972 | Y. Ryabchinskaya, SOV | 2:03.17 |
| 1976 | C. Zirzow, GDR | 2:01.05 |
| 1980 | B. Fischer, GDR | 1:57.96 |
| 1984 | A. Andersson, SWE | 1:58.72 |
| 1988 | V. Gesheva, BUL | 1:55.19 |
| 1992 | B. Schmidt, GER | 1:51.60 |
| 1996 | | |

### WOMEN'S KAYAK PAIRS 500 METERS
*1896-1956 not held*

| | | |
|---|---|---|
| 1960 | M. Chubina, A. Seredina, SOV | 1:54.76 |
| 1964 | R. Esser, A. Zimmermann, GER | 1:56.95 |
| 1968 | R. Esser, A. Zimmermann, GER | 1:56.44 |
| 1972 | L. Pinayeva, E. Kuryshko, SOV | 1:53.50 |
| 1976 | N. Gopova, G. Kreft, SOV | 1:51.15 |
| 1980 | C. Genäuss, M. Bischof, GDR | 1:43.88 |
| 1984 | A. Andersson, A. Olsson, SWE | 1:45.25 |
| 1988 | B. Schmidt (Fischer), A. Nothnagel, GDR | 1:43.46 |
| 1992 | R. Portwich, A. vonSeck, GER | 1:40.29 |
| 1996 | | |

### WOMEN'S KAYAK FOURS 500 METERS
*1896-1980 not held*

| | | |
|---|---|---|
| 1984 | ROM | 1:38.34 |
| 1988 | GDR | 1:40.78 |
| 1992 | HUN | 1:38.32 |
| 1996 | | |

### WOMEN'S KAYAK SLALOM SINGLES
*1896-1968 not held*

| | | |
|---|---|---|
| 1972 | Angelika Bahmann, GDR | |

*1976-1988 not held*

| | | |
|---|---|---|
| 1992 | Elisabeth Micheler, GER | |
| 1996 | | |

## CYCLING

### MEN'S 1000-METER SPRINT (SCRATCH)

| | |
|---|---|
| 1896 | Paul Masson, FRA |
| 1900 | Georges Taillandier, FRA |
| *1904 not held* | |
| 1908 | Final declared void; time limit exceeded |
| *1912 not held* | |
| 1920 | Maurice Peeters, HOL |
| 1924 | Lucien Michard, FRA |
| 1928 | Roger Beaufrand, FRA |
| 1932 | Jacobus van Egmond, HOL |
| 1936 | Toni Merkens, GER |
| 1948 | Mario Ghella, ITA |
| 1952 | Enzo Sacchi, ITA |
| 1956 | Michel Rousseau, FRA |
| 1960 | Sante Gaiardoni, ITA |
| 1964 | Giovanni Pettenella, ITA |
| 1968 | Daniel Morelon, FRA |
| 1972 | Daniel Morelon, FRA |
| 1976 | Anton Tkáč, CZE |
| 1980 | Lutz Hesslich, GDR |
| 1984 | Mark Gorski, USA |
| 1988 | Lutz Hesslich, GDR |
| 1992 | Jans Fiedler, GER |
| 1996 | |

### MEN'S 1000-METER TIME TRIAL
*1896-1924 not held*

| | | |
|---|---|---|
| 1928 | Willy Flack Hansen, DEN | 1:14.40 |
| 1932 | Edgar Gray, AUS | 1:13.00 OR |
| 1936 | Arie van Vliet, HOL | 1:12.00 OR |
| 1948 | Jacques Dupont, FRA | 1:13.50 |
| 1952 | Russell Mockridge, AUS | 1:11.100 OR |
| 1956 | Leandro Faggin, ITA | 1:09.800 OR |
| 1960 | Sante Gaiardoni, ITA | 1:07.270 WR |
| 1964 | Patrick Sercu, BEL | 1:09.590 |
| 1968 | Pierre Trentin, FRA | 1:03.910 WR |
| 1972 | Niels Fredborg, DEN | 1:06.440 |
| 1976 | Klaus-Jürgen Grünke, GDR | 1:05.927 |
| 1980 | Lothar Thoms, GDR | 1:02.955 WR |
| 1984 | Fredy Schmidtke, GER | 1:06.100 |
| 1988 | Aleksandr Kirichenko, SOV | 1:04.499 |
| 1992 | Jose Moreno, SPA | 1:03.342 |
| 1996 | | |

### MEN'S 4000-METER INDIVIDUAL PURSUIT
*1896-1960 not held*

| | | |
|---|---|---|
| 1964 | Jiři Daler, CZE | 5:04.750 |
| 1968 | Daniel Rebillard, FRA | 4:41.710 |
| 1972 | Knut Knudsen, NOR | 4:45.740 |
| 1976 | Gregor Braun, GER | 4:47.610 |
| 1980 | Robert Dill-Bundi, SWI | 4:35.660 |
| 1984 | Steve Hegg, USA | 4:39.350 |
| 1988 | Gintautas Umaras, SOV | 4:32.000 |
| 1992 | Chris Boardman, GBR | 3:21.649 |
| 1996 | | |

### MEN'S 4000-METER TEAM PURSUIT
*1896-1904 not held*

| | | |
|---|---|---|
| 1908 | GER | 2:18.600 |
| *1912 not held* | | |
| 1920 | ITA | 5:20.000 |
| 1924 | ITA | 5:15.000 |

| | | |
|---|---|---|
| 1928 | ITA | 5:01.800 |
| 1932 | ITA | 4:53.000 |
| 1936 | FRA | 4:45.000 |
| 1948 | FRA | 4:57.800 |
| 1952 | ITA | 4:46.100 |
| 1956 | ITA | 4:37.400 |
| 1960 | ITA | 4:30.900 |
| 1964 | GER | 4:35.670 |
| 1968 | DEN | 4:22.440 |
| 1972 | GER | 4:22.140 |
| 1976 | GER | 4:21.060 |
| 1980 | SOV | 4:15.700 |
| 1984 | AUS | 4:25.990 |
| 1988 | SOV | 4:13.310 |
| 1992 | GER | 4:08.791 |
| 1996 | | |

### MEN'S 50-KILOMETER POINTS RACE
*1896-1980 not held*

| | |
|---|---|
| 1984 | Roger Ilegems, BEL |
| 1988 | Dan Frost, DEN |
| 1992 | Giovanni Lombardi, ITA |
| 1996 | |

### MEN'S INDIVIDUAL ROAD RACE

| | | |
|---|---|---|
| 1896 | (87 KM) A. Konstantinidis, GDR | 3:21:10.00 |
| *1900-1908 not held* | | |
| 1912 | (320 KM) R. Lewis, SAF | 10:42:39.00 |
| 1920 | (175 KM) H. Stenqvist, SWE | 4:40:01.80 |
| 1924 | (188 KM) A. Blanchonnet, FRA | 6:20:48.00 |
| 1928 | (168 KM) H. Hansen, DEN | 4:47:18.00 |
| 1932 | (100 KM) A. Pavesi, ITA | 2:28:05.60 |
| 1936 | (100 KM) R. Charpentier, FRA | 2:33:05.00 |
| 1948 | (194.63 KM) J. Beyaert, FRA | 5:18:12.60 |
| 1952 | (190.4 KM) A. Noyelle, BEL | 5:06:03.40 |
| 1956 | (187.73 KM) E. Baldini, ITA | 5:21:17.00 |
| 1960 | (175.38 KM) V. Kapitonov, SOV | 4:20:37.00 |
| 1964 | (194.83 KM) M. Zanin, ITA | 4:39:51.63 |
| 1968 | (196.2 KM) P. Vianelli, ITA | 4:41:25.24 |
| 1972 | (182.4 KM) H. Kuiper, HOL | 4:14:37.00 |
| 1976 | (175 KM) B. Johansson, SWE | 4:46:52.00 |
| 1980 | (189 KM) S. Sukhoruchenkov, SOV | 4:48:28.90 |
| 1984 | (190.2 KM) A. Grewal, USA | 4:59:57.00 |
| 1988 | (196.8 KM) O. Ludwig, GDR | 4:32:22.00 |
| 1992 | (194 KM) F. Casartelli, ITA | 4:35:21.00 |
| 1996 | | |

### MEN'S TEAM TIME TRIAL
*1896-1908 not held*

| | | |
|---|---|---|
| 1912 | (320 KM) SWE | 44:35:33.60 |
| 1920 | (175 KM) FRA | 19:16:43.20 |
| 1924 | (188 KM) FRA | 19:30:14.00 |
| 1928 | (168 KM) DEN | 15:09:14.00 |
| 1932 | (100 KM) ITA | 7:27:15.20 |
| 1936 | (100 KM) FRA | 7:39:16.20 |
| 1948 | (194.63 KM) BEL | 15:58:17.40 |
| 1952 | (190.4 KM) BEL | 15:20:46.60 |
| 1956 | (187.73 KM) FRA | 22 pts. |
| 1960 | (100 KM) ITA | 2:14:33.53 |
| 1964 | (109.89 KM) HOL | 2:26:31.19 |
| 1968 | (104 KM) HOL | 2:07:49.06 |
| 1972 | (100 KM) SOV | 2:11:17.80 |

## CYCLING

| | | |
|---|---|---|
| 1976 (100 KM) SOV | 2:08:53.00 | |
| 1980 (101 KM) SOV | 2:01:21.70 | |
| 1984 (100 KM) ITA | 1:58:28.00 | |
| 1988 (100 KM) GDR | 1:57:47.70 | |
| 1992 (100 KM) GER | 2:01:39.00 | |
| 1996 | | |

**WOMEN'S 1000-METER SPRINT (SCRATCH)**
*1896–1984 not held*
1988 E. Salumäe, SOV
1992 E. Salumäe, EST
1996

**WOMEN'S 3000-METER INDIVIDUAL PURSUIT**
*1896–1988 not held*
1992 Petra Rossner, GER
1996

**WOMEN'S INDIVIDUAL ROAD RACE**
*1896–1980 not held*
1984 (79.2 KM) C. Carpenter-Phinney, USA
                                                    2:11:14
1988 (82 KM) M. Knol, HOL            2:00:52
1992 Kathryn Watt, AUS               2:04:42
1996

## EQUESTRIAN

**THREE-DAY EVENT, INDIVIDUAL**
*1896–1908 not held*
1912 A. Nordlander, SWE
1920 H. Mörner, SWE
1924 A. van der Voort van Zijp, HOL
1928 C. Pahud de Mortanges, HOL
1932 C. Pahud de Mortanges, HOL
1936 L. Stubbendorff, GER
1948 B. Chevallier, FRA
1952 H. von Blixen-Finecke, Jr. SWE
1956 P. Kastenman, SWE
1960 L. Morgan, AUS
1964 M. Checcoli, ITA
1968 J. Guyon, FRA
1972 R. Meade, GBR
1976 E. Coffin, USA
1980 E. Roman, ITA
1984 M. Todd, NZE
1988 M. Todd, NZE
1992 M. Ryan, AUS
1996

**THREE-DAY EVENT, TEAM**
*1896–1908 not held*
1912 SWE
1920 SWE
1924 HOL
1928 HOL
1932 USA
1936 GER
1948 USA
1952 SWE
1956 GER
1960 AUS
1964 ITA
1968 GBR
1972 GBR
1976 USA
1980 SOV
1984 USA
1988 GER
1992 AUS
1996

**JUMPING (PRIX DES NATIONS), INDIVIDUAL**
*1896 not held*
1900 A. Haegeman, BEL
*1904–1908 not held*
1912 J. Cariou, FRA
1920 T. Lequio, ITA
1924 A. Gemuseus, SWI
1928 F. Ventura, CZE
1932 T. Nishi, JPN
1936 K. Hasse, GER
1948 H. Cortés, MEX
1952 P. Jonquères d'Oriola, FRA
1956 H. Winkler, GER
1960 R. D'Inzeo, ITA
1964 P. Jonquères d'Oriola, FRA
1968 W. Steinkraus, USA
1972 G. Mancinelli, ITA
1976 A. Schockemöhle, GER
1980 J. Kowalczyk, POL
1984 J. Fargis, USA
1988 P. Durand, FRA
1992 L. Beerbaum, GER
1996

**JUMPING (PRIX DES NATIONS), TEAM**
*1896–1908 not held*
1912 SWE
1920 SWE
1924 SWE
1928 SPA
1932 *No nation completed the course with three riders*
1936 GER
1948 MEX
1952 GBR
1956 GER
1960 GER
1964 GER
1968 CAN
1972 GER
1976 FRA
1980 SOV
1984 USA
1988 GER
1992 HOL
1996

**DRESSAGE, INDIVIDUAL**
*1896–1908 not held*
1912 C. Bonde, SWE
1920 J. Lundblad, SWE
1924 E. Linder, SWE
1928 C. von Langen-Parow, GER
1932 X. Lesage, FRA
1936 H. Pollay, GER
1948 H. Moser, SWI
1952 H. Saint Cyr, SWE
1956 H. Saint Cyr, SWE
1960 S. Filatov, SOV
1964 H. Chammartin, SWI
1968 I. Kizimov, SOV
1972 L. Linsenhoff, GER
1976 C. Stückelberger, SWI
1980 E. Theurer, AUT
1984 R. Klimke, GER
1988 N. Uphoff, GER
1992 N. Uphoff, GER
1996

**DRESSAGE, TEAM**
*1896–1924 not held*
1928 GER
1932 FRA
1936 GER
1948 SWE
1952 SWE
1956 SWE
*1960 not held*
1964 GER
1968 GER
1972 SOV
1976 GER
1980 SOV
1984 GER
1988 GER
1992 GER
1996

## FENCING

**MEN'S FOIL, INDIVIDUAL**
1896 E. Gravelotte, FRA
1900 E. Coste, FRA
1904 R. Fonst, CUB
*1908 not held*
1912 N. Nadi, ITA
1920 N. Nadi, ITA
1924 R. Ducret, FRA
1928 L. Gaudin, FRA
1932 G. Marzi, ITA
1936 G. Gaudini, ITA
1948 J. Buhan, FRA
1952 C. d'Oriola, FRA
1956 C. d'Oriola, FRA
1960 V. Zhdanovich, SOV
1964 E. Franke, POL
1968 L. Drimbă, ROM
1972 W. Woyda, POL
1976 F. Dal Zotto, ITA
1980 V. Smirnov, SOV
1984 M. Numa, ITA
1988 S. Cerioni, ITA
1992 P. Omnes, FRA
1996

**MEN'S FOIL, TEAM**
*1896–1900 not held*
1904 CUB/USA
*1908–1912 not held*
1920 ITA
1924 FRA
1928 ITA
1932 FRA
1936 ITA
1948 FRA
1952 FRA
1956 ITA
1960 SOV
1964 SOV
1968 FRA
1972 POL
1976 GER
1980 FRA
1984 ITA
1988 SOV
1992 GER
1996

**MEN'S ÉPÉE, INDIVIDUAL**
*1896 not held*
1900 R. Fonst, CUB
1904 R. Fonst, CUB
1908 G. Alibert, FRA
1912 P. Anspach, BEL
1920 A. Massard, FRA
1924 C. Delporte, BEL
1928 L. Gaudin, FRA
1932 G. Cornaggia-Medici, ITA
1936 F. Riccardi, ITA
1948 L. Cantone, ITA
1952 E. Mangiarotti, ITA
1956 C. Pavesi, ITA
1960 G. Delfino, ITA
1964 G. Kriss, SOV
1968 G. Kulcsár, HUN
1972 C. Fenyvesi, HUN
1976 A. Pusch, GER
1980 J. Harmenberg, SWE
1984 P. Boisse, FRA
1988 A. Schmitt, GER
1992 E. Srecki, FRA
1996

**MEN'S ÉPÉE, TEAM**
*1896–1904 not held*
1908 FRA
1912 BEL
1920 ITA
1924 FRA
1928 ITA
1932 FRA
1936 ITA
1948 FRA
1952 ITA
1956 ITA
1960 ITA
1964 HUN
1968 HUN
1972 HUN
1976 SWE
1980 FRA
1984 GER
1988 FRA
1992 GER
1996

**MEN'S SABRE, INDIVIDUAL**
1896 I. Georgiadis, GRE
1900 G. de la Falaise, FRA
1904 M. Diaz, CUB
1908 J. Fuchs, HUN
1912 J. Fuchs, HUN
1920 A. Nadi, ITA
1924 S. Posta, HUN
1928 O. Tersztyánszky, HUN
1932 G. Piller (Jekelfalussy), HUN
1936 E. Kabos, HUN
1948 A. Gerevich, HUN
1952 P. Kovács, HUN
1956 R. Kárpáti, HUN
1960 R. Kárpáti, HUN
1964 T. Pézsa, HUN
1968 J. Pawlowski, POL
1972 V. Sidiak, SOV
1976 V. Krovopuskov, SOV
1980 V. Krovopuskov, SOV
1984 J. Lamour, FRA
1988 J. Lamour, FRA
1992 B. Szabo, HUN
1996

**MEN'S SABRE, TEAM**
*1896–1904 not held*
1908 HUN
1912 HUN
1920 ITA
1924 ITA
1928 HUN
1932 HUN
1936 HUN
1948 HUN
1952 HUN
1956 HUN
1960 HUN
1964 SOV
1968 SOV
1972 ITA
1976 SOV
1980 SOV
1984 ITA
1988 HUN
1992 EUN
1996

**WOMEN'S FOIL, INDIVIDUAL**
*1896–1920 not held*
1924 E. Osiier, DEN
1928 H. Mayer, GER
1932 E. Preis, AUT
1936 I. Schacherer-Elek, HUN
1948 I. Elek, HUN
1952 I. Camber, ITA
1956 G. Sheen, GBR
1960 H. Schmid, GER
1964 I. Ujlaki-Rejtö, HUN
1968 Y. Novikova, SOV
1972 A. Ragno-Lonzi, ITA
1976 I. Schwarczenberger, HUN
1980 P. Trinquet, FRA
1984 L. Jujie, CHN
1988 A. Fichtel, GER
1992 G. Trillini, ITA
1996

**WOMEN'S FOIL, TEAM**
*1896–1956 not held*
1960 SOV
1964 HUN
1968 SOV
1972 SOV
1976 SOV
1980 FRA
1984 GER
1988 GER
1992 ITA
1996

## FIELD HOCKEY

**MEN'S FIELD HOCKEY**
*1896–1904 not held*
1908 GBR
*1912 not held*
1920 GBR
*1924 not held*
1928 IND
1932 IND
1936 IND
1948 IND
1952 IND
1956 IND
1960 PAK
1964 IND
1968 PAK
1972 GER
1976 NZE
1980 IND
1984 PAK
1988 GBR
1992 GER
1996

**WOMEN'S FIELD HOCKEY**
*1896–1976 not held*
1980 ZIM
1984 HOL
1988 AUS
1992 SPA
1996

## FOOTBALL (SOCCER)

| | | |
|---|---|---|
| *1896 not held* | *1932 not held* | 1972 POL |
| 1900 GBR | 1936 ITA | 1976 GDR |
| 1904 CAN | 1948 SWE | 1980 CZE |
| 1908 GBR | 1952 HUN | 1984 FRA |
| 1912 GBR | 1956 SOV | 1988 SOV |
| 1920 BEL | 1960 YUG | 1992 SPA |
| 1924 URU | 1964 HUN | 1996 |
| 1928 URU | 1968 HUN | |

# GYMNASTICS

## MEN'S INDIVIDUAL ALL-AROUND
*1896 not held*
1900 G. Sandras, FRA
1904 J. Lenhart, AUT
1908 A. Braglia, ITA
1912 A. Braglia, ITA
1920 G. Zampori, ITA
1924 L. Štukelj, YUG
1928 G. Miez, SWI
1932 R. Neri, ITA
1936 A. Schwarzmann, GER
1948 V. Huhtanen, FIN
1952 V. Chukarin, SOV
1956 V. Chukarin, SOV
1960 B. Shakhlin, SOV
1964 Y. Endo, JPN
1968 S. Kato, JPN
1972 S. Kato, JPN
1976 N. Andrianov, SOV
1980 A. Dityatin, SOV
1984 K. Gushiken, JPN
1988 V. Artemov, SOV
1992 V. Scherbo, EUN
1996

## MEN'S HORIZONTAL BAR
1896 H. Weingärtner, GER
*1900 not held*
1904 A. Heida, USA
*1908–1920 not held*
1924 L. Štukelj, YUG
1928 G. Miez, SWI
1932 D. Bixler, USA
1936 A. Saarvala, FIN
1948 J. Stalder, SWI
1952 J. Günthard, SWI
1956 T. Ono, JPN
1960 T. Ono, JPN
1964 B. Shakhlin, SOV
1968 A. Nakayama, JPN
1972 M. Tsukahara, JPN
1976 M. Tsukahara, JPN
1980 S. Deltchev, BUL
1984 S. Morisue, JPN
1988 V. Artemov, SOV
1992 T. Dimas, USA
1996

## MEN'S PARALLEL BARS
1896 A. Flatow, GER
*1900 not held*
1904 G. Eyser, USA
*1908–1920 not held*
1924 A. Güttinger, SWI
1928 L. Vácha, CZE
1932 R. Neri, ITA
1936 K. Frey, GER
1948 M. Reusch, SWI
1952 H. Eugster, SWI
1956 V. Chukarin, SOV
1960 B. Shakhlin, SOV
1964 Y. Endo, JPN
1968 A. Nakayama, JPN
1972 S. Kato, JPN
1976 S. Kato, JPN
1980 A. Tkachyov, SOV
1984 B. Conner, USA
1988 V. Artemov, SOV
1992 V. Scherbo, EUN
1996

## MEN'S LONG HORSE VAULT
1896 K. Schumann, GER
*1900 not held*
1904 G. Eyser, USA
*1908–1920 not held*
1924 F. Kriz, USA
1928 E. Mack, SWI
1932 S. Guglielmetti, ITA
1936 A. Schwarzmann, GER
1948 P. Aaltonen, FIN
1952 V. Chukarin, SOV
1956 H. Bantz, GER
1960 T. Ono, JPN
1964 H. Yamashita, JPN
1968 M. Voronin, SOV
1972 K. Köste, GDR
1976 N. Andrianov, SOV
1980 N. Andrianov, SOV
1984 L. Yun, CHN
1988 L. Yun, CHN
1992 V. Scherbo, EUN
1996

## MEN'S SIDE HORSE (POMMELED HORSE)
1896 L. Zutter, SWI
*1900 not held*
1904 A. Heida, USA
*1908–1920 not held*
1924 J. Wilhelm, SWI
1928 H. Hänggi, SWI
1932 I. Pelle, HUN
1936 K. Frey, GER
1948 P. Aaltonen, FIN
1952 V. Chukarin, SOV
1956 B. Shakhlin, SOV
1960 E. Ekman, FIN
1964 M. Cerar, YUG
1972 V. Klimenko, SOV
1976 Z. Magyar, HUN
1980 Z. Magyar, HUN
1984 L. Ning, CHN
1988 D. Bilozerchev, SOV
1992 V. Scherbo, EUN
Pae Gil-Su, PRK (tie)
1996

## MEN'S RINGS
1896 I. Mitropoulos, GRE
*1900 not held*
1904 H. Glass, USA
*1908–1920 not held*
1924 F. Martino, ITA
1928 L. Štukelj, YUG
1932 G. Gulack, USA
1936 A. Hudec, CZE
1948 K. Frei, SWI
1952 G. Shaginyan, SOV
1956 A. Azaryan, SOV
1960 A. Azaryan, SOV
1964 T. Haytta, JPN
1968 A. Nakayama, JPN
1972 A. Nakayama, JPN
1976 N. Andrianov, SOV
1980 A. Dityatin, SOV
1984 K. Gushiken, JPN
1988 H. Behrendt, GDR
1992 V. Scherbo, EUN
1996

## MEN'S FLOOR EXERCISE
*1896–1928 not held*
1932 I. Pelle, HUN
1936 G. Miez, SWI
1948 F. Pataki, HUN
1952 K. W. Thoresson, SWI
1956 V. Muratov, SOV
1960 N. Aihara, JPN
1964 F. Menichelli, ITA
1968 S. Kato, JPN
1972 N. Andrianov, SOV
1976 N. Andrianov, SOV
1980 R. Brückner, GDR
1984 L. Ning. CHN
1988 S. Kharkov, SOV
1992 L. Xiaosahuang, CHN
1996

## MEN'S TEAM COMBINED EXERCISES
*1896–1900 not held*
1904 T. Philadelphia
1908 SWE
1912 ITA
1920 ITA
1924 ITA
1928 SWI
1932 ITA
1936 GER
1948 FIN
1952 SOV
1956 SOV
1960 JPN
1964 JPN
1968 JPN
1972 JPN
1976 JPN
1980 SOV
1984 USA
1988 SOV
1992 EUN
1996

## WOMEN'S ALL-AROUND
*1896–1948 not held*
1952 M. Gorokhovskaya, SOV
1956 L. Latynina, SOV
1960 L. Latynina, SOV
1964 V. Čáslavská, CZE
1968 V. Čáslavská, CZE
1972 L. Tourischeva, SOV
1976 N. Comaneci, ROM
1980 Y. Davydova, SOV
1984 M. Retton, USA
1988 Y. Shushunova, SOV
1992 T. Goutsou, EUN
1996

## WOMEN'S SIDE HORSE VAULT
*1896–1948 not held*
1952 Y. Kalinchuk, SOV
1956 L. Latynina, SOV
1960 M. Nikolayeva, SOV
1964 V. Čáslavská, CZE
1968 V. Čáslavská, CZE
1972 K. Janz, GDR
1976 N. Kim, SOV
1980 N. Shaposhnikova, SOV
1984 E. Szabó, ROM
1988 S. Boginskaya, SOV
1992 H. Onodi, HUN
L. C. Milosovici, ROM (tie)
1996

## WOMEN'S ASYMMETRICAL (UNEVEN) BARS
*1896–1948 not held*
1952 M. Korondi, HUN
1956 Á. Keleti, HUN
1960 P. Astakhova, SOV
1964 P. Astakhova, SOV
1968 V. Čáslavská, CZE
1972 K. Janz, GDR
1976 N. Comaneci, ROM
1980 M. Gnauck, GDR
1984 M. Yanhong, CHN
1988 D. Silivas, ROM
1992 L. Li, CHN
1996

## WOMEN'S BALANCE BEAM
*1896–1948 not held*
1952 N. Bocharova, SOV
1956 Á. Keleti, HUN
1960 E. Bosáková, CZE
1964 V. Čáslavská, CZE
1968 N. Kuchinskaya, SOV
1972 O. Korbut, SOV
1976 N. Comaneci, ROM
1980 N. Comaneci, ROM
1984 S. Pauca, ROM
1988 D. Silivas, ROM

## WOMEN'S FLOOR EXERCISES
*1896–1948 not held*
1952 Á. Keleti, HUN
1956 Á. Keleti, HUN
1960 L. Latynina, SOV
1964 L. Latynina, SOV
1968 V. Čáslavská, CZE
1972 O. Korbut, SOV
1976 N. Kim, SOV
1980 N. Comaneci, ROM
1984 E. Szabó, ROM
1988 D. Silivas, ROM
1992 L. C. Milosovici, ROM
1996

## WOMEN'S TEAM COMBINED EXERCISES
*1896–1924 not held*
1928 HOL
*1932 not held*
1936 GER
1948 CZE
1952 SOV
1956 SOV
1960 SOV
1964 SOV
1968 SOV
1972 SOV
1976 SOV
1980 SOV
1984 ROM
1988 SOV
1992 EUN
1996

## RHYTHMIC ALL-AROUND
*1896–1980 not held*
1984 L. Fung, CAN
1988 M. Lobach, SOV
1992 A. Timoshenko, EUN
1996

# HANDBALL

## MEN'S TEAM HANDBALL
*1896–1932 not held*
1936 GER
*1948–1968 not held*
1972 YUG
1976 SOV
1980 GDR
1984 YUG
1988 SOV
1992 EUN
1996

## WOMEN'S TEAM HANDBALL
*1896–1972 not held*
1976 SOV
1980 SOV
1984 YUG
1988 KOR
1992 KOR
1996

# JUDO

## MEN'S EXTRA-LIGHTWEIGHT
*1896–1976 not held*
1980 T. Rey, FRA
1984 S. Hosokawa, JPN
1988 K. Jae-yup, KOR
1992 N. Gousseinov, EUN
1996

## MEN'S HALF-LIGHTWEIGHT
*1896–1976 not held*
1980 N. Solodukhin, SOV
1984 Y. Matsuoka, JPN
1988 L. Kyung-keun, KOR
1992 R. Sampaio Cardoso, BRA
1996

## MEN'S LIGHTWEIGHT
*1896–1960 not held*
1964 T. Nakatani, JPN
*1968 not held*
1972 T. Kawaguchi, JPN
1976 H. Rodriguez Torres, CUB
1980 E. Gamba, ITA
1984 A. Byeong-keun, KOR
1988 M. Alexandre, FRA
1992 T. Koga, JPN
1996

## MEN'S HALF-MIDDLEWEIGHT
*1896–1968 not held*
1972 T. Nomura, JPN
1976 V. Nevzorov, SOV
1980 S. Khabareli, SOV
1984 F. Wieneke, GER
1988 W. Legień, POL
1992 H. Yosida, JPN
1996

## MEN'S MIDDLEWEIGHT
*1896–1960 not held*
1964 I. Okano, JPN
*1968 not held*
1972 S. Sekine, JPN
1976 I. Sonoda, JPN
1980 J. Röthlisberger, SWI
1984 P. Seisenbacher, AUT
1988 P. Seisenbacher, AUT
1992 W. Legien, POL
1996

## MEN'S HALF-HEAVYWEIGHT
*1896–1968 not held*
1972 S. Chochoshvili, SOV
1976 K. Ninomiya, JPN
1980 R. Van de Walle, BEL
1984 H. Hyoung-zoo, KOR
1988 A. Miguel, BRA
1992 A. Kovacs, HUN
1996

## MEN'S HEAVYWEIGHT
*1896–1960 not held*
1964 I. Inokuma, JPN
*1968 not held*
1972 W. Ruska, HOL
1976 S. Novikov, SOV
1980 A. Parisi, FRA
1984 H. Saito, JPN
1988 H. Saito, JPN
1992 D. Khakhaleichvili, EUN
1996

## WOMEN'S EXTRA-LIGHTWEIGHT
*1896–1988 not held*
1992 C. Nowak, FRA
1996

## WOMEN'S HALF-LIGHTWEIGHT
*1896–1988 not held*
1992 A. Munoz Martinez, SPA
1996

## WOMEN'S LIGHTWEIGHT
*1896–1988 not held*
1992 M. Blasco Soto, SPA
1996

## WOMEN'S HALF-MIDDLEWEIGHT
*1896–1988 not held*
1992 C. Fleury, FRA
1996

## WOMEN'S MIDDLEWEIGHT
*1896–1988 not held*
1992 O. Reve Jimenez, CUB
1996

## WOMEN'S HALF-HEAVYWEIGHT
*1896–1988 not held*
1992 K. M. Jung, KOR
1996

## WOMEN'S HEAVYWEIGHT
*1896–1988 not held*
1992 Z. Xiaoyan, CHN
1996

## MODERN PENTATHLON

**INDIVIDUAL**
*1896–1908 not held*
1912 Gösta Lilliehöök, SWE
1920 Gustaf Dyrssen, SWE
1924 Bo Lindman, SWE
1928 Sven Thofelt, SWE
1932 Johan Oxenstierna, SWE

1936 Gotthardt Handrick, GER
1948 William Grut, SWE
1952 Lars Hall, SWE
1956 Lars Hall, SWE
1960 Férenc Németh, HUN
1964 Ferenc Török, HUN
1968 Björn Ferm, SWE

1972 András Balczó, HUN
1976 Janusz Pyciak-Peciak, POL
1980 Anatoly Starostin, SOV
1984 Daniele Masala, ITA
1988 János Martinek, HUN
1992 A. Skrzypaszek, POL
1996

**TEAM**
*1896–1948 not held*
1952 HUN
1956 SOV
1960 HUN
1964 SOV
1968 HUN

1972 SOV
1976 GBR
1980 SOV
1984 ITA
1988 HUN
1992 POL
1996

## ROWING

**MEN'S SINGLE SCULLS**
*1896 not held*
1900 Henri Barrelet, FRA 7:35.60
1904 Frank Greer, USA 10:08.50
1908 Harry Blackstaffe, GBR 9:26.00
1912 William Kinnear, GBR 7:47.60
1920 John Kelly, Sr., USA 7:35.00
1924 Jack Beresford, GBR 7:49.20
1928 Henry Pearce, AUS 7:11.00
1932 Henry Pearce, AUS 7:44.40
1936 Gustav Schäfer, GER 8:21.50
1948 Mervyn Wood, AUS 7:24.40
1952 Yuri Tyukalov, SOV 8:12.80
1956 Vyacheslav Ivanov, SOV 8:02.50
1960 Vyacheslav Ivanov, SOV 7:13.96
1964 Vyacheslav Ivanov, SOV 8:22.51
1968 Henri Jan Wienese, HOL 7:47.80
1972 Yuri Malishev, SOV 7:10.12
1976 Pertti Karppinen, FIN 7:29.03
1980 Pertti Karppinen, FIN 7:09.61
1984 Pertti Karppinen, FIN 7:00.24
1988 Thomas Lange, GDR 6:49.86
1992 Thomas Lange, GER 6:51.40
1996

**MEN'S DOUBLE SCULLS**
*1896–1900 not held*
1904 USA 10:03.20
*1908–1912 not held*
1920 USA 7:09.00
1924 USA 6:34.00
1928 USA 6:41.40
1932 USA 7:17.40
1936 GBR 7:20.80
1948 GBR 6:51.30
1952 ARG 7:32.20
1956 SOV 7:24.00
1960 CZE 6:47.50
1964 SOV 7:10.66
1968 SOV 6:51.82

1972 SOV 7:01.77
1976 NOR 7:13.20
1980 GDR 6:24.33
1984 USA 6:36.87
1988 HOL 6:21.13
1992 AUS 6:17.32
1996

**MEN'S QUADRUPLE SCULLS**
*1896–1972 not held*
1976 GDR 6:18.65
1980 GDR 5:49.81
1984 GER 5:57.55
1988 ITA 5:53.37
1992 GER 5:45.17
1996

**MEN'S PAIR-OARED SHELL WITHOUT COXSWAIN**
*1896–1900 not held*
1904 USA 10:57.00
1908 GBR 9:41.00
*1912–1920 not held*
1924 HOL 8:19.40
1928 GER 7:06.40
1932 GBR 8:00.00
1936 GER 8:16.10
1948 GBR 7:21.10
1952 USA 8:20.70
1956 USA 7:55.40
1960 SOV 7:02.01
1964 CAN 7:32.94
1968 GDR 7:26.56
1972 GDR 6:53.16
1976 GDR 7:23.31
1980 GDR 6:48.01
1984 ROM 6:45.39
1988 GBR 6:36.84
1992 GBR 6:27.72
1996

**MEN'S PAIR-OARED SHELL WITH COXSWAIN**
*1896 not held*
1900 HOL 7:34.20
*1904–1912 not held*
1920 ITA 7:56.00
1924 SWI 8:39.00
1928 SWI 7:42.60
1932 USA 8:25.80
1936 GER 8:36.90
1948 DEN 8:00.50
1952 FRA 8:28.60
1956 USA 8:26.10
1960 GER 7:29.14
1964 USA 8:21.23
1968 ITA 8:04.81
1972 GDR 7:17.25
1976 GDR 7:58.99
1980 GDR 7:02.54
1984 ITA 7:05.99
1988 ITA 6:58.79
1992 GBR 6:49.83
1996

**MEN'S FOUR-OARED SHELL WITHOUT COXSWAIN**
*1896–1900 not held*
1904 USA 9:05.80
1908 GBR 8:34.00
*1912–1920 not held*
1924 GBR 7:08.60
1928 GBR 6:36.00
1932 GBR 6:58.20
1936 GER 7:01.80
1948 ITA 6:39.00
1952 YUG 7:16.00
1956 CAN 7:08.80
1960 USA 6:26.26
1964 DEN 6:59.30
1968 GDR 6:39.18

1972 GDR 6:24.27
1976 GDR 6:37.42
1980 GDR 6:08.17
1984 NZE 6:03.48
1988 GDR 6:03.11
1992 AUS 5:55.04
1996

**MEN'S FOUR-OARED SHELL WITH COXSWAIN**
*1896 not held*
1900 1st Final FRA 7:11.00
     2nd Final GER 5:59.00
*1904–1908 not held*
1912 GER 6:59.40
1920 SWI 6:54.00
1924 SWI 7:18.40
1928 ITA 6:47.80
1932 GER 7:19.00
1936 GER 7:16.20
1948 USA 6:50.30
1952 CZE 7:33.40
1956 ITA 7:19.40
1960 GER 6:39.12
1964 GER 7:00.44
1968 NZE 6:45.62
1972 GER 6:31.85
1976 SOV 6:40.22
1980 GDR 6:14.51
1984 GBR 6:18.64
1988 GDR 6:10.74
1992 ROM 5:59.37
1996

**MEN'S EIGHT-OARED SHELL WITH COXSWAIN**
*1896 not held*
1900 USA 6:09.80
1904 USA 7:50.00
1908 GBR 7:52.00

1912 GBR 6:15.00
1920 USA 6:02.60
1924 USA 6:33.40
1928 USA 6:03.20
1932 USA 6:37.60
1936 USA 6:25.40
1948 USA 5:56.70
1952 USA 6:25.90
1956 USA 6:35.20
1960 GER 5:57.18
1964 USA 6:18.23
1968 GER 6:07.00
1972 NZE 6:08.94
1976 GDR 5:58.29
1980 GDR 5:49.05
1984 CAN 5:41.32
1988 GER 5:46.05
1992 CAN 5:29.53
1996

**WOMEN'S SINGLE SCULLS**
*1896–1972 not held*
1976 C. Scheiblich, GDR 4:05.56
1980 S. Toma, ROM 3:40.69
1984 V. Račilá, ROM 3:40.68
1988 J. Behrendt, GDR 7:47.19
1992 E. Lipa, ROM 7:25.54
1996

**WOMEN'S DOUBLE SCULLS**
*1896–1972 not held*
1976 BUL 3:44.36
1980 SOV 3:16.27
1984 ROM 3:26.75
1988 GDR 7:00.48
1992 GER 6:49.00
1996

**WOMEN'S QUADRUPLE SCULLS**
*1896–1984 not held*
1988 GDR 6:21.06
1992 GER 6:20.18
1996

**WOMEN'S PAIR-OARED SHELL WITHOUT COXSWAIN**
*1896–1972 not held*
1976 BUL 4:01.22
1980 GDR 3:30.49
1984 ROM 3:32.60
1988 ROM 7:28.13
1992 CAN 7:06.22
1996

**WOMEN'S FOUR-OARED SHELL WITHOUT COXSWAIN**
*1896–1988 not held*
1992 CAN 6:30.85
1996

**WOMEN'S EIGHT-OARED SHELL WITH COXSWAIN**
*1896–1972 not held*
1976 GDR 3:33.32
1980 GDR 3:03.32
1984 USA 2:59.80
1988 GDR 6:15.17
1992 CAN 6:02.62
1996

## SHOOTING

**MEN'S RAPID-FIRE PISTOL**
1896 Ioannis Phrangoudis, GRE
1900 Maurice Larrouy, FRA
*1904 not held*
1908 Paul van Asbroeck, BEL
1912 Alfred Lane, USA
1920 Guilherme Paraense, BRA
1924 Henry Bailey, USA
*1928 not held*
1932 Renzo Morigi, ITA
1936 Cornelius van Oyen, GER
1948 Károly Takács, HUN WR
1952 Károly Takács, HUN
1956 Stefan Petrescu, ROM OR
1960 William McMillan, USA EOR
1964 Pentti Linnosvuo, FIN OR
1968 Józef Zapedzki, POL OR
1972 Józef Zapedzki, POL OR
1976 Norbert Klaar, GDR OR
1980 Corneliu Ion, ROM
1984 Takeo Kamachi, JPN
1988 Afanasi Kuzmin, SOV WR
1992 Ralf Schumann, GER OR
1996

**MEN'S FREE PISTOL**
1896 Sumner Paine, USA
1900 Conrad Karl Röderer, SWI
*1904–1908 not held*
1912 Alfred Lane, USA
1920 Karl Frederick, USA
*1924–1932 not held*
1936 Torsten Ullman, SWE WR
1948 Edwin Vasquez Cam, PER
1952 Huelet Benner, USA OR
1956 Pentti Linnosvuo, FIN OR
1960 Aleksei Gustchin, SOV OR
1964 Väinö Markkanen, FIN OR
1968 Grigory Kossykh, SOV OR
1972 Ragnar Skanåker, SWE OR
1976 Uwe Potteck, GDR WR
1980 Aleksandr Melentev, SOV WR
1984 Xu Haifeng, CHN
1988 Sorin Babii, ROM
1992 Konstantine Loukachik, EUN
1996

**MEN'S AIR PISTOL**
*1896–1984 not held*
1988 Tanue Kiriakov, BUL

1992 Wang Yifu, CHN
1996

**MEN'S SMALL-BORE RIFLE, PRONE**
*1896–1904 not held*
1908 A. A. Carnell, GBR
1912 Frederick Hird, USA
*1920 not held*
1924 Pierre Coquelin de Lisle, FRA
*1928 not held*
1932 Bertil Rönnmark, SWE
1936 Willy Rögeberg, NOR WR
1948 Arthur Cook, USA WR
1952 Iosif Sirbu, ROM EWR
1956 Gerald Ouellette, CAN
1960 Peter Kohnke, GER
1964 László Hammerl, HUN WR
1968 Jan Kurka, CZE EWR
1972 Li Ho-jun, PRK WR
1976 Karlheinz Smieszek, GER EWR
1980 Károly Varga, HUN EWR
1984 Edward Etzel, USA EOR
1988 Miroslav Varga, CZE
1992 Lee Eun-Chul, KOR EOR
1996

**MEN'S SMALL-BORE RIFLE, 3 POSITIONS**
*1896–1948 not held*
1952 Erling Kongshaug, NOR
1956 Anatoly Bogdanov, SOV OR
1960 Viktor Shamburkin, SOV EWR
1964 Lones Wigger, USA WR
1968 Bernd Klingner, GER
1972 John Writer, USA WR
1976 Lanny Bassham, USA
1980 Viktor Vlasov, SOV WR
1984 Malcolm Cooper, GBR EWR
1988 Malcolm Cooper, GBR
1992 Gracha Petikiane, EUN OR
1996

**MEN'S AIR RIFLE**
*1896–1980 not held*
1984 Philippe Heberle, FRA
1988 Goran Maksimović, YUG
1992 Iouri Fedkine, EUN
1996

**MEN'S MOVING TARGET**
*1896 not held*
1900 Louis Debray, FRA
*1904–1968 not held*
1972 Lakov Zhelezniak, SOV WR
1976 Aleksandr Gazov, SOV WR
1980 Igor Sokolov, SOV WR
1984 Li Yuwei, CHN
1988 Tor Heiestad, NOR
1992 Michael Jakosits, GER OR
1996

**WOMEN'S SPORT PISTOL**
*1896–1980 not held*
1984 Linda Thom, CAN
1988 Nino Salukvadke, SOV
1992 Marina Logvinenko, EUN
1996

**WOMEN'S AIR PISTOL**
*1896–1984 not held*
1988 Jasna Šekarić, YUG WR
1992 Marina Logvinenko, EUN OR
1996

## SHOOTING

**WOMEN'S SMALL-BORE RIFLE, 3 POSITIONS**
*1896–1900 not held*
1984 Wu Xiaoxuan, CHN
1988 Sylvia Sperber, GER
1992 Launi Meili, USA
1996

**WOMEN'S AIR RIFLE**
*1896–1980 not held*
1984 Pat Spurgin, USA
1988 Irina Shilova, SOV
1992 Yeo Kab-Soon, KOR
1996

**MIXED TRAP SHOOTING**
*1896 not held*
1900 Roger de Barbarin, FRA

*1904 not held*
1908 Walter Ewing, CAN
1912 James Graham, USA
1920 Mark Arie, USA
1924 Gyula Halasy, HUN                OR
*1928–1948 not held*
1952 George Généreux, CAN
1956 Galliano Rossini, ITA            OR
1960 Ion Dumitrescu, ROM
1964 Ennio Mattarelli, ITA            OR

1968 John Braithwaite, GBR    EWR
1972 Angelo Scalzone, ITA     WR
1976 Donald Haldeman, USA
1980 Luciano Giovannetti, ITA
1984 Luciano Giovannetti, ITA
1988 Dmitri Monakov, SOV
1992 Petr Hrdlicka, TCH        OR
1996

**SKEET SHOOTING**
*1896–1964 not held*
1968 Yevgeny Petrov, SOV       EWR
1972 Konrad Wirnhier, GER
1976 Josef Panaček, CZE        EOR
1980 Hans Kjeld Rasmussen, DEN
1984 Matthew Dryke, USA        EOR
1988 Axel Wegner, GDR
1992 Zhang Shan, CHN           OR
1996

## SWIMMING AND DIVING

**MEN'S 50-METER FREESTYLE**
*1896–1900 not held*
1904 Zoltán Halmay, HUN          0:28.00
*1908–1984 not held*
1988 Matthew Biondi, USA         0:22.14  WR
1992 Aleksandr Popov, EUN        0:21.91  OR
1996

**MEN'S 100-METER FREESTYLE**
1896 Alfréd Hajós, HUN           1:22.20  OR
*1900 not held*
1904 Zoltán Halmay, HUN          1:02.80
1908 Charles Daniels, USA        1:05.60  WR
1912 Duke Paoa Kahanamoku, USA   1:03.40
1920 Duke Paoa Kahanamoku, USA   1:00.40  WR
1924 Johnny Weissmuller, USA     0:59.00  OR
1928 Johnny Weissmuller, USA     0:58.60  OR
1932 Yasuji Miyazaki, JPN        0:58.20
1936 Ferenc Csík, HUN            0:57.60
1948 Walter Ris, USA             0:57.30  OR
1952 Clarke Scholes, USA         0:57.40
1956 Jon Henricks, AUS           0:55.40  OR
1960 John Devitt, USA            0:55.20  OR
1964 Donald Schollander, USA     0:53.40  OR
1968 Michael Wenden, AUS         0:52.20  WR
1972 Mark Spitz, USA             0:51.22  WR
1976 Jim Montgomery, USA         0:49.99  WR
1980 Jörg Woithe, GDR            0:50.40
1984 Ambrose Gaines, USA         0:49.80  OR
1988 Matthew Biondi, USA         0:48.63  OR
1992 Aleksandr Popov, EUN        0:49.02
1996

**MEN'S 200-METER FREESTYLE**
*1896 not held*
1900 Frederick Lane, AUS         1:25.20  OR
1904 Charles Daniels, USA        2:44.20
*1908–1964 not held*
1968 Michael Wenden, AUS         1:55.20  OR
1972 Mark Spitz, USA             1:52.78  WR
1976 Bruce Furniss, USA          1:50.29  WR
1980 Sergei Kopliakov, SOV       1:49.81  OR
1984 Michael Gross, GER          1:47.44  WR
1988 Duncan Armstrong, AUS       1:47.25  WR
1992 Evgueni Sadovyi, EUN        1:46.70  OR
1996

**MEN'S 400-METER FREESTYLE**
1896 Paul Neumann, AUT           8:12.60
*1900 not held*
1904 Charles Daniels, USA        6:16.20
1908 Henry Taylor, GBR           5:36.80
1912 George Hodgson, CAN         5:24.40
1920 Norman Ross, USA            5:26.80
1924 Johnny Weissmuller, USA     5:04.20  OR
1928 Alberto Zorilla, ARG        5:01.60  OR
1932 Clarence Crabbe, USA        4:48.40  OR
1936 Jack Medica, USA            4:44.50  OR
1948 William Smith, USA          4:41.00  OR
1952 Jean Boiteux, FRA           4:30.70  OR
1956 Murray Rose, AUS            4:27.30  OR
1960 Murray Rose, AUS            4:18.30  OR
1964 Donald Schollander, USA     4:12.20  WR
1968 Michael Burton, USA         4:09.00  OR
1972 Bradford Cooper, AUS        4:00.27  OR
1976 Brian Goodell, USA          3:51.93  WR

1980 Vladimir Salnikov, SOV      3:51.31  OR
1984 George DiCarlo, USA         3:51.23  OR
1988 Uwe Dassler, GDR            3:46.95  WR
1992 Evgueni Sadovyi, EUN        3:45.00  WR
1996

**MEN'S 1500-METER FREESTYLE**
1896 Alfréd Hajós, HUN           18:22.20*
1900 John Arthur Jarvis, GBR     13:40.20*
1904 Emil Rausch, GER            27:18.20*
1908 Henry Taylor, GBR           22:48.40  WR
1912 George Hodgson, CAN         22:00.00  WR
1920 Norman Ross, USA            22:23.20
1924 Andrew Charlton, AUS        20:06.60  WR
1928 Arne Borg, SWE              19:51.80  OR
1932 Kusuo Kitamura, JPN         19:12.40  OR
1936 Noboru Terada, JPN          19:13.70
1948 James McLane, USA           19:18.50
1952 Ford Konno, USA             18:30.30  OR
1956 Murray Rose, AUS            17:58.90
1960 Jon Konrads, AUS            17:19.60  OR
1964 Robert Windle, AUS          17:01.70  OR
1968 Michael Burton, USA         16:38.90  OR
1972 Michael Burton, USA         15:52.58  WR
1976 Brian Goodell, USA          15:02.40  WR
1980 Vladimir Salnikov, SOV      14:58.27  WR
1984 Michael O'Brien, USA        15:05.20
1988 Vladimir Salnikov, SOV      15:00.40
1992 Kieren Perkins, AUS         14:43.48  WR
1996

**MEN'S 100-METER BACKSTROKE**
*1896–1900 not held*
1904 Walter Brack, GER           1:16.80*
1908 Arno Bieberstein, GER       1:24.60  WR
1912 Harry Hebner, USA           1:21.20
1920 Warren Paoa Kealoha, USA    1:15.20
1924 Warren Paoa Kealoha, USA    1:13.20  OR
1928 George Kojac, USA           1:08.20
1932 Masaji Kiyokawa, JPN        1:08.60
1936 Adolf Kiefer, USA           1:05.90  OR
1948 Allen Stack, USA            1:06.40
1952 Yoshinobu Oyakawa, USA      1:05.40  OR
1956 David Theile, AUS           1:02.20  OR
1960 David Theile, AUS           1:01.90  OR
*1964 not held*
1968 Roland Matthes, GDR         0:58.70  OR
1972 Roland Matthes, GDR         0:56.58  OR
1976 John Naber, USA             0:55.49  WR
1980 Bengt Baron, SWE            0:56.33
1984 Richard Carey, USA          0:55.79
1988 Daichi Suzuki, JPN          0:55.05
1992 Mark Tewksburg, CAN         0:53.98  OR
1996

**MEN'S 200-METER BACKSTROKE**
*1896 not held*
1900 Ernst Hoppenberg, GER       2:47.00
*1904–1960 not held*
1964 Jed Graef, USA              2:10.30  WR
1968 Roland Matthes, GDR         2:09.60  OR
1972 Roland Matthes, GDR         2:02.82EWR
1976 John Naber, USA             1:59.19  WR
1980 Sándor Wladár, HUN          2:01.93

1984 Richard Carey, USA          2:00.23
1988 Igor Poliansky, SOV         1:59.37
1992 Martin Lopez-Zubero, SPA    1:58.47  OR
1996

**MEN'S 100-METER BREASTSTROKE**
*1896–1964 not held*
1968 Donald McKenzie, USA        1:07.70  OR
1972 Nobutaka Taguchi, JPN       1:04.94  WR
1976 John Hencken, USA           1:03.11  WR
1980 Duncan Goodhew, GBR         1:03.44
1984 Steve Lundquist, USA        1:01.65  WR
1988 Adrian Moorhouse, GBR       1:02.04
1992 Nelson Diebel, USA          1:01.50  OR
1996

**MEN'S 200-METER BREASTSTROKE**
*1896–1904 not held*
1908 Frederick Holman, GBR       3:09.20  WR
1912 Walter Bathe, GER           3:01.80  OR
1920 Håkan Malmroth, SWE         3:04.40
1924 Robert Skelton, USA         2:56.60
1928 Yoshiyuki Tsuruta, JPN      2:48.80  OR
1932 Yoshiyuki Tsuruta, JPN      2:45.40
1936 Tetsuo Hamuro, JPN          2:41.50  OR
1948 Joseph Verdeur, USA         2:39.30  OR
1952 John Davies, AUS            2:34.40  OR
1956 Masaru Furukawa, JPN        2:34.70  OR
1960 William Mulliken, USA       2:37.40
1964 Ian O'Brien, AUS            2:27.80  WR
1968 Felipe Múñoz, MEX           2:28.70
1972 John Hencken, USA           2:21.55  WR
1976 David Wilkie, GBR           2:15.11  WR
1980 Robertas Zhulpa, SOV        2:15.85
1984 Victor Davis, CAN           2:13.34  WR
1988 József Szabó, HUN           2:13.52
1992 Mike Barrowman, USA         2:10.16  WR
1996

**MEN'S 100-METER BUTTERFLY**
*1896–1964 not held*
1968 Douglas Russell, USA        0:55.90  OR
1972 Mark Spitz, USA             0:54.27  WR
1976 Matt Vogel, USA             0:54.35
1980 Pär Arvidsson, SWE          0:54.92
1984 Michael Gross, GER          0:53.08  WR
1988 Anthony Nesty, SUR          0:53.00  OR
1992 Pablo Morales, USA          0:53.32
1996

**MEN'S 200-METER BUTTERFLY**
*1896–1952 not held*
1956 William Yorzyk, USA         2:19.30  OR
1960 Michael Troy, USA           2:12.80  WR
1964 Kevin Berry, AUS            2:06.60  WR
1968 Carl Robie, USA             2:08.70
1972 Mark Spitz, USA             2:00.70  WR
1976 Mike Bruner, USA            1:59.23  WR
1980 Sergei Fesenko, SOV         1:59.76
1984 Jon Sieben, AUS             1:57.04  WR
1988 Michael Gross, GER          1:56.94  WR
1992 Melvin Stewart, USA         1:56.26  OR
1996

**MEN'S 200-METER INDIVIDUAL MEDLEY**
*1896–1964 not held*
1968 Charles Hickcox, USA        2:12.00  OR

1972 Gunnar Larsson, SWE         2:07.17  WR
*1976–1980 not held*
1984 Alex Baumann, CAN           2:01.42  WR
1988 Tamás Darnyi, HUN           2:00.17  WR
1992 Tamás Darnyi, HUN           2:00.76
1996

**MEN'S 400-METER INDIVIDUAL MEDLEY**
*1896–1960 not held*
1964 Richard Roth, USA           4:45.40  WR
1968 Charles Hickcox, USA        4:48.40
1972 Gunnar Larsson, SWE         4:31.98  OR
1976 Rod Strachan, USA           4:23.68  WR
1980 Aleksandr Sidorenko, SOV    4:22.89  WR
1984 Alex Baumann, CAN           4:17.41  WR
1988 Tamás Darnyi, HUN           4:14.75  WR
1992 Tamás Darnyi, HUN           4:14.23  OR
1996

**MEN'S 4 X 100-METER FREESTYLE RELAY**
*1896–1960 not held*
1964 USA                         3:32.20  WR
1968 USA                         3:31.70  WR
1972 USA                         3:26.42  WR
*1976–1980 not held*
1984 USA                         3:19.03  WR
1988 USA                         3:16.53  WR
1992 USA                         3:16.74
1996

**MEN'S 4 X 200-METER FREESTYLE RELAY**
*1896–1904 not held (*distances varried)*
1908 GBR                         10:55.60  WR
1912 AUS/NZE                      10:11.60  WR
1920 USA                         10:04.40  WR
1924 USA                          9:53.40  WR
1928 USA                          9:36.20  WR
1932 JPN                          8:58.40  WR
1936 JPN                          8:51.50  WR
1948 USA                          8:46.00  WR
1952 USA                          8:31.10  OR
1956 AUS                          8:23.60  WR
1960 USA                          8:10.20  WR
1964 USA                          7:52.10  WR
1968 USA                          7:52.33
1972 USA                          7:35.78  WR
1976 USA                          7:23.22  WR
1980 SOV                          7:23.50
1984 USA                          7:15.69  WR
1988 USA                          7:12.51  WR
1992 EUN                          7:11.95  WR
1996

**MEN'S 4 X 100-METER MEDLEY RELAY**
*1896–1956 not held*
1960 USA                         4:05.40  WR
1964 USA                         3:58.40  WR
1968 USA                         3:54.90  WR
1972 USA                         3:48.16  WR
1976 USA                         3:42.22  WR
1980 AUS                         3:45.70
1984 USA                         3:39.30  WR
1988 USA                         3:36.93  WR
1992 USA                         3:36.93EWR
1996

## SWIMMING AND DIVING

### MEN'S SPRINGBOARD DIVING
*1896-1904 not held*

1908 Albert Zürner, GER
1912 Paul Günther, GER
1920 Louis Kuehn, USA
1924 Albert White, USA
1928 Ulise Desjardins, USA
1932 Michael Galitzen (Riley), USA
1936 Richard Degener, USA
1948 Bruce Harlan, USA
1952 David Browning, USA
1956 Robert Clotworthy, USA
1960 Gary Tobian, USA
1964 Kenneth Sitzberger, USA
1968 Bernard Wrightson, USA
1972 Vladimir Vasin, SOV
1976 Philip Boggs, USA
1980 Aleksandr Portnov, SOV
1984 Gregory Louganis, USA
1988 Gregory Louganis, USA
1992 Mark Lenzi, USA
1996

### MEN'S PLATFORM DIVING
*1896-1900 not held*

1904 George Sheldon, USA
1908 Hjalmar Johansson, SWE
1912 Erik Adlerz, SWE
1920 Clarence Pinkston, USA
1924 Albert White, USA
1928 Ulise Desjardins, USA
1932 Harold Smith, USA
1936 Marshall Wayne, USA
1948 Samuel Lee, USA
1952 Samuel Lee, USA
1956 Joaquin Capilla Pérez, MEX
1960 Robert Webster, USA
1964 Robert Webster, USA
1968 Klaus Dibiasi, ITA
1972 Klaus Dibiasi, ITA
1976 Klaus Dibiasi, ITA
1980 Falk Hoffmann, GDR
1984 Gregory Louganis, USA
1988 Gregory Louganis, USA
1992 Sun Shuwei, CHN
1996

### WATER POLO
*1896 not held*

| | | | |
|---|---|---|---|
| 1900 | GBR | 1952 | HUN |
| 1904 | USA | 1956 | HUN |
| 1908 | GBR | 1960 | ITA |
| 1912 | GBR | 1964 | HUN |
| 1920 | GBR/IRL | 1968 | YUG |
| 1924 | FRA | 1972 | SOV |
| 1928 | GER | 1976 | HUN |
| 1932 | HUN | 1980 | SOV |
| 1936 | HUN | 1984 | YUG |
| 1948 | ITA | 1988 | YUG |
| | | 1992 | ITA |
| | | 1996 | |

### WOMEN'S 50-METER FREESTYLE
*1896-1984 not held*

1988 Kristin Otto, GDR          0:25.49 OR
1992 Yang Wenyi, CHN           0:24.79 WR
1996

### WOMEN'S 100-METER FREESTYLE
*1896-1908 not held*

1912 Fanny Durack, AUS          1:22.20
1920 Ethelda Bleibtrey, USA     1:13.60 WR
1924 Ethel Lackie, USA          1:12.40
1928 Albina Osipowich, USA      1:11.00 OR
1932 Helene Madison, USA        1:06.80 OR
1936 Hendrika Mastenbroek, HOL  1:05.90 OR
1948 Greta Andersen, DEN        1:06.30
1952 Katalin Szöke, HUN         1:06.80
1956 Dawn Fraser, AUS           1:02.00 WR
1960 Dawn Fraser, AUS           1:01.20 OR
1964 Dawn Fraser, AUS           0:59.50 OR
1968 Jan Henne, USA             1:00.00
1972 Sandra Neilson, USA        0:58.59 OR

1976 Kornelia Ender, GDR        0:55.65 WR
1980 Barbara Krause, GDR        0:54.79 WR
1984 Nancy Hogshead, USA        0:55.92
1988 Kristin Otto, GDR          0:54.93
1992 Zhuang Yong, CHN           0:54.65 OR
1996

### WOMEN'S 200-METER FREESTYLE
*1896-1964 not held*

1968 Deborah Meyer, USA         2:10.50 OR
1972 Shane Gould, AUS           2:03.56 WR
1976 Kornelia Ender, GDR        1:59.26 WR
1980 Barbara Krause, GDR        1:58.33 OR
1984 Mary Wayte, USA            1:59.23
1988 Heike Friedrich, GDR       1:57.65 OR
1992 Nicole Haislett, USA       1:57.90
1996

### WOMEN'S 400-METER FREESTYLE
*1896-1912 not held*

1920 Ethelda Bleibtrey, USA     4:34.00 WR
1924 Martha Norelius, USA       6:02.20 OR
1928 Martha Norelius, USA       5:42.80 WR
1932 Helene Madison, USA        5:28.50 WR
1936 Hendrika Mastenbroek, HOL  5:26.40 OR
1948 Ann Curtis, USA            5:17.80 OR
1952 Valéria Gyenge, HUN        5:12.10 OR
1956 Lorraine Crapp, AUS        4:54.60 OR
1960 S. Christine Von Saltza, USA 4:50.60 OR
1964 Virginia Duenkel, USA      4:43.30 OR
1968 Debbie Meyer, USA          4:31.80 OR
1972 Shane Gould, AUS           4:19.44 WR
1976 Petra Thümer, GDR          4:09.89 WR
1980 Ines Diers, GDR            4:08.76 OR
1984 Tiffany Cohen, USA         4:07.10 OR
1988 Janet Evans, USA           4:03.85 WR
1992 Dagmar Hase, GER           4:07.18
1996

### WOMEN'S 800-METER FREESTYLE
*1896-1964 not held*

1968 Deborah Meyer, USA         9:24.00 OR
1972 Keena Rothhammer, USA      8:53.68 WR
1976 Petra Thümer, GDR          8:37.14 WR
1980 Michelle Ford, AUS         8:28.90 OR
1984 Tiffany Cohen, USA         8:24.95 OR
1988 Janet Evans, USA           8:20.20 OR
1992 Janet Evans, USA           8:25.52
1996

### WOMEN'S 100-METER BACKSTROKE
*1896-1920 not held*

1924 Sybil Bauer, USA           1:23.20 OR
1928 Maria Braun, HOL           1:22.00
1932 Eleanor Holm, USA          1:19.40
1936 Dina Senff, HOL            1:18.90
1948 Karen-Margrete Harup, DEN  1:14.40 OR
1952 Joan Harrison, SAF         1:14.30
1956 Judith Grinham, GBR        1:12.90 OR
1960 Lynn Burke, USA            1:09.30 OR
1964 Cathy Ferguson, USA        1:07.70 WR
1968 Kaye Hall, USA             1:06.20 WR
1972 Melissa Belote, USA        1:05.78 OR
1976 Ulrike Richter, GDR        1:01.83 OR
1980 Rica Reinisch, GDR         1:00.86 WR
1984 Theresa Andrews, USA       1:02.55
1988 Kristin Otto, GDR          1:00.89
1992 Krisztina Egerszegi, HUN   1:00.68 OR
1996

### WOMEN'S 200-METER BACKSTROKE
*1896-1964 not held*

1968 Lillian Watson, USA        2:24.80 OR
1972 Melissa Belote, USA        2:19.19 WR
1976 Ulrike Richter, GDR        2:13.43 OR
1980 Rica Reinisch, GDR         2:11.77 WR
1984 Jolanda de Rover, HOL      2:12.38
1988 Krisztina Egerszegi, HUN   2:09.29 OR
1992 Krisztina Egerszegi, HUN   2:07.06 OR
1996

### WOMEN'S 100-METER BREASTSTROKE
*1896-1964 not held*

1968 Djurdjica Bjedov, YUG      1:15.80 OR
1972 Catherine Carr, USA        1:13.58 WR
1976 Hannelore Anke, GDR        1:11.16
1980 Ute Geweniger, GDR         1:10.22
1984 Petra van Staveren, HOL    1:09.88 OR
1988 Tania Dangalakova
       (Bogomilova), BUL        1:07.95 OR
1992 Elena Roudkovskaia, EUN    1:08.00
1996

### WOMEN'S 200-METER BREASTSTROKE
*1896-1920 not held*

1924 Lucy Morton, GBR           3:33.20 OR
1928 Hildegard Schrader, GER    3:12.60
1932 Clare Dennis, AUS          3:06.30 OR
1936 Hideko Maehata, JPN        3:03.60
1948 Petronella van Vliet, HOL  2:57.20
1952 Êva Székely, HUN           2:51.70 OR
1956 Ursula Happe, GER          2:53.10 OR
1960 Anita Lonsbrough, GBR      2:49.50 WR
1964 Galina Prozumenshikova, SOV 2:46.40 OR
1968 Sharon Wichman, USA        2:44.40 OR
1972 Beverley Whitfield, AUS    2:41.71 OR
1976 Marina Koshevaia, SOV      2:33.35 WR
1980 Lina Kačiušte, SOV         2:29.54 OR
1984 Anne Ottenbrite, CAN       2:30.38
1988 Silke Hörner, GDR          2:26.71 WR
1992 Kyoko Iwasaki, JPN         2:26.65 OR
1996

### WOMEN'S 100-METER BUTTERFLY
*1896-1952 not held*

1956 Shelly Mann, USA           1:11.00 OR
1960 Carolyn Schuler, USA       1:09.50 OR
1964 Sharon Stouder, USA        1:04.70 WR
1968 Lynette McClements, AUS    1:05.50
1972 Mayumi Aoki, JPN           1:03.34 WR
1976 Kornelia Ender, GDR        1:00.13 EWR
1980 Caren Metschuck, GDR       1:00.42
1984 Mary T. Meagher, USA       0:59.26
1988 Kristin Otto, GDR          0:59.00 OR
1992 Qian Hong, CHN             0:58.62 OR
1996

### WOMEN'S 200-METER BUTTERFLY
*1896-1964 not held*

1968 Ada Kok, HOL               2:24.70 OR
1972 Karen Moe, USA             2:15.57 WR
1976 Andrea Pollack, GDR        2:11.41 OR
1980 Ines Geissler, GDR         2:10.44 OR
1984 Mary T. Meagher, USA       2:06.90 OR
1988 Kathleen Nord, GDR         2:09.51
1992 Summer Sanders, USA        2:08.67
1996

### WOMEN'S 200-METER INDIVIDUAL MEDLEY
*1896-1964 not held*

1968 Claudia Kolb, USA          2:24.70 OR
1972 Shane Gould, AUS           2:23.07 WR
*1976-1980 not held*
1984 Tracy Caulkins, USA        2:12.64 OR
1988 Daniela Hunger, GDR        2:12.59 OR
1992 Lin Li, CHN                2:11.65 OR
1996

### WOMEN'S 400-METER INDIVIDUAL MEDLEY
*1896-1960 not held*

1964 Donna De Varona, USA       5:18.70 OR
1968 Claudia Kolb, USA          5:08.50 OR
1972 Gail Neall, AUS            5:02.97 WR
1976 Ulrike Tauber, GDR         4:42.77 WR
1980 Petra Schneider, GDR       4:36.29 WR
1984 Tracy Caulkins, USA        4:39.24
1988 Janet Evans, USA           4:37.76
1992 Krisztina Egerszegi, HUN   4:36.54
1996

### WOMEN'S 4 X 100-METER FREESTYLE RELAY
*1896-1908 not held*

| | | | |
|---|---|---|---|
| 1912 | GBR | 5:52.80 | WR |
| 1920 | USA | 5:11.60 | WR |
| 1924 | USA | 4:58.80 | WR |
| 1928 | USA | 4:47.60 | WR |
| 1932 | USA | 4:38.00 | WR |
| 1936 | HOL | 4:36.00 | WR |
| 1948 | USA | 4:29.20 | WR |
| 1952 | HUN | 4:24.40 | WR |
| 1956 | AUS | 4:17.10 | WR |
| 1960 | USA | 4:08.90 | WR |
| 1964 | USA | 4:03.80 | WR |
| 1968 | USA | 4:02.50 | OR |
| 1972 | USA | 3:55.19 | WR |
| 1976 | USA | 3:44.82 | WR |
| 1980 | GDR | 3:42.71 | WR |
| 1984 | USA | 3:43.43 | |
| 1988 | GDR | 3:40.63 | OR |
| 1992 | USA | 3:39.46 | WR |
| 1996 | | | |

### WOMEN'S 4 X 100-METER MEDLEY RELAY
*1896-1956 not held*

| | | | |
|---|---|---|---|
| 1960 | USA | 4:41.10 | WR |
| 1964 | USA | 4:33.90 | WR |
| 1968 | USA | 4:28.30 | OR |
| 1972 | USA | 4:20.75 | WR |
| 1976 | GDR | 4:07.95 | WR |
| 1980 | GDR | 4:06.67 | WR |
| 1984 | USA | 4:08.34 | |
| 1988 | GDR | 4:03.74 | OR |
| 1992 | USA | 4:02.54 | OR |
| 1996 | | | |

### WOMEN'S SYNCHRONIZED SWIMMING: SOLO
*1896-1980 not held*

1984 Tracie Ruiz, USA
1988 Carolyn Waldo, CAN
1992 Kristen Babb-Sprague, USA
1996

### WOMEN'S SYNCHRONIZED SWIMMING: DUET
*1896-1980 not held*

1984 Candy Costie, Tracie Ruiz, USA
1988 Michelle Cameron, Carolyn Waldo, CAN
1992 Karen Josephson, Sarah Josephson, USA
1996

### WOMEN'S SPRINGBOARD DIVING
*1896-1912 not held*

1920 Aileen Riggin, USA
1924 Elizabeth Becker, USA
1928 Helen Meany, USA
1932 Georgia Coleman, USA
1936 Marjorie Gestring, USA
1948 Victoria Draves, USA
1952 Patricia McCormick, USA
1956 Patricia McCormick, USA
1960 Ingrid Krämer, GDR
1964 Ingrid Engel-Krämer, GDR
1968 Sue Gossick, USA
1972 Maxine King, USA
1976 Jennifer Chandler, USA
1980 Irina Kalinina, SOV
1984 Sylvie Bernie, CAN
1988 Gao Min, CHN
1992 Gao Min, CHN
1996

### WOMEN'S PLATFORM DIVING
*1896-1908 not held*

1912 Greta Johansson, SWE
1920 Stefani Fryland-Clausen, DEN
1924 Caroline Smith, USA
1928 Elizabeth Becker Pinkston, USA
1932 Dorothy Poynton, USA
1936 Dorothy Poynton Hill, USA
1948 Victoria Draves, USA
1952 Patricia McCormick, USA
1956 Patricia McCormick, USA
1960 Ingrid Krämer, GDR
1964 Lesley Bush, USA

## SWIMMING AND DIVING

| | | | |
|---|---|---|---|
| 1968 | Milena Duchková, CZE | 1984 | Zhou Jihong, CHN |
| 1972 | Ulrika Knape, SWE | 1988 | Xu Yanmei, CHN |
| 1976 | Elena Vaytsekhovskaya, SOV | 1992 | Fu Mingxia, CHN |
| 1980 | Martina Jäschke, GDR | 1996 | |

## TABLE TENNIS

### MEN'S SINGLES
*1896–1984 not held*
1988 Yoo Nam-kyu, KOR
1992 Jan Waldner, SWE
1996

### WOMEN'S TABLE TENNIS SINGLES
*1896–1984 not held*
1988 Chen Jing, CHN
1992 Deng Yaping, CHN
1996

### MEN'S TABLE TENNIS DOUBLES
*1896–1984 not held*
1988 C. Longcan, W. Qingguang, CHN
1992 L. Lin, Wong Tao, CHN
1996

### WOMEN'S TENNIS DOUBLES
*1896–1984 not held*
1988 H. Jung-hwa, Y. Young-ja, KOR
1992 Deng Yaping, Qiao Hong, CHN
1996

## TENNIS

### MEN'S TENNIS SINGLES
1896 John Boland, GBR/IRL
1900 Hugh Doherty, GBR
1904 Beals Wright, USA
1908 Josiah Ritchie, GBR
1908 Arthur Gore, GBR (ICt)
1912 Charles Winslow, SAF
1912 André Gobert, FRA (ICt)
1920 Louis Raymond, SAF
1924 Vincent Richards, USA
*1928–1984 not held*
1988 Miloslav Mečíř, CZE
1992 Marc Rosset, SWI
1996

### MEN'S TENNIS DOUBLES
1896 J. Borland, F. Traun, GBR/IRL
1900 R. Doherty, H. Doherty, GBR
1904 E. Leonard, B. Wright, USA
1908 G. Hillyard, R. Doherty, GBR
1908 A. Gore, H. Barrett, GBR (ICt)
1912 C. Winslow, H. Kitson, SAF
1912 A. Gobert, M. Germot, FRA (ICt)
1920 O. Turnbull, M. Woosnam, GBR
1924 V. Richards, F. Hunter, USA
*1928–1984 not held*
1988 K. Flach, R. Seguso, USA
1992 B. Becker, M. Stich, GER
1996

### WOMEN'S TENNIS SINGLES
*1896 not held*
1900 Charlotte Cooper, GBR
*1904 not held*
1908 Gwendoline Eastlake-Smith, GBR (ICt)
1912 Marguerite Broquedis, FRA
1912 Edith Hannam, GBR (ICt)
1920 Suzanne Lenglen, FRA
1924 Helen Wills, USA
*1928–1984 not held*
1988 Stefanie Graf, GER
1992 Jennifer Capriati, USA
1996

### WOMEN'S TENNIS DOUBLES
*1896–1912 not held*
1920 W. McNair, K. McKane, GBR
1924 H. Wightman, H. Willis, USA
*1928–1984 not held*
1988 P. Shriver, Z. Garrison, USA
1992 G. Fernandez, M. J. Fernandez, USA
1996

## TRACK AND FIELD • MEN

### 100-METER RUN
| | | | |
|---|---|---|---|
| 1896 | Thomas Burke, USA | 12.00 | |
| 1900 | Frank W. Jarvis, USA | 11.00 | |
| 1904 | Archie Hahn, USA | 11.00 | |
| 1908 | Reginald Walker, SAF | 10.80 | EOR |
| 1912 | Ralph Craig, USA | 10.80 | |
| 1920 | Charles Paddock, USA | 10.80 | |
| 1924 | Harold Abrahams, GBR | 10.60 | EOR |
| 1928 | Percy Williams, CAN | 10.80 | |
| 1932 | Eddie Tolan, USA | 10.30 | OR |
| 1936 | Jesse Owens, USA | 10.30 | |
| 1948 | Harrison Dillard, USA | 10.30 | EOR |
| 1952 | Lindy Remigino, USA | 10.40 | |
| 1956 | Bobby Morrow, USA | 10.50 | |
| 1960 | Armin Hary, GER | 10.20 | OR |
| 1964 | Hayes, USA | 10.00 | EWR |
| 1968 | Jim Hines, USA | 9.95 | WR |
| 1972 | Valery Borzov, SOV | 10.14 | |
| 1976 | Hasely Crawford, TRI | 10.06 | |
| 1980 | Allan Wells, GBR | 10.25 | |
| 1984 | Carl Lewis, USA | 9.99 | |
| 1988 | Carl Lewis, USA | 9.92 | OR |
| 1992 | Linford Christie, GBR | 9.96 | |
| 1996 | | | |

### 200-METER RUN
*1896 not held*
| | | | |
|---|---|---|---|
| 1900 | Walter Tewksbury, USA | 22.20 | |
| 1904 | Archie Hahn, USA | 21.60 | OR |
| 1908 | Robert Kerr, CAN | 22.60 | |
| 1912 | Ralph Craig, USA | 21.70 | |
| 1920 | Allen Woodring, USA | 22.00 | |
| 1924 | Jackson Scholz, USA | 21.60 | |
| 1928 | Percy Williams, CAN | 21.80 | |
| 1932 | Eddie Tolan, USA | 21.20 | OR |
| 1936 | Jesse Owens, USA | 20.70 | OR |
| 1948 | Mel Patton, USA | 21.10 | |
| 1952 | Andrew Stanfield, USA | 20.70 | |
| 1956 | Bobby Morrow, USA | 20.60 | OR |
| 1960 | Livio Berruti, ITA | 20.50 | EWR |
| 1964 | Henry Carr, USA | 20.30 | OR |
| 1968 | Tommie Smith, USA | 19.83 | WR |
| 1972 | Valery Borzov, SOV | 20.00 | |
| 1976 | Donald Quarrie, JAM | 20.23 | |
| 1980 | Pietro Mennea, ITA | 20.19 | |
| 1984 | Carl Lewis, USA | 19.80 | OR |
| 1988 | Joe DeLoach, USA | 19.75 | OR |
| 1992 | Mike Marsh, USA | 20.01 | |
| 1996 | | | |

### 400-METER RUN
| | | | |
|---|---|---|---|
| 1896 | Thomas Burke, USA | 54.20 | |
| 1900 | Maxey Long, USA | 49.40 | OR |
| 1904 | Harry Hillman, USA | 49.20 | OR |
| 1908 | Wyndham Halswelle, GBR, | 50.00 | |
| 1912 | Charles Reidpath, USA | 48.20 | OR |
| 1920 | Bevil Rudd, SAF | 49.60 | |
| 1924 | Eric Liddell, GBR | 47.60 | OR |
| 1928 | Ray Barbuti, USA | 47.80 | |
| 1932 | William Carr, USA | 46.20 | WR |
| 1936 | Archie Williams, USA | 46.50 | |
| 1948 | Arthur Wint, JAM | 46.20 | |
| 1952 | George Rhoden, JAM | 45.90 | OR |
| 1956 | Charles Jenkins, USA | 46.70 | |
| 1960 | Otis Davis, USA | 44.90 | WR |
| 1964 | Michael Larrabee, USA | 45.10 | |
| 1968 | Lee Evans, USA | 43.80 | WR |
| 1972 | Vincent Matthews, USA | 44.66 | |
| 1976 | Alberto Juantorena, CUB | 44.26 | |
| 1980 | Viktor Markin, SOV | 44.60 | |
| 1984 | Alonzo Babers, USA | 44.27 | |
| 1988 | Steven Lewis, USA | 43.87 | |
| 1992 | Quincy Watts, USA | 44.21 | |
| 1996 | | | |

### 800-METER RUN
| | | | |
|---|---|---|---|
| 1896 | Edwin Flack, AUS | 2:11.00 | |
| 1900 | Alfred Tysoe, GBR | 2:01.20 | |
| 1904 | James Lightbody, USA | 1:56.00 | OR |
| 1908 | Mel Sheppard, USA | 1:52.80 | WR |
| 1912 | James Meredith, USA | 1:51.90 | WR |
| 1920 | Albert Hill, GBR | 1:53.40 | |
| 1924 | Douglas Lowe, GBR | 1:52.40 | |
| 1928 | Douglas Lowe, GBR | 1:51.80 | OR |
| 1932 | Thomas Hampson, GBR | 1:49.70 | WR |
| 1936 | John Woodruff, USA | 1:52.90 | |
| 1948 | Mal Whitfield, USA | 1:49.20 | OR |
| 1952 | Mal Whitfield, USA | 1:49.20 | EOR |
| 1956 | Thomas Courtney, USA | 1:47.70 | OR |
| 1960 | Peter Snell, NZE | 1:46.30 | OR |
| 1964 | Peter Snell, NZE | 1:45.10 | OR |
| 1968 | Ralph Doubell, AUS | 1:44.30 | EWR |
| 1972 | Dave Wottle, USA | 1:45.90 | |
| 1976 | Alberto Juantorena, CUB | 1:43.50 | WR |
| 1980 | Steve Ovett, GBR | 1:45.40 | |
| 1984 | Joaquim Cruz, BRA | 1:43.00 | OR |
| 1988 | Paul Ereng, KEN | 1:43.45 | |
| 1992 | William Tanui, KEN | 1:43.66 | |
| 1996 | | | |

### 1500-METER RUN
| | | | |
|---|---|---|---|
| 1896 | Edwin Flack, AUS | 4:33.20 | |
| 1900 | Charles Bennett, GBR | 4:06.20 | WR |
| 1904 | James Lightbody, USA | 4:05.40 | WR |
| 1908 | Mel Sheppard, USA | 4:03.40 | OR |
| 1912 | Arnold Jackson, GBR | 3:56.80 | OR |
| 1920 | Albert Hill, GBR | 4:01.80 | |
| 1924 | Paavo Nurmi, FIN | 3:53.60 | OR |
| 1928 | Harry Larva, FIN | 3:53.20 | |
| 1932 | Luigi Beccali, ITA | 3:51.20 | OR |
| 1936 | Jack Lovelock, NZE | 3:47.80 | WR |
| 1948 | Henri Eriksson, SWE | 3:49.80 | |
| 1952 | Josef Barthel, LUX | 3:45.10 | OR |
| 1956 | Ron Delany, IRL | 3:41.20 | OR |
| 1960 | Herbert Elliott, AUS | 3:35.60 | WR |
| 1964 | Peter Snell, NZE | 3:38.10 | |
| 1968 | Kipchoge Keino, KEN | 3:34.90 | OR |
| 1972 | Pekka Vasala, FIN | 3:36.30 | |
| 1976 | John Walker, NZE | 3:39.17 | |
| 1980 | Sebastian Coe, GBR | 3:38.40 | |
| 1984 | Sebastian Coe, GBR | 3:32.53 | OR |
| 1988 | Peter Rono, KEN | 3:35.96 | |
| 1992 | Fermin Cacho Ruiz, SPA | 3:40.12 | |
| 1996 | | | |

### 3000-METER STEEPLECHASE
*1896 not held*
| | | | |
|---|---|---|---|
| 1900 | George Orton, CAN | 7:34.40 | |
| 1904 | James Lightbody, USA | 7:39.60 | |
| 1908 | Arthur Russell, GBR | 10:47.80 | |
| *1912 not held* | | | |
| 1920 | Percy Hodge, GBR | 10:00.40 | OR |
| 1924 | Vilho Ritola, FIN | 9:33.60 | OR |
| 1928 | Toivo Loukola, FIN | 9:21.80 | WR |
| 1932 | Volmari Iso-Hollo, FIN | 10:33.40 | |
| | *(About 3,450 mtrs. extra lap by error)* | | |
| 1936 | Volmari Iso-Hollo, FIN | 9:03.80 | WR |
| 1948 | Thore Sjöstrand, SWE | 9:04.60 | |
| 1952 | Horace Ashenfelter, USA | 8:45.40 | WR |
| 1956 | Chris Brasher, GBR | 8:41.20 | OR |
| 1960 | Zdzislaw Krzyszkowiak, POL | 8:34.20 | OR |
| 1964 | Gaston Roelants, BEL | 8:30.80 | OR |
| 1968 | Amos Biwott, KEN | 8:51.00 | |
| 1972 | Kipchoge Keino, KEN | 8:23.60 | OR |
| 1976 | Anders Gärderud, SWE | 8:08.20 | WR |
| 1980 | Bronislaw Malinowski, POL | 8:09.70 | |
| 1984 | Julius Korir, KEN | 8:11.80 | |
| 1988 | Julius Kariuki, KEN | 8:05.51 | OR |
| 1992 | Matthew Birer, KEN | 8:08.84 | |
| 1996 | | | |

### 5000-METER RUN
*1896–1908 not held*
| | | | |
|---|---|---|---|
| 1912 | Hannes Kolehmainen, FIN | 14:36.60 | WR |
| 1920 | Joseph Guillemot, FRA | 14:55.60 | |
| 1924 | Paavo Nurmi, FIN | 14:31.20 | OR |
| 1928 | Vilho Ritola, FIN | 14:38.00 | |
| 1932 | Lauri Lehtinen, FIN | 14:30.00 | OR |
| 1936 | Gunnar Höckert, FIN | 14:22.20 | OR |
| 1948 | Gaston Reiff, BEL | 14:17.60 | OR |
| 1952 | Emil Zátopek, CZE | 14:06.60 | OR |
| 1956 | Vladimir Kuts, SOV | 13:39.60 | OR |
| 1960 | Murray Halberg, NZE | 13:43.40 | |
| 1964 | Bob Schul, USA | 13:48.80 | |
| 1968 | Mohamed Gammoudi, TUN | 14:05.00 | |
| 1972 | Lasse Viren, FIN | 13:26.40 | OR |
| 1976 | Lasse Viren, FIN | 13:24.76 | |
| 1980 | Miruts Yifter, ETH | 13:21.00 | |
| 1984 | Said Aouita, MOR | 13:05.59 | OR |
| 1988 | John Ngugi, KEN | 13:11.70 | |
| 1992 | Dieter Baumann, GER | 13:12.52 | |
| 1996 | | | |

### 10000-METER RUN
*1896–1908 not held*
| | | | |
|---|---|---|---|
| 1912 | Hannes Kolehmainen, FIN | 31:20.80 | |
| 1920 | Paavo Nurmi, FIN | 31:45.80 | |
| 1924 | Vilho Ritola, FIN | 30:23.20 | WR |
| 1928 | Paavo Nurmi, FIN | 30:18.80 | OR |
| 1932 | Janusz Kusociński, POL | 30:11.40 | OR |
| 1936 | Ilmari Salminen, FIN | 30:15.40 | |
| 1948 | Emil Zátopek, CZE | 29:59.60 | OR |
| 1952 | Emil Zátopek, CZE | 29:17.00 | OR |
| 1956 | Vladimir Kuts, SOV | 28:45.60 | OR |
| 1960 | Pyotr Bolotnikov, SOV | 28:32.20 | OR |
| 1964 | Billy Mills, USA | 28:24.40 | OR |
| 1968 | Naftali Temu, KEN | 29:27.40 | |
| 1972 | Lasse Viren, FIN | 27:38.40 | WR |
| 1976 | Lasse Viren, FIN | 27:40.38 | |
| 1980 | Miruts Yifter, ETH | 27:42.70 | |
| 1984 | Alberto Cova, ITA | 27:47.54 | |
| 1988 | Brahim Boutaib, MOR | 27:21.46 | OR |
| 1992 | Khalid Skah, MOR | 27:46.70 | |
| 1996 | | | |

### MARATHON
| | | | |
|---|---|---|---|
| 1896 | Spiridon Loues, GRE | 2:58:50.0 | |
| 1900 | Michel Théato, FRA | 2:59:45.0 | |
| 1904 | Thomas Hicks, USA | 3:28:53.0 | |
| 1908 | John J. Hayes, USA | 2:55:18.4 | OR |
| 1912 | Kenneth McArthur, SAF | 2:36:54.8 | |
| 1920 | Hannes Kolehmainen, FIN | 2:32:35.8 | WB |
| 1924 | Albin Stenroos, FIN | 2:41:22.6 | |
| 1928 | A. B. El Ouafi, FRA | 2:32:57.0 | |
| 1932 | Juan Zabala, ARG | 2:31:36.0 | OR |
| 1936 | Sohn Kee-chung, KOR | 2:29:19.2 | OR |
| 1948 | Delfo Cabrera, ARG | 2:34:51.6 | |
| 1952 | Emil Zátopek, CZE | 2:23:03.2 | OR |
| 1956 | Alain Mimoun, FRA | 2:25:00.0 | |
| 1960 | Abebe Bikila, ETH | 2:15:16.2 | WB |
| 1964 | Abebe Bikila, ETH | 2:12:11.2 | WB |
| 1968 | Mamo Wolde, ETH | 2:20:26.4 | |
| 1972 | Frank Shorter, USA | 2:12:19.8 | |
| 1976 | Waldemar Cierpinski, GDR | 2:09:55.0 | OR |
| 1980 | Waldemar Cierpinski, GDR | 2:11:03.0 | |
| 1984 | Carlos Lopes, POR | 2:09:21.0 | OR |
| 1988 | Gelindo Bordin, ITA | 2:10:32.0 | |
| 1992 | Hwang Young-Cho, KOR | 2:13:23.0 | |
| 1996 | | | |

### 20-KILOMETER WALK
*1896–1952 not held*
| | | | |
|---|---|---|---|
| 1956 | Leonid Spirin, SOV | 1:31:27.4 | |
| 1960 | Vladimir Golubnichiy, SOV | 1:34:07.2 | |
| 1964 | Kenneth Mathews, GBR | 1:29:34.0 | OR |
| 1968 | Vladimir Golubnichiy, SOV | 1:33:58.4 | |
| 1972 | Peter Frenkel, GDR | 1:26:42.4 | OR |
| 1976 | Daniel Bautista, MEX | 1:24:40.6 | OR |
| 1980 | Maurizio Damilano, ITA | 1:23:35.5 | OR |
| 1984 | Ernesto Canto, MEX | 1:23:13.0 | OR |
| 1988 | Josef Pribilinec, CZE | 1:19:57.0 | OR |

## TRACK AND FIELD · MEN

| 1992 | Daniel Plaza Montero, SPA | 1:21:45.0 | |
| 1996 | | | |

### 50-KILOMETER WALK
*1896-1928 not held*

| 1932 | Thomas W. Green, GBR | 4:50:10.0 | |
| 1936 | Harold Whitlock, GBR | 4:30:41.4 | OR |
| 1948 | John Ljunggren, SWE | 4:41:52.0 | |
| 1952 | Giuseppe Dordoni, ITA | 4:28:07.8 | OR |
| 1956 | Norman Read, NZE | 4:30:42.8 | |
| 1960 | Donald Thompson, GBR | 4:25:30.0 | OR |
| 1964 | Abdon Pamich, ITA | 4:11:12.4 | OR |
| 1968 | Christoph Höhne, GDR | 4:20:13.6 | |
| 1972 | Bernd Kannenberg, GER | 3:56:11.6 | OR |
| *1976 not held* | | | |
| 1980 | Hartwig Gauder, GDR | 3:49:24.0 | OR |
| 1984 | Raúl González, MEX | 3:47:26.0 | OR |
| 1988 | Vyacheslav Ivanenko, SOV | 3:38:29.0 | OR |
| 1992 | Andrei Perlov, EUN | 3:50:13.0 | |
| 1996 | | | |

### 110-METER HURDLES

| 1896 | Thomas Curtis, USA | 17.60 | |
| 1900 | Alvin Kraenzlein, USA | 15.40 | OR |
| 1904 | Frederick Schule, USA | 16.00 | |
| 1908 | Forrest Smithson, USA | 15.00 | WR |
| 1912 | Frederick Kelly, USA | 15.10 | |
| 1920 | Earl Thomson, CAN | 14.80 | WR |
| 1924 | Daniel Kinsey, USA | 15.00 | |
| 1928 | Sydney Atkinson, SAF | 14.80 | |
| 1932 | George Saling, USA | 14.60 | |
| 1936 | Forrest Towns, USA | 14.20 | |
| 1948 | William Porter, USA | 13.90 | OR |
| 1952 | Harrison Dillard, USA | 13.70 | OR |
| 1956 | Lee Calhoun, USA | 13.50 | OR |
| 1960 | Lee Calhoun, USA | 13.80 | |
| 1964 | Hayes Jones, USA | 13.60 | |
| 1968 | Willie Davenport, USA | 13.33 | OR |
| 1972 | Rod Milburn, USA | 13.24 | EWR |
| 1976 | Guy Drut, FRA | 13.30 | |
| 1980 | Thomas Munkelt, GDR | 13.39 | |
| 1984 | Roger Kingdom, USA | 13.20 | OR |
| 1988 | Roger Kingdom, USA | 12.98 | OR |
| 1992 | Mark McCoy, CAN | 13.12 | |
| 1996 | | | |

### 400-METER HURDLES
*1896 not held*

| 1900 | J. W. Tewksbury, USA | 57.60 | |
| 1904 | Harry Hillman, USA | 53.00 | |
| 1908 | Charles Bacon, USA | 55.00 | WR |
| 1920 | Frank Loomis, USA | 54.00 | WR |
| 1924 | F. Morgan Taylor, USA | 52.60 | |
| 1928 | David Burghley, GBR | 53.40 | OR |
| 1932 | Robert Tisdall, IRL | 51.70 | |
| 1936 | Glenn Hardin, USA | 52.40 | |
| 1948 | Roy Cochran, USA | 51.10 | OR |
| 1952 | Charles Moore, USA | 50.80 | OR |
| 1956 | Glenn Davis, USA | 50.10 | EOR |
| 1960 | Glenn Davis, USA | 49.30 | OR |
| 1964 | Rex Cawley, USA | 49.60 | |
| 1968 | Dave Hemery, GBR | 48.12 | WR |
| 1972 | John Akii-Bua, UGA | 47.82 | WR |
| 1976 | Edwin Moses, USA | 47.64 | WR |
| 1980 | Volker Beck, GDR | 48.70 | |
| 1984 | Edwin Moses, USA | 47.75 | |
| 1988 | Andre Phillips, USA | 47.19 | OR |
| 1992 | Kevin Young, USA | 46.78 | OR |
| 1996 | | | |

### HIGH JUMP

| 1896 | Ellery Clark, USA | 5ft. 11 1/4in. | |
| 1900 | Irving Baxter, USA | 6ft. 2 3/4 in.OR | |
| 1904 | Samuel Jones, USA | 5ft. 11 in. | |
| 1908 | Harry Porter, USA | 6ft. 3 in. | OR |
| 1912 | Alma Richards, USA | 6ft. 4 in. | OR |
| 1920 | Richmond Landon, USA | 6ft. 4 in. | EOR |
| 1924 | Harold Osborn, USA | 6ft. 6 in. | OR |
| 1928 | Robert W. King, USA | 6ft. 4 1/2 in. | |
| 1932 | Duncan McNaughton, CAN | 6ft. 5 1/2 in. | |
| 1936 | Cornelius Johnson, USA | 6ft. 8 in. | OR |
| 1948 | John L. Winter, AUS | 6ft. 6 in. | |
| 1952 | Walter Davis, USA | 6ft. 8 1/2 in. OR | |
| 1956 | Charles Dumas, USA | 6ft. 11 1/2 in.OR | |
| 1960 | Robert Shavlakadze, SOV | 7ft. 1 in. | OR |
| 1964 | Valery Brumel, SOV | 7ft. 1 3/4 in. | OR |
| 1968 | Dick Fosbury, USA | 7ft. 4 1/4 in. | OR |
| 1972 | Jüri Tarmak, SOV | 7ft. 3 3/4 in. | |
| 1976 | Jacek Wszola, POL | 7ft. 4 1/2 in. | OR |
| 1980 | Gerd Wessig, GDR | 7ft. 8 3/4 in.WR | |
| 1984 | Dietmar Mögenburg, GER | 7ft. 8 1/2 in. | |
| 1988 | Gennady Avdeyenko, SOV | 7ft. 9 3/4 in. | OR |
| 1992 | Javier Sotomayor, CUB | 7ft. 8 in. | |
| 1996 | | | |

### LONG JUMP

| 1896 | Ellery Clark, USA | 20ft. 10 in. | |
| 1900 | Alvin Kraenzlein, USA | 23ft. 6 3/4 in. | OR |
| 1904 | Meyer Prinstein, USA | 24ft. 1 in. | OR |
| 1908 | Frank Irons, USA | 24ft. 6 1/2 in. | OR |
| 1912 | Albert Gutterson, USA | 24ft. 11 1/4 in.OR | |
| 1920 | William Pettersson, SWE | 23ft. 5 1/2 in. | |
| 1924 | DeHart Hubbard, USA | 24ft. 5 in. | |
| 1928 | Edward B. Hamm, USA | 25ft. 4 1/2 in. | OR |
| 1932 | Edward Gordon, USA | 25ft. 3/4 in. | |
| 1936 | Jesse Owens, USA | 26ft. 5 1/2 in. | OR |
| 1948 | William Steele, USA | 25ft. 8 in. | |
| 1952 | Jerome Biffle, USA | 24ft. 10 in. | |
| 1956 | Gregory Bell, USA | 25ft. 8 1/4 in. | |
| 1960 | Ralph Boston, USA | 26ft. 7 3/4 in. | OR |
| 1964 | Lynn Davies, GBR | 26ft. 5 3/4 in. | |
| 1968 | Bob Beamon, USA | 29ft. 2 1/2 in.WR | |
| 1972 | Randy Williams, USA | 27ft. 1/2 in. | |
| 1976 | Arnie Robinson, USA | 27ft. 4 3/4 in. | |
| 1980 | Lutz Dombrowski, GDR | 28ft. 1/4 in. | |
| 1984 | Carl Lewis, USA | 28ft. 1/4 in. | |
| 1988 | Carl Lewis, USA | 28ft. 7 1/4 in. | |
| 1992 | Carl Lewis, USA | 28ft. 5 1/2 in. | |
| 1996 | | | |

### 400-METER RELAY
*1896-1908 not held*

| 1912 | GBR | 42.40 | |
| 1920 | USA | 42.20 | WR |
| 1924 | USA | 41.00 | EWR |
| 1928 | USA | 41.00 | EWR |
| 1932 | USA | 40.00 | WR |
| 1936 | USA | 39.80 | WR |
| 1948 | USA | 40.60 | |
| 1952 | USA | 40.10 | |
| 1956 | USA | 39.50 | WR |
| 1960 | GER (USA disqualified) | 39.50 | EWR |
| 1964 | USA | 39.00 | WR |
| 1968 | USA | 38.23 | WR |
| 1972 | USA | 38.19 | WR |
| 1976 | USA | 38.33 | |
| 1980 | SOV | 38.26 | |
| 1984 | USA | 37.83 | WR |
| 1988 | SOV (USA disqualified) | 38.19 | |
| 1992 | USA | 37.40 | OR |
| 1996 | | | |

### 1600-METER RELAY
*1896-1904 not held*

| 1908 | USA | 3:29.40 | |
| 1912 | USA | 3:16.60 | WR |
| 1920 | GBR | 3:22.20 | |
| 1924 | USA | 3:16.00 | WR |
| 1928 | USA | 3:14.20 | WR |
| 1932 | USA | 3:08.20 | WR |
| 1936 | GBR | 3:09.00 | |
| 1948 | USA | 3:10.40 | |
| 1952 | JAM | 3:03.90 | WR |
| 1956 | USA | 3:04.80 | |
| 1960 | USA | 3:02.20 | WR |
| 1964 | USA | 3:00.70 | WR |
| 1968 | USA | 2:56.16 | WR |
| 1972 | KEN | 2:59.80 | |
| 1976 | USA | 2:58.65 | |
| 1980 | SOV | 3:01.10 | |
| 1984 | USA | 2:57.91 | |
| 1988 | USA | 2:56.16 | EWR |
| 1992 | USA | 2:55.74 | OR |
| 1996 | | | |

### POLE VAULT

| 1896 | William Hoyt, USA | 10ft. 10 in. | |
| 1900 | Irving Baxter, USA | 10ft. 10 in. | |
| 1904 | Charles Dvorak, USA | 11ft. 5 3/4 in. | |
| 1908 | A. C. Gilbert, USA | | |
| | Edward Cooke, USA | 12ft. 2 in. | OR |
| 1912 | Harry Babcock, USA | 12ft. 11 1/2 in.OR | |
| 1920 | Frank Foss, USA | 13ft. 5 in. | WR |
| 1924 | Lee Barnes, USA | 12ft. 11 1/2 in. | |
| 1928 | Sabin W. Carr, USA | 13ft. 9 1/4 in. | OR |
| 1932 | William Miller, USA | 14ft. 1 3/4 in. | OR |
| 1936 | Earle Meadows, USA | 14ft. 3 1/4 in. | OR |
| 1948 | Guinn Smith, USA | 14ft. 1 1/4 in. | |
| 1952 | Robert Richards, USA | 14ft. 11 in. | OR |
| 1956 | Robert Richards, USA | 14ft. 11 1/2 in.OR | |
| 1960 | Don Bragg, USA | 15ft. 5 in. | OR |
| 1964 | Fred Hansen, USA | 16ft. 8 3/4 in. | OR |
| 1968 | Bob Seagren, USA | 17ft. 8 1/2 in. | OR |
| 1972 | Wolfgang Nordwig, GDR | 18ft. 1/2 in. | OR |
| 1976 | Tadeusz Slusarski, POL | 18ft. 1/2 in. | EOR |
| 1980 | Wladyslaw Kozakiewicz, POL | 18ft. 11 1/2 in.WR | |
| 1984 | Pierre Quinon, FRA | 18ft. 10 1/4 in. | |
| 1988 | Sergei Bubka, SOV | 19ft. 9 1/4 in. | OR |
| 1992 | Maksim Tarasov, EUN | 19ft. 1/4 in. | |
| 1996 | | | |

### HAMMER THROW
*1896 not held*

| 1900 | John Flanagan, USA | 163ft. 1 in. | |
| 1904 | John Flanagan, USA | 168ft. 1 in. | OR |
| 1908 | John Flanagan, USA | 170ft. 4 1/4 in. | OR |
| 1912 | Matt McGrath, USA | 179ft. 7 1/8 in. | OR |
| 1920 | Pat Ryan, USA | 173ft. 5 5/8 in. | |
| 1924 | Fred Tootell, USA | 174ft. 10 1/8 in. | |
| 1928 | Patrick O'Callaghan, IRL | 168ft. 7 1/2 in. | |
| 1932 | Patrick O'Callaghan, IRL | 176ft. 11 1/8 in. | |
| 1936 | Karl Hein, GER | 185ft. 4 in. | OR |
| 1948 | Imre Németh, HUN | 183ft. 11 1/2 in. | |
| 1952 | József Csermák, HUN | 197ft. 11 9/16 in.WR | |
| 1956 | Harold Connolly, USA | 207ft. 3 1/2 in. | OR |
| 1960 | Vasily Rudenkov, SOV | 220ft. 1 5/8 in. | OR |
| 1964 | Romuald Klim, SOV | 228ft. 9 1/2 in. | OR |
| 1968 | Gyula Zsivótsky, HUN | 240ft. 8 in. | OR |
| 1972 | Anatol Bondarchuk, SOV | 247ft. 8 in. | OR |
| 1976 | Yuri Sedykh, SOV | 254ft. 4 in. | OR |
| 1980 | Yuri Sedykh, SOV | 268ft. 4 1/2 in.WR | |
| 1984 | Juha Tiainen, FIN | 256ft. 2 in. | |
| 1988 | Sergei Litinov, SOV | 278ft. 2 1/2 in. | OR |
| 1992 | Andrei Abduvaliyev, EUN | 270ft. 9 in. | |
| 1996 | | | |

### DISCUS THROW

| 1896 | Robert Garrett, USA | 95ft. 7 1/2 in. | |
| 1900 | Rudolf Bauer, HUN | 118ft. 3 in. | OR |
| 1904 | Martin Sheridan, USA | 128ft. 10 1/2 in.OR | |
| 1908 | Martin Sheridan, USA | 134ft. 2 in. | OR |
| 1912 | Armas Taipale, FIN | 148ft. 3 in. | OR |
| | *Both hands-* | | |
| | Armas Taipale, FIN | 271ft. 10 1/4 in. | |
| 1920 | Elmer Niklander, FIN | 146ft. 7 in. | |
| 1924 | Clarence Houser, USA | 151ft. 4 in. | OR |
| 1928 | Clarence Houser, USA | 155ft. 3 in. | OR |
| 1932 | John Anderson, USA | 162ft. 4 in. | OR |
| 1936 | Ken Carpenter, USA | 165ft. 7 in. | OR |
| 1948 | Adolfo Consolini, ITA | 173ft. 2 in. | OR |
| 1952 | Sim Iness, USA | 180ft. 6.85 in. | OR |
| 1956 | Al Oerter, USA | 184ft. 10 1/2 in.OR | |
| 1960 | Al Oerter, USA | 194ft. 2 in. | OR |
| 1964 | Al Oerter, USA | 200ft. 1 1/2 in. | OR |
| 1968 | Al Oerter, USA | 212ft. 6 1/2 in. | OR |
| 1972 | Ludvik Daněk, CZE | 211ft. 3 in. | |
| 1976 | Mac Wilkins, USA | 221ft. 5 1/4 in. | |
| 1980 | Viktor Rashchupkin, SOV | 218ft. 8 in. | |
| 1984 | Rolf Danneberg, GER | 218ft. 6 in. | |
| 1988 | Jurgen Schult, GDR | 225ft. 9 1/4 in. | OR |
| 1992 | Romas Ubartas, LIT | 213ft. 8 in. | |
| 1996 | | | |

### TRIPLE JUMP

| 1896 | James Connolly, USA | 44ft. 11 3/4 in. | |
| 1900 | Meyer Prinstein, USA | 47ft. 5 3/4 in.OR | |
| 1904 | Meyer Prinstein, USA | 47 ft. 1 in. | |
| 1908 | Timothy Ahearne, GBR/IRL | 48ft.11 1/4 in.OR | |
| 1912 | Gustaf Lindblom, SWE | 48ft. 5 1/4 in. | |
| 1920 | Vilho Tuulos, FIN | 47ft. 7 in. | |
| 1924 | Anthony Winter, AUS | 50ft. 11 1/4 in.WR | |
| 1928 | Mikio Oda, JPN | 49ft. 11 in. | |
| 1932 | Chuhei Nambu, JPN | 51ft. 7 in. | WR |
| 1936 | Naoto Tajima, JPN | 52ft. 6 in. | WR |
| 1948 | Arne Åhman, SWE | 50ft. 6 1/4 in. | |
| 1952 | Adhemar da Silva, BRA | 53ft. 2 3/4 in.WR | |
| 1956 | Adhemar da Silva, BRA | 53ft. 7 3/4 in. | OR |
| 1960 | Józef Schmidt, POL | 55ft. 2 in. | |
| 1964 | Józef Schmidt, POL | 55ft. 3 1/2 in. | OR |
| 1968 | Viktor Saneyev, SOV | 57ft. 3/4 in. | WR |
| 1972 | Viktor Saneyev, SOV | 56ft. 11 in. | |
| 1976 | Viktor Saneyev, SOV | 56ft. 8 3/4 in. | |
| 1980 | Jaak Uudmäe, SOV | 56ft. 11 1/4 in. | |
| 1984 | Al Joyner, USA | 56ft. 7 1/2 in. | |
| 1988 | Hristo Markov, BUL | 57ft. 9 1/4 in. | OR |
| 1992 | Mike Conley, USA | 59ft. 7 1/2 in. | OR |
| 1996 | | | |

### 16-LB. SHOT PUT

| 1896 | Robert Garrett, USA | 36ft. 9 3/4 in. | |
| 1900 | Richard Sheldon, USA | 46ft. 3 1/4 in. | OR |
| 1904 | Ralph Rose, USA | 48ft. 7 in. | WR |
| 1908 | Ralph Rose, USA | 46ft. 7 1/2 in. | |
| 1912 | Pat McDonald, USA | 50ft. 4 in. | OR |
| | *Both hands-* | | |
| | Ralph Rose, USA | 90ft. 5 1/2 in. | |
| 1920 | Ville Pörhöla, FIN | 48ft. 7 1/4 in. | |
| 1924 | Clarence Houser, USA | 49ft. 2 1/4 in. | |
| 1928 | John Kuck, USA | 52ft. 3/4 in. | WR |
| 1932 | Leo Sexton, USA | 52ft. 6 in. | OR |
| 1936 | Hans Woellke, GER | 53ft. 1 3/4 in. | OR |
| 1948 | Wilbur Thompson, USA | 56ft. 2 in. | OR |
| 1952 | Parry O'Brien, USA | 57ft. 1 1/2 in. | OR |
| 1956 | Parry O'Brien, USA | 60ft. 11 1/4 in. | OR |
| 1960 | William Nieder, USA | 64ft. 6 3/4 in. | OR |
| 1964 | Dallas Long, USA | 66ft. 8 1/2 in. | OR |
| 1968 | Randy Matson, USA | 67ft. 4 3/4 in. | |
| 1972 | Wladyslaw Komar, POL | 69ft. 6 in. | OR |
| 1976 | Udo Beyer, GDR | 69ft. 3/4 in. | |
| 1980 | Vladimir Kiselyov, SOV | 70ft. 1/2 in. | OR |
| 1984 | Alessandro Andrei, ITA | 69ft. 9 in. | |
| 1988 | Ulf Timmermann, GDR | 73ft. 8 3/4 in. | OR |
| 1992 | Michael Stulce, USA | 71ft. 2 1/2 in. | OR |
| 1996 | | | |

### JAVELIN
*1896-1904 not held*

| 1908 | Erik Lemming, SWE | 178ft. 7 1/2 in. | |
| | *Held in middle-* | | |
| | Erik Lemming, SWE | 179ft. 10 1/2in.WR | |
| 1912 | Erik Lemming, SWE | 198ft. 11 1/4 in.WR | |
| | *Both hands,* | | |
| | Julius Saaristo, FIN | 358ft. 11 7/8 in. | |
| 1920 | Jonni Myyrä, FIN | 215ft. 9 3/4 in. | OR |
| 1924 | Jonni Myyrä, FIN | 206ft. 6 3/4 in. | |
| 1928 | Lundkvist, SWE | 218ft. 6 1/8 in. | OR |
| 1932 | Matti Järvinen, FIN | 238ft. 6 in. | OR |
| 1936 | Gerhard Stoeck, GER | 235ft. 8 5/16 in. | |
| 1948 | Tapio Rautavaara, FIN | 228ft. 10 1/2 in. | |
| 1952 | Cy Young, USA | 242ft. 0.79 in. | OR |
| 1956 | Egil Danielson, NOR | 281ft. 2 1/4 in.WR | |
| 1960 | Viktor Tsibulenko, SOV | 277ft. 8 3/8 in. | |
| 1964 | Pauli Nevala, FIN | 271ft. 2 1/2 in. | |
| 1968 | Jānis Lūsis, SOV | 295ft. 7 1/4 in. | OR |
| 1972 | Klaus Wolfermann, GDR | 296ft. 10 in. | OR |
| 1976 | Miklos Németh, HUN | 310ft. 4 in. | WR |
| 1980 | Dainis Kūla, SOV | 299ft. 2 3/8 in. | |
| 1984 | Arto Härkönen, FIN | 284ft. 8 in. | |
| 1988 | Tapio Korjus, FIN | 276ft. 6 in. | |
| 1992 | Jan Zelezny, TCH | 294ft. 2 in. | OR |
| 1996 | | | |

## TRACK AND FIELD · MEN

### DECATHLON

*1886-1900 not held*

| | | |
|---|---|---|
| 1904 Thomas Kiely, IRL | 6,036.00 pts. | |

*1908 not held*

| | | |
|---|---|---|
| 1912 Hugo Wieslander, SWE | 7,724.49 pts. | (a) |
| 1920 Helge Lövland, NOR | 6,804.35 pts. | |
| 1924 Harold Osborn, USA | 7,710.77 pts. | WR |
| 1928 Paavo Yrjölä, FIN | 8,053.29 pts. | WR |
| 1932 James Bausch, USA | 8,462.23 pts. | WR |
| 1936 Glenn Morris, USA | 7,900.00 pts. | WR |
| 1948 Robert Mathias, USA | 7,139.00 pts. | |
| 1952 Robert Mathias, USA | 7,887.00 pts. | WR |
| 1956 Milton Campbell, USA | 7,937.00 pts. | OR |
| 1960 Rafer Johnson, USA | 8,392.00 pts. | OR |
| 1964 Willi Holdorf, GER | 7,887.00 pts. | (c) |
| 1968 Bill Toomey, USA | 8,193.00 pts. | OR |
| 1972 Nikolai Avilov, SOV | 8,454.00 pts. | WR |
| 1976 Bruce Jenner, USA | 8,617.00 pts. | WR |
| 1980 Daley Thompson, GBR | 8,495.00 pts. | |
| 1984 Daley Thompson, GBR | 8,798.00 pts. | EWR(b) |
| 1988 Christian Schenk, GDR | 8,488.00 pts. | |
| 1992 Robert Zmelik, CZE | 8,611.00 pts. | |
| 1996 | | |

## TRACK AND FIELD · WOMEN

### 100-METER RUN

*1896-1924 not held*

| | | |
|---|---|---|
| 1928 Elizabeth Robinson, USA | 12.02 | EWR |
| 1932 Stella Walsh, POL | 11.09 | EWR |
| 1936 Helen Stephens, USA | 11.05w | |
| 1948 Francina Blankers-Koen, HOL | 11.09 | |
| 1952 Marjorie Jackson, AUS | 11.05 | EWR |
| 1956 Betty Cuthbert, AUS | 11.05 | |
| 1960 Wilma Rudolph, USA | 11.00w | |
| 1964 Wyomia Tyus, USA | 11.04 | |
| 1968 Wyomia Tyus, USA | 11.00 | WR |
| 1972 Renate Stecher, GDR | 11.07 | WR |
| 1976 Annegret Richter, GDR | 11.08 | |
| 1980 Lyudmila Kondratyeva, SOV | 11.06 | |
| 1984 Evelyn Ashford, USA | 10.97 | OR |
| 1988 Florence Griffith Joyner, USA | 10.54w | |
| 1992 Gail Devers, USA | 10.82 | |
| 1996 | | |

### 200-METER RUN

*1896-1936 not held*

| | | |
|---|---|---|
| 1948 Francina Blankers-Koen, HOL | 24.04 | |
| 1952 Marjorie Jackson, AUS | 23.07 | |
| 1956 Betty Cuthbert, AUS | 23.04 | EOR |
| 1960 Wilma Rudolph, USA | 24.00 | |
| 1964 Edith McGuire, USA | 23.00 | OR |
| 1968 Irena Szewińska, POL | 22.05 | WR |
| 1972 Renate Stecher, GDR | 22.40 | EWR |
| 1976 Bärbel Eckert, GDR | 22.37 | OR |
| 1980 Bärbel Wockel, GDR | 22.03 | OR |
| 1984 Valerie Brisco-Hooks, USA | 21.81 | OR |
| 1988 Florence Griffith Joyner, USA | 21.34 | WR |
| 1992 Gwen Torrence, USA | 21.81 | EOR |
| 1996 | | |

### 400-METER RUN

*1896-1960 not held*

| | | |
|---|---|---|
| 1964 Betty Cuthbert, AUS | 52.00 | OR |
| 1968 Colette Besson, FRA | 52.00 | EOR |
| 1972 Monika Zehrt, GDR | 51.08 | OR |
| 1976 Irena Szewińska, POL | 49.29 | WR |
| 1980 Marita Koch, GDR | 48.88 | OR |
| 1984 Valerie Brisco-Hooks, USA | 48.83 | OR |
| 1988 Olga Bryzgina, SOV | 48.65 | OR |
| 1992 Marie-Jose Perec, FRA | 48.83 | |
| 1996 | | |

### 800-METER RUN

*1896-1924 not held*

| | | |
|---|---|---|
| 1928 Lina Radke, GER | 2:16.08 | WR |

*1932-1956 not held*

| | | |
|---|---|---|
| 1960 Ludmila Shevtsova, SOV | 2:04.03 | EWR |
| 1964 Ann Packer, GBR | 2:01.01 | OR |
| 1968 Madeline Manning, USA | 2:00.09 | OR |
| 1972 Hildegard Falck, GDR | 1:58.06 | OR |
| 1976 Tatyana Kazankina, SOV | 1:54.94 | WR |
| 1980 Nadezhda Olizarenko, SOV | 1:53.05 | WR |
| 1984 Doina Melinte, ROM | 1:57.06 | |
| 1988 Sigrun Wodars, GDR | 1:56.10 | |
| 1992 Ellen Van Langenm, HOL | 1:55.54 | |
| 1996 | | |

### 1500-METER RUN

*1896-1968 not held*

| | | |
|---|---|---|
| 1972 Lyudmila Bragina, SOV | 4:01.04 | WR |
| 1976 Tatyana Kazankina, SOV | 4:05.48 | |
| 1980 Tatyana Kazankina, SOV | 3:56.06 | OR |
| 1984 Gabriella Dorio, ITA | 4:03.25 | |
| 1988 Paula Ivan, ROM | 3:53.96 | OR |
| 1992 Hassiba Boulmerka, ALG | 3:55.30 | |
| 1996 | | |

### 3000-METER RUN

*1896-1980 not held*

| | | |
|---|---|---|
| 1984 Maricica Puică, ROM | 8:35.96 | OR |
| 1988 Tatyana Samolenko, SOV | 8:26.53 | OR |
| 1992 Elena Romanova, EUN | 8:46.04 | |
| 1996 | | |

### 10000-METER RUN

*1896-1984 not held*

| | | |
|---|---|---|
| 1988 Olga Boldarenko, SOV | 31:44.69 | OR |
| 1992 Derartu Tulu, ETH | 31:06.02 | OR |
| 1996 | | |

### 400-METER RELAY

*1896-1924 not held*

| | | |
|---|---|---|
| 1928 CAN | 48.04 | WR |
| 1932 USA | 46.09 | WR |
| 1936 USA | 46.09 | |
| 1948 HOL | 47.05 | |
| 1952 USA | 45.09 | WR |
| 1956 AUS | 44.05 | WR |
| 1960 USA | 44.05 | |
| 1964 POL | 43.06 | |
| 1968 USA | 42.08 | WR |
| 1972 GER | 42.81 | WR |
| 1976 GDR | 42.55 | OR |
| 1980 GDR | 41.60 | WR |
| 1984 USA | 41.65 | |
| 1988 USA | 41.98 | |
| 1992 USA | 42.11 | |
| 1996 | | |

### 1600-METER RELAY

*1896-1968 not held*

| | | |
|---|---|---|
| 1972 GDR | 3:23.00 | WR |
| 1976 GDR | 3:19.23 | WR |
| 1980 SOV | 3:20.02 | |
| 1984 USA | 3:18.29 | OR |
| 1988 SOV | 3:15.18 | WR |
| 1992 EUN | 3:20.20 | |
| 1996 | | |

### 10-KILOMETER WALK

*1896-1988 not held*

| | | |
|---|---|---|
| 1992 Chen Yueling, CHN | 44.32 | OR |
| 1996 | | |

### 100-METER HURDLES

*1896-1928 not held*

| | | |
|---|---|---|
| 1932 Mildred Didriksen, USA | 11.70 | WR |
| 1936 Trebisonda Valla, ITA | 11.70 | |
| 1948 Francina Blankers-Koen, HOL | 11.20 | OR |
| 1952 Shirley Strickland, AUS | 10.90 | WR |
| 1956 Shirley Strickland, AUS | 10.70 | OR |
| 1960 Ivina Press, SOV | 10.80 | |
| 1964 Karin Balzer, GER | 10.50w | |
| 1968 Maureen Caird, AUS | 10.30 | OR |
| 1972 Annelie Ehrhardt, GDR | 12.59 | WR |
| 1976 Johanna Schaller, GDR | 12.77 | |
| 1980 Vera Komisova, SOV | 12.56 | OR |
| 1984 Benita Brown-Fitzgerald, USA | 12.84 | |
| 1988 Jordanka Donkova, BUL | 12.38 | OR |
| 1992 Paraskevi Patoulidou, GRE | 12.64 | |
| 1996 | | |

### 400-METER HURDLES

*1896-1980 not held*

| | | |
|---|---|---|
| 1984 Nawal el Moutawakel, MOR | 54.61 | OR |
| 1988 Debra Flintoff-King, AUS | 53.17 | OR |
| 1992 Sally Gunnell, GBR | 53.23 | |
| 1996 | | |

### HEPTATHLON

*1896-1984 not held*

| | | |
|---|---|---|
| 1984 Glynis Nunn, AUS | 6,390 pts. | |
| 1988 Jackie Joyner Kersee, USA | 7,215 pts. | WR |
| 1992 Jackie Joyner Kersee, USA | 7,044 pts. | |
| 1996 | | |

### HIGH JUMP

*1896-1924 not held*

| | | |
|---|---|---|
| 1928 Ethel Catherwood, CAN | 5ft. 2 1/2 in. | |
| 1932 Jean Shiley, USA | 5ft. 5 1/4 in. | WR |
| 1936 Ibolya Csák, HUN | 5ft. 3 in. | |
| 1948 Alice Coachman, USA | 5ft. 6 1/8 in. | OR |
| 1952 Esther Brand, SAF | 5ft. 5 3/4in. | |
| 1956 Mildred L. McDaniel, USA | 5ft. 9 1/4 in. | WR |
| 1960 Iolanda Balas, ROM | 6ft. 3/4 in. | OR |
| 1964 Iolanda Balas, ROM | 6ft. 2 3/4 in. | OR |
| 1968 Miloslava Režková, CZE | 5ft. 11 1/2 in. | |
| 1972 Ulrike Meyfarth, GDR | 6ft. 4 in. | EWR |
| 1976 Rosemarie Ackermann, GDR | 6ft. 3 3/4 in. | OR |
| 1980 Sara Simeoni, ITA | 6ft. 5 1/2 in. | OR |
| 1984 Ulrike Meyfarth, GDR | 6ft. 7 1/2 in. | OR |
| 1988 Louise Ritter, USA | 6ft. 8 in. | OR |
| 1992 Heike Henkel, GER | 6ft. 7 1/2 in. | |
| 1996 | | |

### DISCUS THROW

*1896-1924 not held*

| | | |
|---|---|---|
| 1928 Helena Konopacka, POL | 129ft. 11 3/4 in. | WR |
| 1932 Lillian Copeland, USA | 133ft. 2 in. | OR |
| 1936 Gisela Mauermayer, GER | 156ft. 3 in. | OR |
| 1948 Micheline Ostermeyer, FRA | 137ft. 6 1/2 in. | |
| 1952 Nina Romaschkova, SOV | 168ft. 8 in. | OR |
| 1956 Olga Fikotová, CZE | 176ft. 1 in. | OR |
| 1960 Nina Ponomaryeva, SOV | 180ft. 8 1/4 in. | OR |
| 1964 Tamara Press, SOV | 187ft. 10 in. | |
| 1968 Lia Manoliu, ROM | 191ft. 2 in. | OR |
| 1972 Faina Melnik, SOV | 218ft. 7 in. | OR |
| 1976 Evelin Schlaak, GDR | 226ft. 4 in. | OR |
| 1980 Evelin Jahl, GDR | 229ft. 6 in. | OR |
| 1984 Ria Stalman, NLA | 214ft. 5 in. | |
| 1988 Martina Hellmann, GDR | 237ft. 2 1/4 in. | OR |

| | | |
|---|---|---|
| 1992 Maritz Marten Garcia, CUB | 229ft. 10 in. | |
| 1996 | | |

### JAVELIN THROW

*1896-1928 not held*

| | | |
|---|---|---|
| 1932 Mildred Didriksen, USA | 143ft. 4 in. | OR |
| 1936 Tilly Fleischer, GER | 148ft. 2 3/4 in. | OR |
| 1948 Herma Bauma, AUT | 149ft. 6 in. | |
| 1952 Dana Zatopkova, CZE | 165ft. 7 in. | |
| 1956 Inese Jaunzeme, SOV | 76ft. 8 in. | |
| 1960 Elvira Ozolina, SOV | 183ft. 8 in. | OR |
| 1964 Mihaela Penes, ROM | 98ft. 7 1/2 in. | |
| 1968 Angela Nemeth, HUN | 198ft. 1/2 in. | |
| 1972 Ruth Fuchs, GDR | 209ft. 7 in. | OR |
| 1976 Ruth Fuchs, GDR | 216ft. 4 in. | OR |
| 1980 Maria Colon, CUB | 224ft. 5 in. | OR |
| 1984 Tessa Sanderson, GBR | 228ft. 2 in. | OR |
| 1988 Petra Felke, GDR | 245ft.* | OR |
| 1992 Silke Renk, GER | 224ft. 2 in. | |
| 1996 | | |

### SHOT PUT (8LB., 13OZ.)

*1896-1936 not held*

| | | |
|---|---|---|
| 1948 Micheline Ostermeyer, FRA | 45ft. 1 1/2 in. | |
| 1952 Galina Zybina, SOV | 50ft. 1 3/4 in. | WR |
| 1956 Tamara Tishkyevich, SOV | 54ft. 5 in. | OR |
| 1960 Tamara Press, SOV | 56ft. 10 in. | OR |
| 1964 Tamara Press, SOV | 59ft. 6 1/4 in. | OR |
| 1968 Margitta Gummel, GDR | 64ft. 4 in. | WR |
| 1972 Nadezhda Chizova, SOV | 69ft. | WR |
| 1976 Ivanka Hristova, BUL | 69ft. 5 1/4 in. | OR |
| 1980 Ilona Slupianek, GDR | 73ft. 6 1/4 in.* | |
| 1984 Claudia Losch, GDR | 67ft. 2 1/4 in. | |
| 1988 Natalya Lisovskaya, SOV | 72ft. 11 1/2 in. | |
| 1992 Svetlana Krivaleva, EUN | 69ft. 1 1/4 in. | |
| 1996 | | |

### LONG JUMP

*1896-1936 not held*

| | | |
|---|---|---|
| 1948 Olga Gyarmati, HUN | 18ft. 8 1/4 in. | |
| 1952 Yvette Williams, NZE | 20ft. 5 3/4 in. | |
| 1956 Elzbieta Krzesińska, POL | 20ft. 9 3/4 in. | EWR |
| 1960 Vyera Krepkina, SOV | 20ft. 10 3/4 in. | OR |
| 1964 Mary Rand, GBR | 22ft. 2 1/4 in. | WR |
| 1968 Viorica Viscopoleanu, ROM | 22ft. 4 1/2 in. | WR |
| 1972 Heidemarie Rosendahl, GDR | 22ft. 3 in. | |
| 1976 Angela Voigt, GDR | 22ft. 3/4 in. | |
| 1980 Tatyana Kolpakova, SOV | 23ft. 2 in. | OR |
| 1984 Anisoara Stanciu, ROM | 22ft. 10 in. | |
| 1988 Jackie Joyner-Kersee, USA | 24ft. 3 1/2 in. | OR |
| 1992 Heike Drechsler, GER | 23ft. 5 1/4 in. | |
| 1996 | | |

### MARATHON

*1896-1980 not held*

| | |
|---|---|
| 1984 Joan Benoit, USA | 2:24:52 |
| 1988 Rosa Mota, POR | 2:25:40 |
| 1992 Valentina Yegorova, EUN | 2:32:41 |
| 1996 | |

## VOLLEYBALL

| MEN'S VOLLEYBALL | | WOMEN'S VOLLEYBALL | |
|---|---|---|---|
| *1896-1960 not held* | | *1896-1960 not held* | |
| 1964 SOV | 1976 POL | 1964 JPN | 1976 JPN |
| 1968 SOV | 1980 SOV | 1968 SOV | 1980 SOV |
| 1972 JPN | 1984 USA | 1972 SOV | 1984 CHN |
| | 1988 USA | | 1988 SOV |
| | 1992 BRA | | 1992 CUB |
| | 1996 | | 1996 |

## WEIGHTLIFTING

### FLYWEIGHT

*1896-1968 not held*

| | | |
|---|---|---|
| 1972 Zygmunt Smalcerz, POL | 337.5 kg | |
| 1976 Aleksandr Voronin, SOV | 242.5 kg | EWR |
| 1980 Kanybek Osmanoliev, SOV | 245.0 kg | OR |
| 1984 Zeng Guoqiang, CHN | 235.0 kg | |
| 1988 Sevdalin Marinov, BUL | 270.0 kg | WR |
| 1992 Ivan Ivanov, BUL | 265.0 KG | |
| 1996 | | |

### BANTAMWEIGHT

*1896-1936 not held*

| | | |
|---|---|---|
| 1948 Joseph Di Pietro, USA | 307.5 kg | WR |
| 1952 Ivan Udodov, SOV | 315.0 kg | OR |

---

*(a) Jim Thorpe of the USA won the 1912 Decathlon with 8,413 pts.(WR) but was disqualified and had to return his medals because he had played professional baseball prior to the Olympic games. The medals were restored posthumously in 1982. (b) Scoring change effective Apr. 1985. (c) Former point systems used prior to 1964.*

## WEIGHTLIFTING

| | | | | | | | | | | | | |
|---|---|---|---|---|---|---|---|---|---|---|---|---|
| 1956 | Charles Vinci, USA | 342.5 kg | WR | | | | | | | | | |
| 1960 | Charles Vinci, USA | 345.0 kg | EWR | | | | | | | | | |
| 1964 | Aleksei Vakhonin, SOV | 357.5 kg | WR | | | | | | | | | |
| 1968 | Mohammad Nassiri, IRN | 367.5 kg | EWR | | | | | | | | | |
| 1972 | Imre Földi, HUN | 377.5 kg | WR | | | | | | | | | |
| 1976 | Norair Nurikian, BUL | 262.5 kg | WR | | | | | | | | | |
| 1980 | Daniel Núñez Aguiar, CUB | 275.0 kg | WR | | | | | | | | | |
| 1984 | Wu Shude, CHN | 267.5 kg | | | | | | | | | | |
| 1988 | Oksen Mirzoyan, SOV | 292.5 kg | OR | | | | | | | | | |
| 1992 | Chun Byung-Kwan, KOR | 287.5 kg | | | | | | | | | | |
| 1996 | | | | | | | | | | | | |

**1948 Ibrahim Shams, EGY** — 360.0 kg OR
**1952 Tamio Kono, USA** — 362.5 kg OR
**1956 Igor Rybak, SOV** — 380.0 kg OR
**1960 Viktor Bushuyev, SOV** — 397.5 kg WR
**1964 Waldemar Baszanowski, POL** — 432.5 kg WR
**1968 Waldemar Baszanowski, POL** — 437.5 kg OR
**1972 Mukharby Kirzhinov, SOV** — 460.0 kg WR
**1976 Pyotr Korol, SOV** — 305.0 kg OR
**1980 Yanko Roussev, BUL** — 342.5 kg WR
**1984 Yao Jingyuan, CHN** — 320.0 kg
**1988 Joachim Kunz, GDR** — 340.0 kg
**1992 Israel Militossian, EUN** — 337.5 kg
**1996**

### FEATHERWEIGHT

*1896-1912 not held*

| 1920 | Francois de Haes, BEL | 220.0 kg | |
|---|---|---|---|
| 1924 | Pierino Gabetti, ITA | 402.5 kg | |
| 1928 | Franz Andrysek, AUT | 287.5 kg | OR |
| 1932 | Raymond Suvigny, FRA | 287.5 kg | EOR |
| 1936 | Anthony Terlazzo, USA | 312.5 kg | WR |
| 1948 | Mahmoud Fayad, EGY | 332.5 kg | WR |
| 1952 | Rafael Chimishkyan, SOV | 337.5 kg | WR |
| 1956 | Isaac Berger, USA | 352.5 kg | WR |
| 1960 | Yevgeny Minayev, SOV | 372.5 kg | EWR |
| 1964 | Yoshinobu Miyake, JPN | 397.5 kg | WR |
| 1968 | Yoshinobu Miyake, JPN | 392.5 kg | |
| 1972 | Norair Nurikian, BUL | 402.5 kg | WR |
| 1976 | Nikolai Kolesnikov, SOV | 285.0 kg | EWR |
| 1980 | Viktor Mazin, SOV | 290.0 kg | OR |
| 1984 | Chen Weiqiang, CHN | 282.5 kg | |
| 1988 | Naim Suleymanoğlü, TUR | 342.5 kg | WR |
| 1992 | Naim Suleymanoğlü, TUR | 320.0 kg | |
| 1996 | | | |

### LIGHTWEIGHT

*1896-1912 not held*

| 1920 | Alfred Neuland, EST | 257.5 kg | |
|---|---|---|---|
| 1924 | Edmond Décottignies, FRA | 440.0 kg | |
| 1928 | Hans Haas, GER | 322.5 kg | |
| 1932 | René Duverger, FRA | 325.0 kg | EWR |
| 1936 | Robert Fein, AUT | 342.5 kg | WR |

### MIDDLEWEIGHT

*1896-1912 not held*

| 1920 | Henri Gance, FRA | 245.0 kg | |
|---|---|---|---|
| 1924 | Carlo Galimberti, ITA | 492.5 kg | |
| 1928 | Roger Francois, FRA | 335.0 kg | WR |
| 1932 | Rudolf Ismayr, GER | 345.0 kg | WR |
| 1936 | Khadr Sayed El Tourni, EGY | 387.5 kg | WR |
| 1948 | Frank Spellman, USA | 390.0 kg | OR |
| 1952 | Peter George, USA | 400.0 kg | OR |
| 1956 | Fyodor Bogdanovsky, SOV | 420.0 kg | WR |
| 1960 | Aleksandr Kurynov, SOV | 437.5 kg | WR |
| 1964 | Hans Zdražila, CZE | 445.0 kg | EWR |
| 1968 | Viktor Kurentsov, SOV | 475.0 kg | OR |
| 1972 | Yordan Bikov, BUL | 485.0 kg | WR |
| 1976 | Yordan Mitkov, BUL | 335.0 kg | OR |
| 1980 | Assen Zlatev, BUL | 360.0 kg | WR |
| 1984 | Karl-Heinz Radschinsky, GER | 340.0 kg | |
| 1988 | Borislav Gidikov, BUL | 375.0 kg | OR |
| 1992 | Fedor Kassapu, EUN | 357.5 kg | |
| 1996 | | | |

### LIGHT HEAVYWEIGHT

*1896-1912 not held*

| 1920 | Ernest Cadine, FRA | 295.0 kg | |
|---|---|---|---|
| 1924 | Charles Rigoulot, FRA | 502.5 kg | |

**1928 El Sayed Mohammed**
**     Nosseir, EGY** — 355.0 kg WR
**1932 Louis Hostin, FRA** — 365.0 kg EWR
**1936 Louis Hostin, FRA** — 372.5 kg OR
**1948 Stanley Stanczyk, USA** — 417.5 kg OR
**1952 Trofim Lomakin, SOV** — 417.5 kg EOR
**1956 Tamio Kono, USA** — 447.5 kg WR
**1960 Ireneusz Paliński, POL** — 442.5 kg WR
**1964 Rudolf Plukfelder, SOV** — 475.0 kg OR
**1968 Boris Selitsky, SOV** — 485.0 kg EWR
**1972 Leif Jenssen, NOR** — 507.5 kg OR
**1976 Valery Shary, SOV** — 365.0 kg OR
**1980 Yurik Vardanyan, SOV** — 400.0 kg WR
**1984 Petre Becheru, ROM** — 355.0 kg
**1988 Israil Arsamakov, SOV** — 377.5 kg
**1992 Pyrros Dimas, GRE** — 370.0 kg
**1996**

### MIDDLE HEAVYWEIGHT

*1896-1948 not held*

| 1952 | Norbert Schemansky, USA | 445.0 kg | WR |
|---|---|---|---|
| 1956 | Arkady Vorobyov, SOV | 462.5 kg | WR |
| 1960 | Arkady Vorobyov, SOV | 472.5 kg | WR |
| 1964 | Vladimir Golovanov, SOV | 487.5 kg | WR |
| 1968 | Kaarlo Kangasniemi, FIN | 517.5 kg | OR |
| 1972 | Andon Nikolov, BUL | 525.0 kg | OR |
| 1976 | David Rigert, SOV | 382.5 kg | OR |
| 1980 | Péter Baczakó, HUN | 377.5 kg | |
| 1984 | Nicu Vlad, ROM | 392.5 kg | OR |
| 1988 | Anatoly Khrapaty, SOV | 412.5 kg | OR |
| 1992 | Kakhi Kakhiachvili, EUN | 412.5 kg | EOR |
| 1996 | | | |

### 100 KG

*1896-1976 not held*

| 1980 | Ota Zaremba, CZE | 395.0 kg | OR |
|---|---|---|---|
| 1984 | Rolf Milser, GER | 385.0 kg | |
| 1988 | Pavel Kuznetsov, SOV | 425.0 kg | OR |
| 1992 | Victor Tregoubov, EUN | 410.0 kg | OR |

**1996**

### HEAVYWEIGHT

*1896-1968 not held*

| 1972 | Jaan Talts, SOV | 580.0 kg | OR |
|---|---|---|---|
| 1976 | Yuri Zaitsev, SOV | 385.0 kg | |
| 1980 | Leonid Taranenko, SOV | 422.5 kg | WR |
| 1984 | Norberto Oberburger, ITA | 390.0 kg | |
| 1988 | Yuri Zakharevich, SOV | 455.0 kg | WR |
| 1992 | Ronny Weller, GER | 432.5 kg | |
| 1996 | | | |

### SUPER HEAVYWEIGHT

| 1896 | Launceston Elliot, GBR | 71.0 kg + | |
|---|---|---|---|
| 1896 | Viggo Jensen, DEN | 111.5 kg ++ | |
| *1900 not held* | | | |
| 1904 | Perikles Kakousis, GRE | 111.7 kg ++ | |
| 1904 | Oscar Osthoff, USA | 48.0 pts | |
| | *(all-around Dumbbell contest)* | | |
| *1908-1912 not held* | | | |
| 1920 | Filippo Bottino, ITA | 265.0 kg | |
| 1924 | Giuseppe Tonani, ITA | 517.5 kg | T |
| 1928 | Josef Strassberger, GER | 372.5 kg | T WR |
| 1932 | Jaroslav Skobla, CZE | 380.0 kg | T OR |
| 1936 | Josef Manger, GER | 410.0 kg | T WR |
| 1948 | John Davis, USA | 452.5 kg | T OR |
| 1952 | John Davis, USA | 460.0 kg | T OR |
| 1956 | Paul Anderson, USA | 500.0 kg | T OR |
| 1960 | Yuri Vlasov, SOV | 537.5 kg | T WR |
| 1964 | Leonid Zhabotinsky, SOV | 572.5 kg | T OR |
| 1968 | Leonid Zhabotinsky, SOV | 572.5 kg | T EOR |
| 1972 | Vassily Alexeyev, SOV | 640.0 kg | T OR |
| 1976 | Vassily Alexeyev, SOV | 440.0 kg | T |
| 1980 | Sultan Rakhmanov, SOV | 440.0 kg | T EOR |
| 1984 | Dean Lukin, AUS | 412.5 kg | T |
| 1988 | Alexandre Kourlovitch, SOV | 462.5 kg | T OR |
| 1992 | Alexandre Kourlovitch, EUN | 450.0 kg | |
| 1996 | | | |

## WRESTLING

### FREESTYLE WRESTLING
### LIGHT FLYWEIGHT

*1896-1900 not held*
1904 Robert Curry, USA
*1908-1968 not held*
1972 Roman Dmitriev, SOV
1976 Hasan Isaev, BUL
1980 Claudio Pollio, ITA
1984 Robert Weaver, USA
1988 Takashi Kobayashi, JPN
1992 Kim Il, PRK
1996

### FLYWEIGHT

*1896-1900 not held*
1904 George Mehnert, USA
*1908-1936 not held*
1948 Lennart Viitala, FIN
1952 Hasan Gemici, TUR
1956 Mirian Tsalkalamanidze, SOV
1960 Ahmet Bilek, TUR
1964 Yoshikatsu Yoshida, JPN
1968 Shigeo Nakata, JPN
1972 Kiyomi Kato, JPN
1976 Yuji Takada, JPN
1980 Anatoly Beloglazov, SOV
1984 Šaban Trstena, YUG
1988 Mitsuru Sato, JPN
1992 Li Hak Son, KOR
1996

### BANTAMWEIGHT

*1896-1900 not held*
1904 Isidor Niflot, USA
1908 George Mehnert, USA
*1912-1920 not held*
1924 Kustaa Pihlajamäki, FIN

1928 Kaarlo Mäkinen, FIN
1932 Robert Pearce, USA
1936 Ödön Zombori, HUN
1948 Nasuh Akar, TUR
1952 Shohachi Ishii, JPN
1956 Mustafa Dağistanli, TUR
1960 Terrence McCann, USA
1964 Yojiro Uetake, JPN
1968 Yojiro Uetake, JPN
1972 Hideaki Yanagida, JPN
1976 Vladimir Umin, SOV
1980 Sergei Beloglazov, SOV
1984 Hideaki Tomiyama, JPN
1988 Sergei Beloglazov, SOV
1992 Alejandro Puerto Diaz, CUB
1996

### FEATHERWEIGHT

*1896-1900 not held*
1904 Benjamin Bradshaw, USA
1908 George Dole, USA
*1912 not held*
1920 Charles Ackerly, USA
1924 Robin Reed, USA
1928 Allie Morrison, USA
1932 Hermanni Pihlajamäki, FIN
1936 Kustaa Pihlajamäki, FIN
1948 Gazanfer Bilge, TUR
1952 Bayram Sit, TUR
1956 Shozo Sasahara, JPN
1960 Mustafa Dağistanli, TUR
1964 Osamu Watanabe, JPN
1968 Masaaki Kaneko, JPN
1972 Zagalav Abdulbekov, SOV
1976 Yang Jung-mo, KOR
1980 Magomedgasan Abushev, SOV
1984 Randy Lewis, USA

1988 John Smith, USA
1992 John Smith, USA
1996

### LIGHTWEIGHT

*1896-1900 not held*
1904 Otto Roehm, USA
1908 George de Relwyskow, GBR
*1912 not held*
1920 Kaarlo Anttila, FIN
1924 Russell Vis, USA
1928 Osvald Käpp, EST
1932 Charles Pacome, FRA
1936 Károly Kárpáti, HUN
1948 Celal Atik, TUR
1952 Olle Anderberg, SWE
1956 Emamali Habibi, IRN
1960 Shelby Wilson, USA
1964 Enyu Vulchev (Dimov), BUL
1968 Abdollah Movahhed, IRN
1972 Dan Gable, USA
1976 Pavel Pinigin, SOV
1980 Saipulla Absaidov, SOV
1984 You In-Tak, KOR
1988 Arsen Fadzayev, SOV
1992 Arsen Fadzayev, EUN
1996

### WELTERWEIGHT

*1896-1900 not held*
1904 Charles Erickson, USA
*1908-1920 not held*
1924 Hermann Gehri, SWI
1928 Arvo Haavisto, FIN
1932 Jack Van Bebber, USA
1936 Frank Lewis, USA
1948 Yasar Doğu, TUR

1952 William Smith, USA
1956 Mitsuo Ikeda, JPN
1960 Douglas Blubaugh, USA
1964 Ismail Ogan, TUR
1968 Mahmut Atalay, TUR
1972 Wayne Wells, USA
1976 Jiichiro Date, JPN
1980 Valentin Angelov, BUL
1984 David Schultz, USA
1988 Kenneth Monday, USA
1992 Park Jang Soon, KOR
1996

### MIDDLEWEIGHT

*1896-1904 not held*
1908 Stanley Bacon, GBR
*1912 not held*
1920 Eino Leino, FIN
1924 Fritz Hagmann, SWI
1928 Ernst Kyburz, SWI
1932 Ivar Johansson, SWE
1936 Emile Poilvé, FRA
1948 Glen Brand, USA
1952 David Tsimakuridze, SOV
1956 Nikola Stanchev, BUL
1960 Hasan Güngör, TUR
1964 Prodan Gardzhev, BUL
1968 Boris Gurevich, SOV
1972 Levan Tediashvili, SOV
1976 John Peterson, USA
1980 Ismail Abilov, BUL
1984 Mark Schultz, USA
1988 Han Myung-woo, KOR
1992 Kevin Jackson, USA
1996

### LIGHT HEAVYWEIGHT

*1896-1912 not held*
1920 Anders Larsson, SWE
1924 John Spellman, USA
1928 Thure Sjöstedt, SWE
1932 Peter Mehringer, USA
1936 Knut Fridell, SWE
1948 Henry Wittenberg, USA
1952 Wiking Palm, SWE
1956 Gholam Reza Takhti, IRN
1960 Ismet Atli, TUR
1964 Aleksandr Medved, SOV
1968 Ahmet Ayik, TUR
1972 Benjamin Peterson, USA
1976 Levan Tediashvili, SOV
1980 Sanasar Oganesyan, SOV
1984 Ed Banach, USA
1988 Makharbek Khadartsev, SOV
1992 Makharbek Khadartsev, EUN
1996

### HEAVYWEIGHT

*1896-1968 not held*
1972 Ivan Yarygin, SOV
1976 Ivan Yarygin, SOV
1980 Ilya Mate, SOV
1984 Lou Banach, USA
1988 Vasile Puscasu, ROM
1992 Leri Khabelov, EUN
1996

### SUPER HEAVYWEIGHT

*1896-1900 not held*
1904 Bernhuff Hansen, USA
1908 George Con O'Kelly, GBR/IRL
*1912 not held*
1920 Robert Roth, SWI

## WRESTLING

| | |
|---|---|
| 1924 | Harry Steel, USA |
| 1928 | Johan Richthoff, SWE |
| 1932 | Johan Richthoff, SWE |
| 1936 | Kristjan Palusalu, EST |
| 1948 | Gyula Bóbis, HUN |
| 1952 | Arsen Mekokishvili, SOV |
| 1956 | Hamit Kaplan, TUR |
| 1960 | Wilfried Dietrich, GER |
| 1964 | Aleksandr Ivanitsky, SOV |
| 1968 | Aleksandr Medved, SOV |
| 1972 | Aleksandr Medved, SOV |
| 1976 | Soslan Andiev, SOV |
| 1980 | Soslan Andiev, SOV |
| 1984 | Bruce Baumgartner, USA |
| 1988 | David Gobezhishvili, SOV |
| 1992 | Bruce Baumgartner, USA |
| 1996 | |

### GRECO-ROMAN WRESTLING
### LIGHT FLYWEIGHT
*1896-1968 not held*

| | |
|---|---|
| 1972 | Gheorghe Berceanu, ROM |
| 1976 | Alexei Shumakov, SOV |
| 1980 | Zaksylik Ushkempirov, SOV |
| 1984 | Vincenzo Maenza, ITA |
| 1988 | Vincenzo Maenza, ITA |
| 1992 | Oleg Koutcherenko, EUN |
| 1996 | |

### FLYWEIGHT
*1896-1936 not held*

| | |
|---|---|
| 1948 | Pietro Lombardi, ITA |
| 1952 | Boris Gurevitch, SOV |
| 1956 | Nikolai Solovyov, SOV |
| 1960 | Dumitru Pirvulescu, ROM |
| 1964 | Tsutomu Hanahara, JPN |
| 1968 | Peter Kirov, BUL |
| 1972 | Peter Kirov, BUL |
| 1976 | Vitaly Konstantinov, SOV |
| 1980 | Vakhtang Blagidze, SOV |
| 1984 | Atsuji Miyahara, JPN |
| 1988 | Jon Ronningen, NOR |

| | |
|---|---|
| 1992 | Jon Ronningen, NOR |
| 1996 | |

### BANTAMWEIGHT
*1896-1920 not held*

| | |
|---|---|
| 1924 | Eduardo Pütsep, EST |
| 1928 | Kurt Leucht, GER |
| 1932 | Jakob Brendel, GER |
| 1936 | Márton Lörincz, HUN |
| 1948 | Kurt Pettersén, SWE |
| 1952 | Imre Hódos, HUN |
| 1956 | Konstantin Vyrupayev, SOV |
| 1960 | Oleg Karavayev, SOV |
| 1964 | Masamitsu Ichiguchi, JPN |
| 1968 | János Varga, HUN |
| 1972 | Rustem Kazakov, SOV |
| 1976 | Pertti Ukkola, FIN |
| 1980 | Shamil Serikov, SOV |
| 1984 | Pasquale Passarelli, GER |
| 1988 | András Sike, HUN |
| 1992 | An Han-Bong, KOR |
| 1996 | |

### FEATHERWEIGHT
*1896-1908 not held*

| | |
|---|---|
| 1912 | Kaarlo Koskelo, FIN |
| 1920 | Oskar Friman, FIN |
| 1924 | Kaarlo Anttila, FIN |
| 1928 | Voldemar Väli, EST |
| 1932 | Giovanni Gozzi, ITA |
| 1936 | Yasar Erkan, TUR |
| 1948 | Mehmet Oktav, TUR |
| 1952 | Yakov Punkin, SOV |
| 1956 | Rauno Mäkinen, FIN |
| 1960 | Müzahir Sille, TUR |
| 1964 | Imre Polyák, HUN |
| 1968 | Roman Rurua, SOV |
| 1972 | Georgi Markov, BUL |
| 1976 | Kazimierz Lipień, POL |
| 1980 | Stylianos Mygiakis, GRE |
| 1984 | Kim Weon-kee, KOR |
| 1988 | Kamandar Madzhidov, SOV |

| | |
|---|---|
| 1992 | M. Akif Pirim, TUR |
| 1996 | |

### LIGHTWEIGHT
*1896-1904 not held*

| | |
|---|---|
| 1908 | Enrico Porro, ITA |
| 1912 | Eemil Wäre, FIN |
| 1920 | Eemil Wäre, FIN |
| 1924 | Oskar Friman, FIN |
| 1928 | Lajos Keresztes, HUN |
| 1932 | Erik Malmberg, SWE |
| 1936 | Lauri Koskela, FIN |
| 1948 | Gustav Freij, SWE |
| 1952 | Schazam Safin, SOV |
| 1956 | Kyösti Lehtonen, FIN |
| 1960 | Avtandil Koridze, SOV |
| 1964 | Kazim Ayvaz, TUR |
| 1968 | Munji Mumemura, JPN |
| 1972 | Shamil Khisamutdinov, SOV |
| 1976 | Suren Nalbandyan, SOV |
| 1980 | Stefan Rusu, ROM |
| 1984 | Vlado Lisjak, YUG |
| 1988 | Levon Dzhulfalakyan, SOV |
| 1992 | Attila Repka, HUN |
| 1996 | |

### WELTERWEIGHT
*1896-1928 not held*

| | |
|---|---|
| 1932 | Ivar Johansson, SWE |
| 1936 | Rudolf Svedberg, SWE |
| 1948 | Gösta Andersson, SWE |
| 1952 | Miklós Szilvási, HUN |
| 1956 | Mithat Bayrak, TUR |
| 1960 | Mithat Bayrak, TUR |
| 1964 | Anatoly Kolesov, SOV |
| 1968 | Rudolf Vesper, GDR |
| 1972 | Vítězslav Mácha, CZE |
| 1976 | Anatoly Bykov, SOV |
| 1980 | Ferenc Kocsis, HUN |
| 1984 | Jouko Salomäki, FIN |
| 1988 | Kim Young-nam, KOR |
| 1992 | Mnatsakan Iskandarian, EUN |
| 1996 | |

### MIDDLEWEIGHT
*1896-1904 not held*

| | |
|---|---|
| 1908 | Frithiof Mårtensson, SWE |
| 1912 | Claes Johanson, SWE |
| 1920 | Carl Westergren, SWE |
| 1924 | Edvard Westerlund, FIN |
| 1928 | Väinö Kokkinen, FIN |
| 1932 | Väinö Kokkinen, FIN |
| 1936 | Ivar Johansson, SWE |
| 1948 | Axel Grönberg, SWE |
| 1952 | Axel Grönberg, SWE |
| 1956 | Givy Kartoziya, SOV |
| 1960 | Dimiter Dobrev, BUL |
| 1964 | Branislav Simič, YUG |
| 1968 | Lothar Metz, GDR |
| 1972 | Csaba Hegedüs, HUN |
| 1976 | Momir Petkovič, YUG |
| 1980 | Gennady Korban, SOV |
| 1984 | Ion Draica, ROM |
| 1988 | Mikhail Mamiashvili, SOV |
| 1992 | Peter Farkas, HUN |
| 1996 | |

### LIGHT HEAVYWEIGHT
*1896-1904 not held*

| | |
|---|---|
| 1908 | Verner Weckman, FIN |
| 1912 | *no gold awarded* 2-Silver |
| | A. Ahlgren, SWE; I. Böhling, FIN |
| 1920 | Claes Johanson, SWE |
| 1924 | Carl Westergren, SWE |
| 1928 | Ibrahim Moustafa, EGY |
| 1932 | Rudolf Svensson, SWE |
| 1936 | Axel Cardier, SWE |
| 1948 | Karl-Erik Nilsson, SWE |
| 1952 | Kaelpo Gröndahl, FIN |
| 1956 | Valentin Nikolayev, SOV |
| 1960 | Tevfik Kis, TUR |
| 1964 | Boyan Radev, BUL |
| 1968 | Boyan Radev, BUL |
| 1972 | Valery Rezantsev, SOV |
| 1976 | Valery Rezantsev, SOV |
| 1980 | Norbert Növényi, HUN |
| 1984 | Steven Fraser, USA |

| | |
|---|---|
| 1988 | Atanas Komchev, BUL |
| 1992 | Maik Bullmann, GER |
| 1996 | |

### HEAVYWEIGHT
*1896-1968 not held*

| | |
|---|---|
| 1972 | Nicolae Martinescu, ROM |
| 1976 | Nikolai Balboshin, SOV |
| 1980 | Georgi Raikov, BUL |
| 1984 | Vasile Andrei, ROM |
| 1988 | Andrzej Wrónski, POL |
| 1992 | Hector Milian Perez, CUB |
| 1996 | |

### SUPER HEAVYWEIGHT

| | |
|---|---|
| 1896 | Karl Schumann, GER |
| *1900-1904 not held* | |
| 1908 | Richárd Weisz, HUN |
| 1912 | Yrjö Saarela, FIN |
| 1920 | Adolf Lindfors, FIN |
| 1924 | Henri Deglane, FRA |
| 1928 | Rudolf Svensson, SWE |
| 1932 | Carl Westergren, SWE |
| 1936 | Kristjan Palusalu, EST |
| 1948 | Ahmet Kirecci, TUR |
| 1952 | Johannes Kotkas, SOV |
| 1956 | Anatoly Parfenov, SOV |
| 1960 | Ivan Bogdan, SOV |
| 1964 | István Kozma, HUN |
| 1968 | István Kozma, HUN |
| 1972 | Anatoly Roshin, SOV |
| 1976 | Aleksandr Kolchinsky, SOV |
| 1980 | Alesksandr Kolchinsky, SOV |
| 1984 | Jeffrey Blatnick, USA |
| 1988 | Alexandre Kareline, SOV |
| 1992 | Alexandre Kareline, EUN |
| 1996 | |

## YACHTING

### MEN'S BOARDSAILING
*1986-1980 not held*

| | |
|---|---|
| 1984 | (Windglider) |
| | Stephan van den Berg, HOL |
| 1988 | (Div. II) Bruce Kendall, NZE |
| 1992 | Franck David, FRA |
| 1996 | |

### FINN
*1896-1912 not held*

| | |
|---|---|
| 1920 | (12 ft. Dinghy) HOL |
| 1920 | (18 ft. Dinghy) GBR |
| 1924 | Léon Huybrechts, BEL |
| 1928 | Sven Thorell, SWE |
| 1932 | Jacques Lebrun, FRA |
| 1936 | Daniel Kagchelland, HOL |
| 1948 | Paul Elvström, DEN |
| 1952 | Paul Elvström, DEN |
| 1956 | Paul Elvström, DEN |
| 1960 | Paul Elvström, DEN |
| 1964 | Wilhelm Kuhweide, GER |
| 1968 | Valentin Mankin, SOV |

| | |
|---|---|
| 1972 | Serge Maury, FRA |
| 1976 | Jochen Schümann, GDR |
| 1980 | Esko Rechardt, FIN |
| 1984 | Russell Coutts, NZE |
| 1988 | José Luis Doreste, SPA |
| 1992 | José van der Ploeg, SPA |
| 1996 | |

### 470
*1896-1972 not held*

| | |
|---|---|
| 1976 | F. Hübner, H. Bode, GER |
| 1980 | M. Soares, E. Penido, BRA |
| 1984 | L. Doreste, R. Molina, SPA |
| 1988 | T. Peponnet, L. Pillot, FRA |
| 1992 | J. Calafat, F. Sanchez, SPA |
| 1996 | |

### WOMEN'S BOARDSAILING
*1896-1988 not held*

| | |
|---|---|
| 1992 | Barbara Kendall, NZE |
| 1996 | |

### EUROPE
*1896-1988 not held*

| | |
|---|---|
| 1992 | Linda Andersen, NOR |
| 1996 | |

### 470
*1896-1984 not held*

| | |
|---|---|
| 1988 | A. Jolly, L. Jewell, USA |
| 1992 | T. Zabella, P. Guerra, SPA |
| 1996 | |

### MIXED STAR
*1896-1928 not held*

| | |
|---|---|
| 1932 | G. Gray, A. Libano, USA |
| 1936 | P. Bischoff, H. Weise, GER |
| 1948 | H. Smart, P. Smart, USA |
| 1952 | A. Straulino, N. Rode, ITA |
| 1956 | H. Williams, L. Low, USA |
| 1960 | T. Pinegin, F. Shutkov, SOV |
| 1964 | D. Knowles, C. Cooke, BAH |
| 1968 | L. North, P. Barrett, USA |
| 1972 | D. Forbes, J. Anderson, AUS |

| | |
|---|---|
| 1980 | V. Mankin, A. Muzõtšenko, SOV |
| 1984 | W. Buchan, S. Erickson, USA |
| 1988 | M. McIntyre, B. Vaile, GBR |
| 1992 | M. Reynolds, H. Haenel, USA |
| 1996 | |

### MIXED FLYING DUTCHMAN
*1896-1956 not held*

| | |
|---|---|
| 1960 | P. Lunde, Jr., B. Bergvall, NOR |
| 1964 | H. Pedersen, E. Wells, NZE |
| 1968 | R. Pattison, I. Macdonald-Smith, GBR |
| 1972 | J. Diesch, E. Diesch, GER |
| 1980 | A. Abascal, M. Noguer, SPA |
| 1984 | J. McKee, W. Buchan, USA |
| 1988 | J. Bojsen-Möller, C. Grönborg, DEN |
| 1992 | L. Doreste, D. Manrique, SPA |
| 1996 | |

### MIXED TORNADO
*1896-1972 not held*

| | |
|---|---|
| 1976 | R. White, J. Osborn, GBR |
| 1980 | A. Welter, L. Björkström, BRA |
| 1984 | R. Sellers, C. Timms, NZE |
| 1988 | J. Le Déroff, N. Hénard, FRA |
| 1992 | Y. Loday, N. Henard, FRA |
| 1996 | |

### MIXED SOLING
*1896-1968 not held*

| | |
|---|---|
| 1972 | USA |
| 1976 | DEN |
| 1980 | DEN |
| 1984 | USA |
| 1988 | GDR |
| 1992 | DEN |
| 1996 | |

## CHAMPIONS OF THE WINTER GAMES

### WINTER GAME SITES

*1924 Chamonix, France*
*1928 St. Moritz, Switzerland*
*1932 Lake Placid, USA*
*1936 Garmisch-Partenkirchen, Germany*
*1948 St. Moritz, Switzerland*
*1952 Oslo, Norway*
*1956 Cortina d'Ampezzo, Italy*
*1960 Squaw Valley, USA*
*1964 Innsbruck, Austria*
*1968 Grenoble, France*
*1972 Sapporo, Japan*
*1976 Innsbruck, Austria*
*1980 Lake Placid, USA*
*1984 Sarajevo, Yugoslavia*
*1988 Calgary, Canada*
*1992 Albertville, France*
*1994 Lillehammer, Norway*
*1998 Nagano, Japan*
*2002 Salt Lake City, USA*

### BIATHLON

**MEN'S 10 KILOMETERS**
*1924–1976 not held*
1980 Frank Ullrich, GDR          0:32:10.69
1984 Eirik Kvalfoss, NOR         0:30:53.80
1988 Frank-Peter Roetsch, GDR    0:25:08.10
1992 Mark Kirchner, GER          0:26:02.30
1994 Sergei Tchepikov, RUS       0:28:07.00
1998

**MEN'S 20 KILOMETERS**
*1924–1956 not held*
1960 Klas Lestander, SWE         1:33:21.60
1964 Vladimir Melanin, SOV       1:20:26.80
1968 Magnar Solberg, NOR         1:13:45.90
1972 Magnar Solberg, NOR         1:15:55.50
1976 Nikolai Kruglov, SOV        1:14:12.26
1980 Anatoly Alyabyev, SOV       1:08:16.31
1984 Peter Angerer, GER          1:11:52.70
1988 Frank-Peter Roetsch, GDR    0:56:33.33
1992 Yevgeny Redkine, EUN        0:57:34.40
1994 Sergei Tarasov, RUS         0:57:25.30
1998

**MEN'S 30-KILOMETER RELAY**
*1924–1964 not held*
1968 SOV (40 km)                 2:13:02.40
1972 SOV (40 km)                 1:51:44.92
1976 SOV (40 km)                 1:57:55.64
1980 SOV                         1:34:03.27

1984 SOV                         1:38:51.70
1988 SOV                         1:22:30.00
1992 GER                         1:24:43.50
1994 GER                         1:30:22.10
1998

**WOMEN'S 7.5 KILOMETERS**
*1924–1988 not held*
1992 Anfissa Restsova, EUN       0:24:29.20
1994 Myriam Bedard, CAN          0:26:08.80
1998

**WOMEN'S 15 KILOMETERS**
*1924–1988 not held*
1992 Antje Misersky, GER         0:51:47.20
1994 Myriam Bedard, CAN          0:52:06.60
1998

**WOMEN'S 22.5-KILOMETER RELAY**
*1924–1988 not held*
1992 FRA                         1:15:55.60
1994
1998

**WOMEN'S 30-KILOMETER RELAY**
*1924–1992 not held*
1994 RUS                         1:47:19.50
1998

### BOBSLEDDING

**4-MAN BOB**
*(Driver in parentheses)*
1924 SWI (Eduard Scherrer)                5:45.54
1928 USA (William Fiske) (5-man)          3:20.50
1932 USA (William Fiske)                  7:53.68
1936 SWI (Pierre Musy)                    5:19.85
1948 USA (Francis Tyler)                  5:20.10
1952 GER (Andreas Ostler)                 5:07.84
1956 SWI (Franz Kapus)                    5:10.44
*1960 not held*
1964 CAN (Victor Emery)                   4:14.46
1968 ITA (Eugenio Monti) (2 races)        2:17.39
1972 SWI (Jean Wicki)                     4:43.07
1976 GDR (Meinhard Nehmer)                3:40.43
1980 GDR (Meinhard Nehmer)                3:59.92
1984 GDR (Wolfgang Hoppe)                 3:20.22
1988 SWI (Ekkehard Fasser)                3:47.51
1992 AUT (Ingo Appelt)                    3:53.90
1994 GER (Wolfgang Hoppe)                 3:27.28
1998

**2-MAN BOB**
*1924–1928 not held*
1932 USA (Hubert Stevens)                 8:14.74
1936 USA (Ivan Brown)                     5:29.29
1948 SWI (Felix Endrich)                  5:29.20
1952 GER (Andreas Ostler)                 5:24.54
1956 ITA (Lamberto Dalla Costa)           5:30.14
*1960 not held*
1964 GBR (Anthony Nash)                   4:21.90
1968 ITA (Eugenio Monti)                  4:41.54
1972 GER (Wolfgang Zimmerer)              4:57.07
1976 GDR (Meinhard Nehmer)                3:44.42
1980 SWI (Erich Schärer)                  4:09.36
1984 GDR (Wolfgang Hoppe)                 3:25.56
1988 SOV (Jānis Kipours)                  3:53.48
1992 SWI (Gustav Weber)                   4:03.26
1994 SWI (Gustav Weber)                   3:30.81
1998

### LUGE

**MEN'S SINGLES**
*1924–1960 not held*
1964 Thomas Köhler, GDR          3:26.770
1968 Manfred Schmid, AUT         2:52.480
1972 Wolfgang Scheidel, GDR      3:27.580
1976 Dettlef Günther, GDR        3:27.688
1980 Bernhard Glass, GDR         2:54.796
1984 Paul Hildgartner, ITA       3:04.258
1988 Jens Müller, GDR            3:05.548
1992 Georg Hackl, GER            3:02.363
1994 Georg Hackl, GER            3:21.571
1998

**MEN'S PAIRS**
*1924–1960 not held*
1964 AUT                         1:41.620
1968 GDR                         1:35.850
1972 ITA, GDR (tie)              1:28.350
1976 GDR                         1:25.604
1980 GDR                         1:19.331
1984 GER                         1:23.620
1988 GDR                         1:31.940
1992 GER                         1:32.053
1994 ITA                         1:36.720
1998

**WOMEN'S SINGLES**
*1924–1960 not held*
1964 Ortrun Enderlein, GER       3:24.670
1968 Erica Lechner, ITA          2:28.660
1972 Anna-Maria Müller, GDR      2:59.180
1976 Margit Schumann, GDR        2:50.621
1980 Vera Zozulya, SOV           2:36.537
1984 Steffi Martin, GDR          2:46.570
1988 Steffi Walter, GDR          3:03.973
1992 Doris Neuner, AUT           3:06.696
1994 Gerda Weissensteiner, ITA   3:15.517
1998

### ICE HOCKEY

| | | | |
|---|---|---|---|
| 1920 CAN▲ | 1948 CAN | 1968 SOV | 1988 SOV |
| 1924 CAN | 1952 CAN | 1972 SOV | 1992 EUN |
| 1928 CAN | 1956 SOV | 1976 SOV | 1994 SWE |
| 1932 CAN | 1960 USA | 1980 USA | 1998 |
| 1936 GBR | 1964 SOV | 1984 SOV | |

### FIGURE SKATING

**MEN'S SINGLES**
1908 Ulrich Salchow, SWE▲
*1912 not held*
1920 Gillis Grafström, SWE▲
1924 Gillis Grafström, SWE
1928 Gillis Grafström, SWE
1932 Karl Schäfer, AUT
1936 Karl Schäfer, AUT
1948 Richard Button, USA
1952 Richard Button, USA
1956 Hayes Alan Jenkins, USA
1960 David W. Jenkins, USA
1964 Manfred Schnelldorfer, GER
1968 Wolfgang Schwarz, AUT
1972 Ondrej Nepela, CZE
1976 John Curry, GBR
1980 Robin Cousins, GBR
1984 Scott Hamilton, USA
1988 Brian Boitano, USA
1992 Viktor Petrenko, EUN
1994 Aleksei Urmanov, RUS
1998

**WOMEN'S SINGLES**
1908 Madge Syers, GBR▲
*1912 not held*
1920 Magda Julin-Mauroy, SWE▲
1924 Herma Planck-Szabó, AUT
1928 Sonja Henie, NOR
1932 Sonja Henie, NOR
1936 Sonja Henie, NOR
1948 Barbara Ann Scott, CAN
1952 Jeanette Altwegg, GBR
1956 Tenley Albright, USA
1960 Carol Heiss, USA
1964 Sjoukje Dijkstra, HOL
1968 Peggy Fleming, USA
1972 Beatrix Schuba, AUT
1976 Dorothy Hamill, USA
1980 Anett Pötzsch, GDR
1984 Katarina Witt, GDR
1988 Katarina Witt, GDR
1992 Kristi Yamaguchi, USA
1994 Oksana Baiul, UKR
1998

**PAIRS**
1908 Anna Hübler & Heinrich Burger, GER▲
*1912 not held*
1920 Ludovika & Walter Jakobsson, FIN▲
1924 Helene Engelman & Alfred Berger, AUT
1928 Andrée Joly & Pierre Brunet, FRA
1932 Andrée Joly & Pierre Brunet, FRA
1936 Maxi Herber & Ernst Baier, GER
1948 Micheline Lannoy & Pierre Baugniet, BEL
1952 Ria & Paul Falk, GER
1956 Elisabeth Schwartz & Kurt Oppelt, AUT
1960 Barbara Wagner & Robert Paul, CAN
1964 Ludmila Beloussova & Oleg Protopopov, SOV
1968 Ludmila Beloussova & Oleg Protopopov, SOV
1972 Irina Rodnina & Alexei Ulanov, SOV
1976 Irina Rodnina & Aleksandr Zaitzev, SOV
1980 Irina Rodnina & Aleksandr Zaitzev, SOV
1984 Elena Valova & Oleg Vassiliev, SOV
1988 Ekaterina Gordeeva & Sergei Grinkov, SOV
1992 Natalia Mishkutienok & Artur Dimitriev, EUN
1994 Ekaterina Gordeeva & Sergei Grinkov, RUS
1998

**ICE DANCING**
*1924–1972 not held*
1976 Ludmila Pakhomova & Aleksandr Gorschkov, SOV
1980 Natalya Linichuk & Gennadi Karponosov, SOV
1984 Jayne Torvill & Christopher Dean, GBR
1988 Natalia Bestemianova & Andrei Bukin, SOV
1992 Marina Klimova & Sergei Ponomarenko, EUN
1994 Oksana Grichtchuk & Yevgeny Platov, RUS
1998

*Photo: Opposite © Duomo.*

## SPEED SKATING

### MEN'S 500 METERS

| | | | |
|---|---|---|---|
| 1924 | Charles Jewtraw, USA | 44.00 | |
| 1928 | Clas Thunberg, FIN | | OR |
| | Bernt Evensen, NOR (tie) | 43.40 | OR |
| 1932 | John Shea, USA | 43.40 | EOR |
| 1936 | Ivar Ballangrud, NOR | 43.40 | EOR |
| 1948 | Finn Helgesen, NOR | 43.10 | OR |
| 1952 | Kenneth Henry, USA | 43.20 | |
| 1956 | Yevgeny Grishin, SOV | 40.20 | EWR |
| 1960 | Yevgeny Grishin, SOV | 40.20 | EWR |
| 1964 | Terry McDermott, USA | 40.10 | OR |
| 1968 | Erhard Keller, GER | 40.30 | |
| 1972 | Erhard Keller, GER | 39.44 | OR |
| 1976 | Yevgeny Kulikov, SOV | 39.17 | OR |
| 1980 | Eric Heiden, USA | 38.03 | OR |
| 1984 | Sergei Fokichev, SOV | 38.19 | |
| 1988 | Uwe-Jens Mey, GDR | 36.45 | WR |
| 1992 | Uwe-Jens Mey, GER | 37.14 | |
| 1994 | Aleksandr Golubev, RUS | 36.33 | OR |
| 1998 | | | |

### MEN'S 1000 METERS
*1924–1972 not held*

| | | | |
|---|---|---|---|
| 1976 | Peter Mueller, USA | 1:19.32 | |
| 1980 | Eric Heiden, USA | 1:15.18 | OR |
| 1984 | Gaétan Boucher, CAN | 1:15.80 | |
| 1988 | Nikolai Gulyaev, SOV | 1:13.03 | OR |
| 1992 | Olaf Zinke, GER | 1:14.85 | |
| 1994 | Dan Jansen, USA | 1:12.43 | WR |
| 1998 | | | |

### MEN'S 1500 METERS

| | | | |
|---|---|---|---|
| 1924 | Clas Thunberg, FIN | 2:20.80 | |
| 1928 | Clas Thunberg, FIN | 2:21.10 | |
| 1932 | John Shea, USA | 2:57.50 | |
| 1936 | Charles Mathisen, NOR | 2:19.20 | OR |
| 1948 | Sverre Farstad, NOR | 2:17.60 | OR |
| 1952 | Hjalmar Andersen, NOR | 2:20.40 | |
| 1956 | Yevgeny Grishin, SOV | | WR |
| | Yuri Mikhailov, SOV (tie) | 2:08.60 | WR |
| 1960 | Roald Aas, NOR | | |
| | Yevgeny Grishin, SOV (tie) | 2:10.40 | |
| 1964 | Ants Anston, SOV | 2:10.30 | |
| 1968 | Cornelis Verkerk, HOL | 2:03.40 | OR |
| 1972 | Ard Schenk, HOL | 2:02.96 | OR |
| 1976 | Jan Egil Storholt, NOR | 1:59.38 | OR |
| 1980 | Eric Heiden, USA | 1:55.44 | OR |
| 1984 | Gaétan Boucher, CAN | 1:58.36 | |
| 1988 | André Hoffmann, GDR | 1:52.06 | WR |
| 1992 | Johann Koss, NOR | 1:54.81 | |
| 1994 | Johann Koss, NOR | 1:51.29 | OR |
| 1998 | | | |

### MEN'S 5000 METERS

| | | | |
|---|---|---|---|
| 1924 | Clas Thunberg, FIN | 8:39.00 | |
| 1928 | Ivar Ballangrud, NOR | 8:50.50 | |
| 1932 | Irving Jaffee, USA | 9:40.80 | |
| 1936 | Ivar Ballangrud, NOR | 8:19.60 | OR |
| 1948 | Reidar Liaklev, NOR | 8:29.40 | |
| 1952 | Hjalmar Andersen, NOR | 8:10.60 | OR |
| 1956 | Boris Shilkov, SOV | 7:48.70 | OR |
| 1960 | Viktor Kosichkin, SOV | 7:51.30 | |
| 1964 | Knut Johannesen, NOR | 7:38.40 | OR |
| 1968 | Anton Maier, NOR | 7:22.40 | WR |
| 1972 | Ard Schenk, HOL | 7:23.61 | |
| 1976 | Sten Stensen, NOR | 7:24.48 | |
| 1980 | Eric Heiden, USA | 7:02.29 | OR |
| 1984 | Tomas Gustafson, SWE | 7:12.28 | |
| 1988 | Tomas Gustafson, SWE | 6:44.63 | OR |
| 1992 | Geir Karlstad, NOR | 6:59.97 | |
| 1994 | Johann Koss, NOR | 6:34.96 | OR |
| 1998 | | | |

### MEN'S 10000 METERS

| | | | |
|---|---|---|---|
| 1924 | Julius Skutnabb, FIN | 18:04.80 | |
| 1928 | *Event not held, thawing of ice* | | |
| 1932 | Irving Jaffee, USA | 19:13.60 | |
| 1936 | Ivar Ballangrud, NOR | 17:24.30 | OR |
| 1948 | Åke Seyffarth, SWE | 17:26.30 | |
| 1952 | Hjalmar Andersen, NOR | 16:45.80 | OR |
| 1956 | Sigvard Ericsson, SWE | 16:35.90 | OR |

| | | | |
|---|---|---|---|
| 1960 | Knut Johannesen, NOR | 15:46.60 | WR |
| 1964 | Jonny Nilsson, SWE | 15:50.10 | |
| 1968 | Johnny Höglin, SWE | 15:23.60 | OR |
| 1972 | Ard Schenk, HOL | 15:01.35 | OR |
| 1976 | Piet Kleine, HOL | 14:50.59 | OR |
| 1980 | Eric Heiden, USA | 14:28.13 | |
| 1984 | Igor Malkov, SOV | 14:39.90 | |
| 1988 | Tomas Gustafson, SWE | 13:48.20 | WR |
| 1992 | Bart Veldkamp, HOL | 14:12.12 | |
| 1994 | Johann Koss, NOR | 13:30.55 | OR |
| 1998 | | | |

### WOMEN'S 500 METERS
*1924–1956 not held*

| | | | |
|---|---|---|---|
| 1960 | Helga Haase, GDR | 45.90 | |
| 1964 | Lydia Skoblikova, SOV | 45.00 | OR |
| 1968 | Ludmila Titova, SOV | 46.10 | |
| 1972 | Anne Henning, USA | 43.33 | OR |
| 1976 | Sheila Young, USA | 42.76 | OR |
| 1980 | Karin Enke, GDR | 41.78 | OR |
| 1984 | Christa Rothenburger, GDR | 41.02 | OR |
| 1988 | Bonnie Blair, USA | 39.10 | WR |
| 1992 | Bonnie Blair, USA | 40.33 | |
| 1994 | Bonnie Blair, USA | 39.25 | |
| 1998 | | | |

### WOMEN'S 1000 METERS
*1924–1956 not held*

| | | | |
|---|---|---|---|
| 1960 | Klara Guseva, SOV | 1:34.10 | |
| 1964 | Lydia Skoblikova, SOV | 1:33.20 | OR |
| 1968 | Carolina Geijssen, HOL | 1:32.60 | OR |
| 1972 | Monika Pflug, GER | 1:31.40 | OR |
| 1976 | Tatiana Averina, SOV | 1:28.43 | OR |
| 1980 | Natalya Petruseva, SOV | 1:24.10 | OR |
| 1984 | Karin Enke, GDR | 1:21.61 | OR |
| 1988 | Christa Rothenburger, GDR | 1:17.65 | WR |
| 1992 | Bonnie Blair, USA | 1:21.90 | |
| 1994 | Bonnie Blair, USA | 1:18.74 | |
| 1998 | | | |

### WOMEN'S 1500 METERS
*1924–1956 not held*

| | | | |
|---|---|---|---|
| 1960 | Lydia Skoblikova, SOV | 2:52.20 | WR |
| 1964 | Lydia Skoblikova, SOV | 2:22.60 | OR |
| 1968 | Kaija Mustonen, FIN | 2:22.40 | OR |
| 1972 | Dianne Holum, USA | 2:20.85 | OR |
| 1976 | Galina Stepanskaya, SOV | 2:16.58 | OR |
| 1980 | Anne Borckink, HOL | 2:10.95 | OR |
| 1984 | Karin Enke, GDR | 2:03.42 | WR |
| 1988 | Yvonne van Gennip, HOL | 2:00.68 | OR |
| 1992 | Jacqueline Boerner, GER | 2:05.87 | |
| 1994 | Emese Hunyady, AUS | 2:02.19 | |
| 1998 | | | |

### WOMEN'S 3000 METERS
*1924–1956 not held*

| | | | |
|---|---|---|---|
| 1960 | Lydia Skoblikova, SOV | 5:14.30 | |
| 1964 | Lydia Skoblikova, SOV | 5:14.90 | |
| 1968 | Johanna Schut, HOL | 4:56.20 | OR |
| 1972 | Christina Baas-Kaiser, HOL | 4:52.14 | OR |
| 1976 | Tatiana Averina, SOV | 4:45.19 | OR |
| 1980 | Bjorg Eva Jensen, NOR | 4:32.13 | OR |
| 1984 | Andrea Schöne, GDR | 4:24.79 | OR |
| 1988 | Yvonne van Gennip, HOL | 4:11.94 | WR |
| 1992 | Gunda Niemann, GER | 4:19.90 | |
| 1994 | Svetlana Bazhanova, RUS | 4:17.43 | |
| 1998 | | | |

### WOMEN'S 5000 METERS
*1924–1984 not held*

| | | | |
|---|---|---|---|
| 1988 | Yvonne van Gennip, HOL | 7:14.13 | WR |
| 1992 | Gunda Niemann, GER | 7:31.57 | |
| 1994 | Claudia Pechstein, GER | 7:14.37 | |
| 1998 | | | |

## ALPINE SKIING

### MEN'S DOWNHILL
*1924–1944 not held*

| | | | |
|---|---|---|---|
| 1948 | Henri Oreiller, FRA | 2:55.00 | |
| 1952 | Zeno Colò, ITA | 2:30.80 | |
| 1956 | Anton Sailer, AUT | 2:52.20 | |
| 1960 | Jean Vuarnet, FRA | 2:06.00 | |
| 1964 | Egon Zimmermann, AUT | 2:18.16 | |
| 1968 | Jean-Claude Killy, FRA | 1:59.85 | |
| 1972 | Bernhard Russi, SWI | 1:51.43 | |
| 1976 | Franz Klammer, AUT | 1:45.73 | |
| 1980 | Leonhard Stock, AUT | 1:45.50 | |
| 1984 | Bill Johnson, USA | 1:45.59 | |
| 1988 | Pirmin Zurbriggen, SWI | 1:59.63 | |
| 1992 | Patrick Ortlieb, AUT | 1:50.37 | |
| 1994 | Tommy Moe, USA | 1:45.75 | |
| 1998 | | | |

### MEN'S SUPER GIANT SLALOM
*1924–1984 not held*

| | | | |
|---|---|---|---|
| 1988 | Franck Piccard, FRA | 1:39.66 | |
| 1992 | Kjetil-Andre Aamodt, NOR | 1:13.04 | |
| 1994 | Markus Wasmeier, GER | 1:32.53 | |
| 1998 | | | |

### MEN'S GIANT SLALOM
*1924–1948 not held*

| | | | |
|---|---|---|---|
| 1952 | Stein Eriksen, NOR | 2:25.00 | |
| 1956 | Anton Sailer, AUT | 3:00.10 | |
| 1960 | Roger Staub, SWI | 1:48.30 | |
| 1964 | Francois Bonlieu, FRA | 1:46.71 | |
| 1968 | Jean-Claude Killy, FRA | 3:29.28 | |
| 1972 | Gustav Thöni, ITA | 3:09.62 | |
| 1976 | Heini Hemmi, SWI | 3:26.97 | |
| 1980 | Ingemar Stenmark, SWE | 2:40.74 | |
| 1984 | Max Julen, SWI | 2:41.18 | |
| 1988 | Alberto Tomba, ITA | 2:06.37 | |
| 1992 | Alberto Tomba, ITA | 2:06.98 | |
| 1994 | Markus Wasmeier, GER | 2:52.46 | |
| 1998 | | | |

### MEN'S SLALOM
*1924–1936 not held*

| | | | |
|---|---|---|---|
| 1948 | Edi Reinalter, SWI | 2:10.30 | |
| 1952 | Othmar Schneider, AUT | 2:00.00 | |
| 1956 | Anton Sailer, AUT | 3:14.70 | |
| 1960 | Ernst Hinterseer, AUT | 2:08.90 | |
| 1964 | Josef Stiegler, AUT | 2:11.13 | |
| 1968 | Jean-Claude Killy, FRA | 1:39.73 | |
| 1972 | Francisco Fernandez Ochoa, SPA | 1:49.27 | |
| 1976 | Piero Gros, ITA | 2:03.29 | |
| 1980 | Ingemar Stenmark, SWE | 1:44.26 | |
| 1984 | Phil Mahre, USA | 1:39.41 | |
| 1988 | Alberto Tomba, ITA | 1:39.47 | |
| 1992 | Finn Christian Jagge, NOR | 1:44.39 | |
| 1994 | Thomas Stangassinger, AUT | 2:02.02 | |
| 1998 | | | |

### MEN'S COMBINED
*1924–1932 not held*

| | | | |
|---|---|---|---|
| 1936 | Franz Pfnür, GER | 99.25 pts. | |
| 1948 | Henri Oreiller, FRA | 3.27 pts. | |
| *1952–1984 not held* | | | |
| 1988 | Hubert Strolz, AUT | 36.55 pts. | |
| 1992 | Josef Polig, ITA | 14.58 pts. | |
| 1994 | Lasse Kjus, NOR | 14.58 pts. | |
| 1998 | | | |

### WOMEN'S DOWNHILL
*1924–1936 not held*

| | | | |
|---|---|---|---|
| 1948 | Hedi Schlunegger, SWI | 2:28.30 | |
| 1952 | Trude Jochum-Beiser, AUT | 1:47.10 | |
| 1956 | Madeleine Berthod, SWI | 1:40.70 | |
| 1960 | Heidi Biebl, GER | 1:37.60 | |
| 1964 | Christl Haas, AUT | 1:55.39 | |
| 1968 | Olga Pall, AUT | 1:40.87 | |
| 1972 | Marie-Theres Nadig, SWI | 1:36.68 | |
| 1976 | Rosi Mittermaier, GER | 1:46.16 | |
| 1980 | Annemarie Moser-Pröll, AUT | 1:37.52 | |
| 1984 | Michela Figini, SWI | 1:13.36 | |
| 1988 | Marina Kiehl, GER | 1:25.86 | |
| 1992 | Kerrin Lee-Gartner, CAN | 1:52.55 | |
| 1994 | Katja Seizinger, GER | 1:35.93 | |
| 1998 | | | |

### WOMEN'S SUPER GIANT SLALOM
*1924–1984 not held*

| | | | |
|---|---|---|---|
| 1988 | Sigrid Wolf, AUT | 1:19.03 | |
| 1992 | Deborah Compagnoni, ITA | 1:21.22 | |
| 1994 | Diann Roffe-Steinrotter, USA | 1:22.15 | |
| 1998 | | | |

### WOMEN'S GIANT SLALOM
*1924–1948 not held*

| | | | |
|---|---|---|---|
| 1952 | Andrea Mead Lawrence, USA | 2:06.80 | |
| 1956 | Ossi Reichert, GER | 1:56.50 | |
| 1960 | Yvonne Rüegg, SWI | 1:39.90 | |
| 1964 | Marielle Goitschel, FRA | 1:52.24 | |
| 1968 | Nancy Greene, CAN | 1:51.97 | |
| 1972 | Marie-Theres Nadig, SWI | 1:29.90 | |
| 1976 | Kathy Kreiner, CAN | 1:29.13 | |
| 1980 | Hanni Wenzel, LIE (2 runs) | 2:41.66 | |
| 1984 | Debbie Armstrong, USA | 2:20.98 | |
| 1988 | Vreni Schneider, SWI | 2:06.49 | |
| 1992 | Pernilla Wiberg, SWE | 2:12.74 | |
| 1994 | Deborah Compagnoni, ITA | 2:30.97 | |
| 1998 | | | |

### WOMEN'S SLALOM
*1924–1936 not held*

| | | | |
|---|---|---|---|
| 1948 | Gretchen Fraser, USA | 1:57.20 | |
| 1952 | Andrea Mead Lawrence, USA | 2:10.60 | |
| 1956 | Renée Colliard, SWI | 1:52.30 | |
| 1960 | Anne Heggtveit, CAN | 1:49.60 | |
| 1964 | Christine Goitschel, FRA | 1:29.86 | |
| 1968 | Marielle Goitschel, FRA | 1:25.86 | |
| 1972 | Barbara Cochran, USA | 1:31.24 | |
| 1976 | Rosi Mittermaier, GER | 1:30.54 | |
| 1980 | Hanni Wenzel, LIE | 1:25.09 | |
| 1984 | Paoletta Magoni, ITA | 1:36.47 | |
| 1988 | Vreni Schneider, SWI | 1:36.69 | |
| 1992 | Petra Kronberger, AUT | 1:32.68 | |
| 1994 | Vreni Schneider, SWI | 1:56.01 | |
| 1998 | | | |

### WOMEN'S COMBINED
*1924–1932 not held*

| | | | |
|---|---|---|---|
| 1936 | Christl Cranz, GER | 97.06 pts. | |
| 1948 | Trude Beiser, AUT | 6.58 pts. | |
| *1952–1984 not held* | | | |
| 1988 | Anita Wachter, AUT | 29.25 pts. | |
| 1992 | Petra Kronberger, AUT | 2.55 pts. | |
| 1994 | Pernilla Wiberg, SWE | 3:05.16 | |
| 1998 | | | |

## FREESTYLE SKIING

### MEN'S MOGULS
*1924–1988 not held*

| | |
|---|---|
| 1992 | Edgar Grospiron, FRA |
| 1994 | Jean-Luc Brassard, CAN |
| 1998 | |

### MEN'S AERIALS
*1924–1992 not held*

| | |
|---|---|
| 1994 | Andreas Schoenbaechler, SWI |
| 1998 | |

### WOMEN'S MOGULS
*1924–1988 not held*

| | |
|---|---|
| 1992 | Donna Weinbrecht, USA |
| 1994 | Stine Lise Hattestad, NOR |
| 1998 | |

### WOMEN'S AERIALS
*1924–1992 not held*

| | |
|---|---|
| 1994 | Lina Tcherjazova, UZB |

## CROSS-COUNTRY SKIING · MENS

**10 KILOMETERS**
*1924–1988 not held*
| | | |
|---|---|---|
| 1992 | Vegard Ulvang, NOR | 0:27:36.00 |
| 1994 | Bjørn Daehlie, NOR | 0:24:20.10 |
| 1998 | | |

**15 KILOMETERS**
| | | |
|---|---|---|
| 1924 | Thorleif Haug, NOR | 1:14:31.00 |
| 1928 | Johan Gröttumsbråten, NOR | 1:37:01.00 |
| 1932 | Sven Utterström, SWE | 1:23:07.00 |
| 1936 | Erik-August Larsson, SWE | 1:14:38.00 |
| 1948 | Martin Lundström, SWE | 1:13:50.00 |
| 1952 | Hallgeir Brenden, NOR | 1:01:34.00 |
| 1956 | Hallgeir Brenden, NOR | 0:49:39.00 |
| 1960 | Håkon Brusveen, NOR | 0:51:55.50 |
| 1964 | Eero Mäntyranta, FIN | 0:50:54.10 |
| 1968 | Harald Grönningen, NOR | 0:47:54.20 |
| 1972 | Sven-Ake Lundbäck, SWE | 0:45:28.24 |
| 1976 | Nikolai Bazhukov, SOV | 0:43:58.47 |
| 1980 | Thomas Wassberg, SWE | 0:41:57.63 |
| 1984 | Gunde Svan, SWE | 0:41:25.60 |
| 1988 | Mikhail Devyatyarov, SOV | 0:41:18.90 |
| 1992 | Bjørn Daehlie, NOR | 0:38:01.90 |
| 1994 | Bjørn Daehlie, NOR | 0:35:48.80 |
| 1998 | | |

*(Note: approx. 18-km. course 1924–1952)*

**30 KILOMETERS**
*1924–1952 not held*
| | | |
|---|---|---|
| 1956 | Veikko Hakulinen, FIN | 1:44:06.00 |
| 1960 | Sixten Jernberg, SWE | 1:51:03.90 |
| 1964 | Eero Mäntyranta, FIN | 1:30:50.70 |
| 1968 | Franco Nones, ITA | 1:35:39.20 |
| 1972 | Vyacheslav Vedenine, SOV | 1:36:31.15 |
| 1976 | Sergei Saveliev, SOV | 1:30:29.38 |
| 1980 | Nikolai Zimyatov, SOV | 1:27:02.80 |
| 1984 | Nikolai Zimyatov, SOV | 1:28:56.30 |
| 1988 | Aleksei Prokurorov, SOV | 1:24:26.30 |
| 1992 | Vegard Ulvang, NOR | 1:22:27.80 |
| 1994 | Thomas Alsgaard, NOR | 1:12:26.40 |
| 1998 | | |

**50 KILOMETERS**
| | | |
|---|---|---|
| 1924 | Thorleif Haug, NOR | 3:44:32.00 |
| 1928 | Per Erik Hedlund, SWE | 4:52:03.00 |
| 1932 | Veli Saarinen, FIN | 4:28:00.00 |
| 1936 | Elis Wiklund, SWE | 3:30:11.00 |
| 1948 | Nils Karlsson, SWE | 3:47:48.00 |
| 1952 | Veikko Hakulinen, FIN | 3:33:33.00 |
| 1956 | Sixten Jernberg, SWE | 2:50:27.00 |
| 1960 | Kalevi Hämäläinen, FIN | 2:59:06.30 |
| 1964 | Sixten Jernberg, SWE | 2:43:52.60 |
| 1968 | Ole Ellefsaeter, NOR | 2:28:45.80 |
| 1972 | Pål Tyldum, NOR | 2:43:14.75 |
| 1976 | Ivar Formo, NOR | 2:37:30.05 |
| 1980 | Nikolai Zimyatov, SOV | 2:27:24.60 |
| 1984 | Thomas Wassberg, SWE | 2:15:55.80 |
| 1988 | Gunde Svan, SWE | 2:04:30.90 |
| 1992 | Bjørn Daehlie, NOR | 2:03:41.50 |
| 1994 | Vladimir Smirnov, KAZ | 2:07:20.30 |
| 1998 | | |

**40 KILOMETERS RELAY**
*1924–1932 not held*
| | | |
|---|---|---|
| 1936 | FIN | 2:41:33.00 |
| 1948 | SWE | 2:32:08.00 |
| 1952 | FIN | 2:20:16.00 |
| 1956 | SOV | 2:15:30.00 |
| 1960 | FIN | 2:18:45.60 |
| 1964 | SWE | 2:18:34.60 |
| 1968 | NOR | 2:08:33.50 |
| 1972 | SOV | 2:04:47.94 |
| 1976 | FIN | 2:07:59.72 |
| 1980 | SOV | 1:57:03.46 |
| 1984 | SWE | 1:55:06.30 |
| 1988 | SWE | 1:43:58.60 |
| 1992 | NOR | 1:39:26.00 |
| 1994 | ITA | 1:41:15.00 |
| 1998 | | |

**COMBINED CROSS-COUNTRY & JUMPING**
| | |
|---|---|
| 1924 | Thorleif Haug, NOR |
| 1928 | Johan Gröttumsbråten, NOR |
| 1932 | Johan Gröttumsbråten, NOR |
| 1936 | Oddbjörn Hagen, NOR |
| 1948 | Heikki Hasu, FIN |
| 1952 | Simon Slåttvik, NOR |
| 1956 | Sverre Stenersen, NOR |
| 1960 | Georg Thoma, GER |
| 1964 | Tormod Knutsen, NOR |
| 1968 | Franz Keller, GER |
| 1972 | Ulrich Wehling, GDR |
| 1976 | Ulrich Wehling, GDR |
| 1980 | Ulrich Wehling, GDR |
| 1984 | Tom Sandberg, NOR |
| 1988 | Hippolyt Kempf, SWI |
| 1992 | Fabrice Guy, FRA |
| 1994 | Fred Barre Lundberg, NOR |
| 1998 | |

## CROSS-COUNTRY SKIING · WOMENS

**5 KILOMETERS**
*1924–1960 not held*
| | | |
|---|---|---|
| 1964 | Claudia Boyarskikh, SOV | 17:50.500 |
| 1968 | Toini Gustafsson, SWE | 16:45.200 |
| 1972 | Galina Koulacova, SOV | 17:00.500 |
| 1976 | Helena Takalo, FIN | 15:48.690 |
| 1980 | Raisa Smetanina, SOV | 15:06.920 |
| 1984 | Marja-Liisa Hämäläinen, FIN | 17:04.000 |
| 1988 | Marjo Matikainen, FIN | 15:04.000 |
| 1992 | Marjut Lukkarinen, FIN | 14:13.800 |
| 1994 | Ljubov Egorova, RUS | 14:08.815 |
| 1998 | | |

**10 KILOMETERS**
*1924–1948 not held*
| | | |
|---|---|---|
| 1952 | Lydia Wideman, FIN | 41:40.00 |
| 1956 | Lyubov Kosyreva, SOV | 38:11.00 |
| 1960 | Maria Gusakova, SOV | 39:46.60 |
| 1964 | Claudia Boyarskikh, SOV | 40:24.30 |
| 1968 | Toini Gustafsson, SWE | 36:46.50 |
| 1972 | Galina Koulacova, SOV | 34:17.82 |
| 1976 | Raisa Smetanina, SOV | 30:13.41 |
| 1980 | Barbara Petzold, GDR | 30:31.54 |
| 1984 | Marja-Liisa Hämäläinen, FIN | 31:44.20 |
| 1988 | Vida Venciene, SOV | 30:08.30 |
| 1992 | Lyubov Egorova, EUN | 25:53.70 |
| 1994 | Lyubov Egorova, RUS | 27:30.10 |
| 1998 | | |

**16 KILOMETERS**
*1924–1988 not held*
| | | |
|---|---|---|
| 1992 | Lyubov Egorova, EUN | 42:20.80 |

**20 KILOMETERS**
*1924–1980 not held*
| | | |
|---|---|---|
| 1984 | Marja-Liisa Hämäläinen, FIN | 1:01:45.00 |
| 1988 | Tamara Tikhonova, SOV | 0:55:53.60 |

**30 KILOMETERS**
*1924–1988 not held*
| | | |
|---|---|---|
| 1992 | Stefania Belmondo, ITA | 1:22:30.10 |
| 1994 | Manuela Di Centa, ITA | 1:25:41.60 |
| 1996 | | |

Also listed:
| | | |
|---|---|---|
| 1994 | Manuela Di Centa, ITA | 0:39:44.50 |
| 1998 | | |

**20 KILOMETERS RELAY**
*1924–1952 not held*
| | | |
|---|---|---|
| 1956 | FIN (15 km.) | 1:09:01.00 |
| 1960 | SWE (15 km.) | 1:04:21.40 |
| 1964 | SOV (15 km.) | 0:59:20.20 |
| 1968 | NOR (15 km.) | 0:57:30.00 |
| 1972 | SOV (15 km.) | 0:48:46.15 |
| 1976 | SOV | 1:07:49.75 |
| 1980 | GDR | 1:02:11.10 |
| 1984 | NOR | 1:06:49.70 |
| 1988 | SOV | 0:59:51.10 |
| 1992 | EUN | 0:59:34.80 |
| 1994 | RUS | 0:57:12.50 |
| 1998 | | |

## SKI JUMPING

**TEAM SKI JUMPING**
*1924–1984 not held*
| | |
|---|---|
| 1988 | FIN |
| 1992 | FIN |
| 1994 | GER |
| 1998 | |

**SKI JUMPING, LARGE HILL***
| | |
|---|---|
| 1924 | Jacob Thams, NOR |
| 1928 | Alfred Andersen, NOR |
| 1932 | Birger Ruud, NOR |
| 1936 | Birger Ruud, NOR |
| 1948 | Petter Hugsted, NOR |
| 1952 | Arnfinn Bergmann, NOR |
| 1956 | Antti Hyvärinen, FIN |
| 1960 | Helmut Recknagel, GDR |
| 1964 | Toralf Engan, NOR |
| 1968 | Vladimir Beloussov, SOV |
| 1972 | Wojciech Fortuna, POL |
| 1976 | Karl Schnabl, AUT |
| 1980 | Jouko Törmänen, FIN |
| 1984 | Matti Nykänen, FIN |
| 1988 | Matti Nykänen, FIN |
| 1992 | Toni Nicminen, FIN |
| 1994 | Jens Weissflog, GER |
| 1998 | |

**TEAM NORDIC COMBINED**
*1924–1984 not held*
| | |
|---|---|
| 1988 | GDR |
| 1992 | JPN |
| 1994 | JPN |
| 1998 | |

**SKI JUMPING, NORMAL HILL**
*1924–1960 not held*
| | |
|---|---|
| 1964 | Veikko Kankkonen, FIN |
| 1968 | Jiri Raska, CZE |
| 1972 | Yukio Kasaya, JPN |
| 1976 | Hans-Georg Aschenbach, GDR |
| 1980 | Anton Innauer, AUT |
| 1984 | Jens Weissflog, GDR |
| 1988 | Matti Nykänen, FIN |
| 1992 | Ernst Vettori, AUT |
| 1994 | Espen Bredesen, NOR |
| 1998 | |

**NORDIC COMBINED, INDV.**
| | |
|---|---|
| 1924 | Thorleif Haug, NOR |
| 1928 | Johan Grottumsbråten, NOR |
| 1932 | Johan Grottumsbråten, NOR |
| 1936 | Oddbjörn Hagen, NOR |
| 1948 | Heikki Hasu, FIN |
| 1952 | Simon Slåttvik, NOR |
| 1956 | Sverre Stenersen, NOR |
| 1960 | Georg Thoma, GER |
| 1964 | Tormod Knutsen, NOR |
| 1968 | Franz Keller, GER |
| 1972 | Ulrich Wehling, GDR |
| 1976 | Ulrich Wehling, GDR |
| 1980 | Ulrich Wehling, GDR |
| 1984 | Tom Sandberg, NOR |
| 1988 | Hippolyt Kempf, SWI |
| 1992 | Fabrice Guy, FRA |
| 1994 | Fred Barre Lundberg, NOR |
| 1998 | |

## SHORT TRACK SPEEDSKATING

**MEN'S 1000 METERS**
*1924–1960 not held*
| | | |
|---|---|---|
| 1992 | Kim Ki-Hoon, KOR | 1:30.76 |
| 1994 | Kim Ki-Hoon, KOR | 1:34.57 |
| 1998 | | |

**MEN'S 5000-METER RELAY**
*1924–1988 not held*
| | | |
|---|---|---|
| 1992 | KOR | 7:14.02 |
| 1994 | ITA | 7:11.74 |
| 1998 | | |

**WOMEN'S 500 METERS**
*1924–1988 not held*
| | | |
|---|---|---|
| 1992 | Cathy Turner, USA | 0:47:04 |
| 1994 | Cathy Turner, USA | 0:45.98 |
| 1998 | | |

**WOMEN'S 3000-METER RELAY**
*1924–1988 not held*
| | | |
|---|---|---|
| 1992 | CAN | 4:36.62 |
| 1994 | KOR | 4:26.64 |
| 1998 | | |

# INDEX

## ACKNOWLEDGMENTS

Tehabi Books gratefully acknowledges the generous support and contributions provided by the following individuals to *The Olympic Spirit*. Without their commitment this project would not have been possible. Tom Angelillo, Southern Progress Corporation; Bruce Akin, Dianne Mooney, Carolyn Smith and Rebecca Fitzgerald, *Southern Living* Books; Fernando Riba, Jean-Francois Pahud, Dr. Doris Vanhove, Claude Jaccard, Catherine Fasel, and Sylvia de Techtermann, Olympic Museum, Lausanne, Switzerland; Jenny Barry, Maura Carey Damacion and Jenny Collins, Collins Publishers San Francisco; Carlos Duran, Galeria Senda, Barcelona, Spain; Dr. Vladimir Mateveyeu, Hermitage Museum, Saint Petersburg, Russia; Bernard Knox, Center for Hellenic Studies, Washington, D.C.; Walt Wilson and the staff of the USOC's Center for Sports Technology, and Barry King, Maxine Fleming and the staff at the USOC's Public Information Office, Colorado Springs, Colorado; George Ortiz and Laurentia Leon of The George Ortiz Collection, Switzerland; Dr. Alfred Bernhard-Walcher and Dr. Tscrwantner, Kunsthistorisches Museum, Austria; Professor Ruurd B. Halbertsma, Rijks Museum, Holland; Amy Freehour and the Sculpture Society, New York; Todd Toth and GT Bicycles, Santa Ana, California; Steve Sutton and Andy Kiss, Duomo Photography, New York; Allsport Photography, Los Angeles; Maggie Lavin, ISL Marketing, Atlanta; Andrew Clarke, Leo Chu and Raymond Shing, Mandarin Offset, Washington, D.C. and Hong Kong; Sanjay Sakhuja, Scott Runcorn, Maria Sota, Luke VanMeter and the staff at Digital Pre-Press International, San Francisco; Greg della Stua, PrintNet, San Francisco; Andy Gutierrez, Kara Thoman and Kathleen Wilkinson.

## SELECTED BIBLIOGRAPHY

Carlson, Lewis H., and Fogarty, John J. *Tales of Gold*. Chicago: Contemporary Books, 1987.

Coe, Sebastian. *The Olympians*. London: Pavilion Michael Joseph, 1984.

Connors, Martin; Dupuis, Diane L.; and Morgan, Brad. *The Olympics Factbook*. Detroit: Visible Ink Press, 1992.

Finley, M.I., and Pleket, H.W. *The Olympic Games: The First Thousand Years*. New York: The Viking Press, 1976.

Guttmann, Allen. *The Olympics: A History of the Modern Games*. Urbana and Chicago: University of Illinois Press, 1992.

Pausanias. *Guide to Greece*. Translated by Peter Levi, S.J. Harmondsworth. Middlesex, England: Penguin Books, Ltd., 1971.

*Suite Olympic Centennial: A History of Modern Olympism*. Barcelona: Editorial Centennial, 1992.

Schaap, Richard. *An Illustrated History of the Olympics*. New York: Alfred A. Kopf, 1963.

Schöbel, Heinz. *The Ancient Olympic Games*. London: Studio Vista Limited, 1966.

Sweet, Waldo E. *Sport and Recreation in Ancient Greece*. New York: Oxford University Press, 1987.

Wallechinsky, David. *The Complete Book of the Olympics*. Boston: Little, Brown and Company, 1992.